Country Bairns
Growing Up 1900–1930

EDINBURGH EDUCATION AND SOCIETY SERIES
General Editor: Colin Bell

Country Bairns
Growing Up 1900–1930

———————

LYNN JAMIESON
and
CLAIRE TOYNBEE

EDINBURGH UNIVERSITY PRESS

The order of authors is alphabetical. Both
authors contributed equally to this work.
© Lynn Jamieson and Claire Toynbee, 1992

Edinburgh University Press
22 George Square, Edinburgh

Typeset in Linotron Baskerville and
printed in Great Britain by
Redwood Press, Melksham, Wiltshire

A CIP record for this book is available
from the British Library.

ISBN 0 7486 0373 5

The Publisher gratefully acknowledges subsidy from the
Scottish Arts Council towards the publication of this volume.

To our parents
Isabella (Ella) Brotherstone White Toynbee
Helen Rae Dalziel Jamieson
William (Bill) Lauren Paton Jamieson
and in memory of
William (Bill) Toynbee

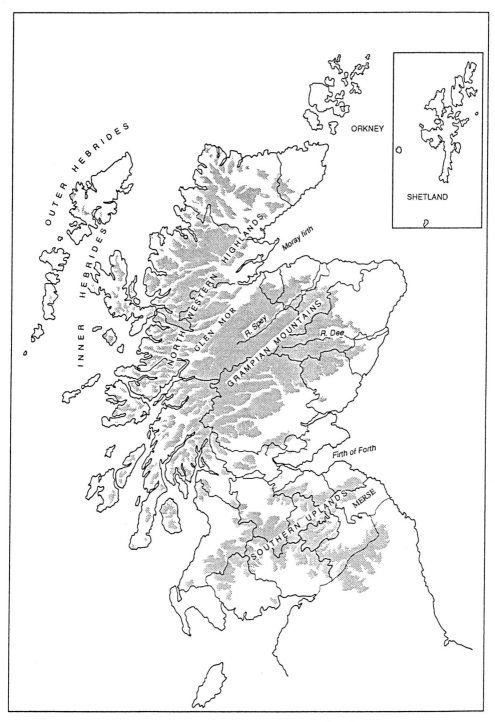

MAP 1   Topographical map of Scotland

Contents

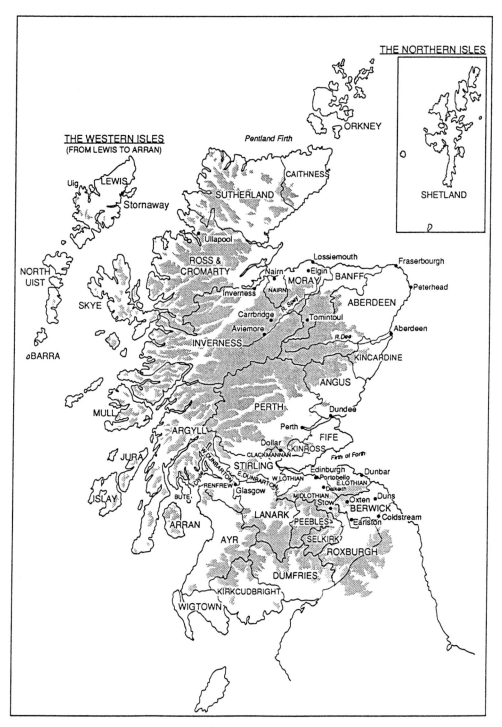

MAP 2 The counties of Scotland (including towns named by interviewees).

Preface

BOTH AUTHORS have been engaged in research on the nature of family life in the first decades of the twentieth century for some years and have made this the subject of their respective Ph.D.s, one at Edinburgh University and the other at the Victoria University of Wellington in New Zealand. Both are lecturers in the sociology departments of their respective universities and have used their material for teaching purposes over a number of years. Response to articles published on the basis of the research, and comments by others, indicate that there is a wide interest in the nature of family life in past time.

While work on the Ph.Ds. began totally independently, in both cases it was a response to discovering the value of oral history through the reading of Paul Thompson's *The Edwardians*. The writers met when Claire Toynbee, who was born in Scotland, returned to spend her first Christmas there in twenty-five years. On what would otherwise have been a very brief visit to the Sociology Department of Edinburgh University, she met Lynn Jamieson and discovered the very close overlap in their interests. Claire's first sabbatical leave from July 1986 to January 1987 was based in Edinburgh, where the fieldwork on which this book is based was jointly planned and launched. A number of other papers have been written and published either jointly or independently.

Acknowledgements

CLOSE FRIENDS AND FAMILY encouraged and sustained our enthusiasm for this research. Apart from the emotional support they gave us, they also made it possible for the interviewing to take place in remote areas by providing free bed, board, and Highland and Borders hospitality.

The people whom we interviewed were, of course, crucial to the whole enterprise and we owe special thanks to them. The hospitality and warmth of our respondents everywhere made the whole thing not only possible, but enjoyable. Thanks are also due to those who helped put us in touch with them.

All the photographs come from the Scottish Ethnological Archive, National Museums of Scotland. We thank the staff for their help, the National Trust for Scotland, Angus Folk Museum, for permission to reproduce Figure 4.3, and those members of the public who donated the photographs and provided written descriptions of them.

We also have a debt to our universities. Many people – too many to mention individually – have been involved in advising and encouraging us whether in departments of Sociology, Anthropology, Social and Economic History, History, Education, Scottish Studies or Computing Services.

Several people have helped us by reading the manuscript, providing constructive criticism and suggesting amendments of various kinds. We are especially indebted to Emeritus Professor Ian Gordon of Victoria University of Wellington for his considerable assistance with the many Scots accents and dialects with which we have had to grapple. We also wish to thank Sarah White of the

ACKNOWLEDGEMENTS

University of East Anglia, Richard Anthony of the Social and Economic History Department at Edinburgh University, and Barbara Robertson, of Edinburgh.

Lynn Jamieson
Claire Toynbee

Introduction

——————

IN THE LAST TWENTY YEARS there has been a revival of interest in the use of oral history. Interviews with elderly people have greatly expanded our knowledge and understanding of the everyday lives of ordinary people, women especially, and those whose accomplishments and experiences have rarely occupied the attention of historians of previous generations.

It is only now that we are beginning to learn about what it meant to be a child in past time. We still know very little about children's personal lives, since few writers have been specifically concerned with the ways in which children have been involved with their parents or with other people in the community. There is little published work of a sociological nature dealing with Scottish rural childhood during the early twentieth century. Our purpose in writing this book is to start to fill this gap.

This book is based on memories of childhood and youth. Interviewers took elderly people back to their young days and explored particular aspects of their lives at that time. Life is described from the perspective of children and young people, although it is a remembered, rather than a living, childhood and youth. We present the accounts of these early lives in the words of the people themselves, in the form either of full interviews, or of extracts illustrating specific cases of family and community life. Readers should note that the interview material is presented in Scots, together with notes explaining dialect and archaic terms where we think this is necessary.

One of our tasks as sociologists is to interpret these individuals' experiences within a historical and sociological framework in a manner designed to interest the general reader. A basic tenet of sociology is that lives are socially constructed. Throughout life any individual has to interact with other people continually and work within the ways in which others organise and define situations. This is the case whether a person is engaging in economic activity, like working a croft, or enjoying a cultural pursuit, like telling a story. In some aspects of how things are done, the rules are laid down long before birth. The pre-existing features of the immediate social environment put limits on individual experience. Even our private view of the self is profoundly shaped by, not just the physical world, but the social world of what other people think and do. Throughout this book, it is taken for granted that being born into very different social scenes results in different kinds of lives. We illustrate and explore how this 'social shaping' occurred for a group of men and women growing up in rural Scotland in the early 1900s.

The interviews selected for full transcription include a son and a daughter from crofting households, a son and a daughter from households in which the father was a farm worker, and a son and a daughter of farmer fathers. The inclusion of both sons and daughters allows consideration of the different experiences and destinies of boys and girls. Different occupational groupings are included to allow consideration of such factors as social class background, material wellbeing and standing in the community, as well as the effects of the particular occupation on the household. Clearly these occupational groupings – crofter, farm labourer and farmer – do not cover the full cast of characters which made up rural life at the beginning of the century. However, they were key categories and stand in sufficient contrast to each other to make comparison fruitful. A fuller description of how and why particular people were interviewed is given in an appendix on our methodology (Appendix One).

The interviewees describe their economic circumstances, the strategies of housekeeping, and ways of making a living employed by members of their household. Our questions were geared to finding out how their household worked in terms of producing a particular standard of living for its members and what part, if any, they played as a child or young person in maintaining this. The relationship between the interviewee as a child or young adult and his or her parents was a central theme in the interview. We wanted to know how close parents and children were and whether this differed for boys and girls in different economic circumstances. The interviewees also described their social and cultural context, their relationships to neighbours and the wider community, and the nature of commonly-held views about relationships between boys and girls and their mothers and fathers. Hence, it is possible to look for different types of parent/child relationship in different economic and cultural contexts.

We were also interested in the background factors affecting individuals' educational history and first occupation after schooling. Clearly some 'got on' and others did not. Again, interviewees' descriptions of the economic and social circumstances of their family households were crucial parts of the story, as were their parents' attitudes to education and the quality of their relationships with their parents. One well-known sociologist has distinguished between what he calls 'private ills' and 'public issues' (Mills, 1970). The private ills with which we are concerned are the frustrations faced by bright and ambitious children from backgrounds where there was little or no encouragement for anything other than basic education. The associated public issue, then, is unequal access to public education.

Regardless of the dominant view of education and the realities of work prospects, there are always the exceptions for whom more seems desirable and possible. At the level of individual life stories, some accident of biography, idiosyncratic influences, 'quirks of fate', – a mother who had some secondary schooling before she married and became downwardly mobile, the encouragement of the bookish spinster aunt – can sometimes be heard above the voices of the background culture. Indeed, there is a danger of becoming lost in the unique details of individual lives and losing sight of the pressures and constraints people shared with their neighbours. We hope that our style of presentation in this book gives a flavour of both.

While the book is intended for the general reader, advanced school pupils and first-year social science students, it will be of interest to scholars. It may provoke the interest of educational researchers and policy-makers who wish to explore the interrelationships between biography, history and structure.

Families, Households and Significant Contexts

Although this work is based on interviews with individuals, much of the focus is on their homes and families in childhood and youth. Our central questions are: what was the part played by the children and young people in the everyday life of family households?; what kind of relationship did they have with their mothers and fathers, and why?; what happened to them once they were too old for compulsory schooling, and why? We look for systematic differences, and their causes, between boys and girls, and between those with fathers in different occupational groups.

The term 'the family'[1] is often used as a shorthand for parents and children living together, that is, a particular type of family household, although 'the family' is also used to refer to the entirety of a person's biological and affinal kin. Until recently, sociologists, using 'the family' as shorthand for the dominant type of family household, tended to write about entities called 'the pre-industrial family' and 'the modern family', suggesting a simple dichotomy between past and present. Since the late 1960s, however, there has been a great blossoming of historical and demographic research on household composition and family structure in past time. This work has demonstrated both continuity between the past and present, and variation between family households in any given period. We can no longer assume one particular type of family characterised a particular period of history. Even when family households look similar in terms of such factors as their size, age structure or means of earning a living, their members might behave towards each other in very different ways. For example, people whose family households share very similar economic circumstances can have very different lives. Paul Thompson has pointed to the role of religious beliefs in the contrast between the rather authoritarian style of parent/child relationships in the crofting communities of the Western Isles and the more egalitarian style of parents in the Northern Isles of Shetland.

Ideas, then, are as important as economic circumstances. Before television became part of everyday life, ideas were primarily communicated in everyday interaction. But not all family households were equally open to communication. While some family households had very tenuous ties with other people in their neighbourhoods, others were embedded in daily interaction with kin, neighbours and local organisations. There were few social isolates in crofting communities. Most crofting parents in both the Western Isles and Shetland had cultural support for the way they treated their children – the assurance that they were doing things the way others did them.

In lived lives, economic and cultural factors are interwoven. For example, hard facts, like how much land and labour was available in a crofting household, tell us little about how life was lived if they are not informed by knowledge of custom concerning who does what, and when, to the land. Ideas, as well as material realities, open and limit possibilities in everyday lives.

Researchers working on both historical and contemporary societies have documented how ideas about what girls and women, boys and men, can and cannot do, constrain both divisions of labour within family households and the take-up of jobs outside the home. But ideas about gender interact with economic circumstance in complex ways.

For example, many authors have noted that men's dominance within the household has been supported by the norm of the 'breadwinner' husband/father with dependent wife and children. This norm in turn depended on economic circumstances, including better opportunities for paid work for men than women and the difficulty of combining childcare and paid employment, as well as ideas about who should do paid work and domestic work. Historians and sociologists have documented the privileges extended to male breadwinners in many households at the turn of the century: the best food, the largest portion, the best chair, the most spending money. But they have also noted many households in which women took complete charge of all finances and were effectively the boss of the house.

Most family households in western societies today earn their living by the wage-earning of adult members; in the late twentieth century, married women are almost as likely to be in paid employment as their husbands. Since the Second World War, claiming state benefit is also a significant means by which adults acquire household income. Before there was a developed welfare state, more households provided for themselves without the intermediary of money wages or benefits. In respect of our own research, it is clear that very different ways of life prevailed. Not all our interviewees were wholly integrated into a capitalist system of economic production or a money economy (Toynbee & Jamieson, 1989). Getting a living was not the sole responsibility of adults, nor did it depend exclusively on a relationship to an employer or the state. Many households generating their livelihood from the land were distant from the norm of a money-earning husband/father with dependent wife and children.

According to the size of the croft or farm, a greater or lesser amount of food was provided directly for the household. And particularly on crofts and small farms, the responsibility for providing was not exclusively that of the husband/father or men of the household; women and children contributed their labour. Even in the case of the farm-worker husband/father who was the main wage-earner, wages were paid partially in food and rights to grow food rather than in money, and women and children participated in this self-provisioning.

It is only since the advent of widespread access to radio and television that we can speak of the influence of mass communications. In the average western household today, images, ideas and styles of life other than those of the occupants are watched on television screens for several hours a day. While forms of mass media have become more pervasive and invasive, the influence of the clergy or religion in everyday life has been reduced, though the relationship is by no means a simple one. One of our Border interviewees reflected that when he was young, you were considered strange if you didn't go to church, whereas today you are considered strange if you do. We might add that one's neighbours are less likely to comment – or care – either way.

Organisation of Chapters

The main body of the book is organised into chapters dealing with the childhood experiences of the children of crofters, farm workers and farmers respectively. In each case, there is a general background section, followed by a section containing two or three full transcriptions of interviews. Some readers may prefer to skip the more general chapters and go straight to the interview material.

NOTE

1. See comments made by Rapp, 1982, and Wilson and Pahl, 1988.

CHAPTER ONE

Scottish Society and Country Bairns

THIS CHAPTER provides some very general background to everyday life in rural Scotland in the early decades of the twentieth century. It places rural life in the context of an industrial, urbanising society, and discusses briefly trends in fertility and mortality, housing and domestic technology, and developments in the education system. The chapter ends with some general discussion of farming and crofting. Some readers may wish to go straight to this section. More specific background to crofting, farm labouring and farming is given in the relevant subsequent chapters; some readers may wish to skip straight to these.

Industrialisation and its Impact on Rural Family Life

One of the most important background factors to be considered is the fact that we are discussing rural lives in the context of an industrial, not a rural, society. The minimal definition of industrialisation is an increase in the proportion of the workforce engaged in industry – in manufacture or, more loosely, in production processes other than agriculture. Industrialisation is associated with a quickening of the pace of technological innovation, increased production capacity and national income, larger workforces subjected to new techniques of management, and concentration of employment in urban centres.

The most intense period of British industrialisation is conventionally dated as lasting from the late eighteenth to the mid nineteenth century, although it is now accepted that economic growth was slower than previously believed (Crafts, 1988). It is generally accepted that the process of industrialisation in Scotland and England was simultaneous, sharing a common set of causes (Kendrick, 1983; Smout, 1972, p. 224).

In the mid nineteenth century Scottish industry was concentrated in the Central Belt (the low-lying land between Edinburgh and Glasgow), although spread more widely than it now is within that region. While towns had been growing rapidly since the start of the nineteenth century, much industry was still rural. Machines had not yet superseded hand work in some industries, and many machines were still water-powered. It should not be thought that factory production was the norm. Large proportions of the workforce were engaged in small establishments, using primitive equipment (Samuel, 1977). The rise in the scale of production, the technical changes, and the changes in the organisation of the labour process continued at an uneven pace in different industries into the twentieth century (Levitt & Smout, 1979).

Industrialisation is a process which brings with it accelerating population movement from rural to urban areas (urbanisation), the sprawl of inner city slums, and later, suburbs which engulf what was once countryside and farmland. Although rural depopulation and industrialisation go hand in hand, the link is not as simple as is often imagined. Smout (1986, p. 61) suggests that urbanisation and technical innovation in agriculture were mutually reinforcing trends. As agricultural workers left the land for industrial jobs, farmers were both increasingly forced to compete with wage levels in industry, and encouraged to replace workers with machines; as jobs and prospects shrank for workers on the land, more were encouraged to leave for the towns. However, this remains contentious. Collins (1987) argues, albeit with respect to England, that there was little evidence in the nineteenth century of farmers trying to reduce the size of their workforce with machines.

As late as 1861, when industrialisation was well under way, the majority of the Scottish population lived outside of towns with populations of 5,000 or above (Levitt & Smout, 1979, p. 6; Devine, 1988, p. 31). By the time of the 1911 Census, the population distribution was much closer to that of the present day. Thirty per cent of the Scottish population lived in the four cities of Glasgow, Edinburgh, Dundee and Aberdeen, while over 50 per cent of the population lived in towns of more than 10,000 inhabitants. The largest Scottish town of Glasgow was approaching a population of

FIGURE 1.1: Horse-drawn binders being used along with hand tools, Kinrosshire, *c.* 1900.

800,000 by 1911. Over the fifty-year period of 1861–1911, the profile of the rural population was shifting towards one in which the elderly were over-represented and young women particularly under-represented in rural areas, as the young people and especially young females sought employment elsewhere.

Since most of our farming and crofting interviewees had been recruited in rural areas, those who had resisted or been oblivious to the pull of the towns and cities were probably over-represented. But our interviewees also included some who took it for granted that they had to go away to the towns to get work when they were old enough to leave school. Those who stayed in the countryside and went into farming work had lives partially removed from changes associated with industrialisation. Many of their tools and techniques of work had been the same for generations. The tractor, which was to make such an impact on the later rural scene, was not a feature of childhood before the Second World War.

Industrialisation was associated with a rise in national income and a proliferation in the variety of goods and services available for purchase relative to previous times.[1] However, most of our rural interviewees show little evidence of having benefited from the fruits of industrial society. Apart from farmers near the top end of the rural social ladder, there seems to have been little spending of money on anything other than the bare essentials. Crofters and small farmers relying on their own labour had very little money to make use of on a day-to-day basis. Money was required for the rent, for boots, tools and food which could not be produced at home. Agricultural workers also had very modest disposable incomes. While they earned money wages and bought some of their supplies from itinerant merchants, part of their earnings came in the form of perquisites such as potatoes, milk or a tied house. The general economic backwardness of rural and remote areas of Scotland – a recurrent theme of this book – is testimony to the unevenness of change.

Industrialisation, Fertility and Mortality

Industrialisation in western societies was associated with a long-term decline in family size. This started in Britain in the second half of the nineteenth century, declining sharply in the 1880s, with the most dramatic fall occurring between 1911 and 1939. The national

birth rate did not decline until the 1860s, but this average con-
cealed considerable variation by social class. The upper-class birth
rate declined even before 1860, and this was followed by a fall in the
middle-class birth rate in the last two decades of the century. The
working-class birth rate generally declined much later. The largest
families throughout this period were found among miners and
'agricultural labourers' – the term used by the census to cover all
farm workers. However, the correlation of fertility with social class
is by no means perfect; for example, the family size of textile
workers had been low during most of the nineteenth century.

The causes behind the decline and the reasons for variation in
fertility behaviour and family size are a matter of considerable
debate among social demographers (Banks, 1954, 1981; Gilloran,
1985; Kemmer, 1990; Woods 1982, pp. 112–30). But most analysts
relate fertility behaviour to economic factors. The fertility of farm
workers remained higher than average and we consider this in
relation to their economic situation again in our final chapter.

Family limitation is generally related to improvements in standards of living. Such changes are associated with a rise in parental
aspirations for children. Industrialisation brought with it better
wages and a general rise in the standard of living, especially for
those with smaller families. The conditions of bringing up children
and settling them in some means of gaining a livelihood changed as
industrial capitalism encroached into the furthest reaches of Scotland, transforming the occupational structure and the relationship
between town and country.

Demographic imbalance – problems created by having too many
mouths to feed and too little productive land, or too few hands to
work the land – could have severely disruptive consequences for
both parents and children. Too many non-earning children made it
difficult for parents to feed and clothe them. On the other hand,
older children could contribute to bringing in food and/or money.
On small farms, too few children made it difficult for parents to run
a farm without bringing in paid workers which they could ill afford.
When an older son left school, a hired hand would be redundant,
not only on small, poor farms but on some larger ones as well.
Among farm workers it was often necessary for children to leave
home either to take jobs locally or, where none were available, to
leave the area, sometimes at as young as 13 years old.

During the nineteenth century, there was a fall in mortality in

Britain generally owing to improvements in public health in urban areas and because of dramatically improved control of epidemic disease; however, infant mortality remained high, particularly in poor urban districts, into the twentieth century. Class differences in mortality were marked and persistent. In 1911, for example, children of fathers in the Registrar-General's class v (e.g. general labourers) were twice as likely to die before they were one year old than those in class 1 (Banks, 1981, p. 123).

Problems of sanitation were not as acute in rural areas, hence the spread of certain diseases was less of a problem. Also, the chronic lack of fresh air and sunshine experienced by many city children was not a feature of rural life. Diet was probably better; country children were generally taller and heavier than their city peers (Smout, 1986, p. 80). Nevertheless, rural poverty was not at all wholesome. Overcrowded, damp, cold housing, primitive facilities (see the Royal Commission on Housing, 1917) and a limited, occasionally inadequate diet were features of life. Of the infectious diseases particularly rife in the cities, tuberculosis was the biggest killer of all. TB was not endemic in the Highlands until the late nineteenth century, but once introduced, it proved hard to eradicate (Smout, 1986, p. 120).

Housing and Domestic Technology

It is important to note that the modernisations and conveniences of domestic life associated with advanced industrial capitalism were slow in coming to the households of ordinary people, both urban and rural. By the late nineteenth century, middle-class and working-class families lived in different parts of the towns in very different housing situations. While the middle class had several rooms, the urban working-class majority typically lived in just one or two. The 1901 Census indicates that 58 per cent of Scottish families were living in dwellings of no more than two rooms. In 1911, 62 per cent of Glasgow's population lived in such dwellings. While urban middle-class households had their own piped water and water closet, in many working-class tenements several families shared a sink and privy.

Smout speaks of the worst rural housing being transformed between the 1880s and the 1930s (1986, p. 79). However, there was not much evidence in our interviews of what we would regard today as basic domestic facilities. Differences in size of house and facilities were clearly related to class position among our interviewees. Many of the crofters' cottages had been built by ancestors and their neighbours or kin using local stone. These had been added to as the family grew, sometimes by previous generations of the family. Most of the crofters had byres for the cattle under the same roof as the family's own dwelling. Facilities were basic.

While there were many regional variations, married farm servants generally had small tied cottages, necessitating the sharing of rooms and beds by variable numbers of children; single men working on large farms were allocated sleeping space in a bothy, outhouse or loft. By contrast, some employers were agreeably housed, a couple in mansions surrounded by large gardens, others with solid, stone houses situated close to the farm buildings, but quite separate from those of their married employees and the single men. The physical arrangements of housing clearly symbolised the organisation of work, its social relationships and the rewards associated with each of these social contexts.

While domestic technology was not very advanced in either urban or rural working-class homes, it remained basic for longer in the country. Keeping the house, and clothes and bodies clean was a low-technology, labour-intensive business. In every household water had to be carried, and wood had to be cut. In 'modern' farm cottages there was a solid fuel range for heating water and cooking – an enclosed fire incorporating a water tank, oven and hot plate. But in many houses, particularly in the Highlands, all cooking and water heating was done in vessels suspended over an open fire.

Our interviewees suggest that convenience foods were simply not available and in more remote areas there was no possibility of buying bread. Turning the limited range of available ingredients into a decent diet required considerable skill and effort. In the Highlands and Islands, regularly baked scones and oatcakes were the staple, rather than bread. These were baked on a griddle on an open hearth. Hunter suggests that by the 1930s mechants' vans were regularly visiting most crofting townships and 'there was jam, sugar, tea, bacon, canned beef, scones and biscuits where once there had been only oatmeal, herrings, potatoes and milk'. Interviewees suggest, however, that jam and scones were generally homemade rather than bought ready-made, and tinned meat and biscuits remained a luxury.

FIGURE 1.2:   Oatcakes on a griddle hanging from a device called a swey.

Education

The question of access to higher education and equal opportunity to gain qualifications has only become a public issue since the Second World War. Scots often take it for granted that their educational system has always allowed children of ability to do well. Historical research on the Scottish education system has exposed the mythical quality of this widely-acclaimed tradition of egalitarianism. The hero of the egalitarian version of the past is the 'lad of pairts' – the outstanding pupil who went from local school to university and beyond, despite an 'ordinary' background and the absence of state provision of universal secondary schooling and student grants. While such lads existed, they were likely to have had rather extraordinary family backgrounds which fostered learning and achievement, to have been nurtured in one of the outstanding schools, and to have been singled out by an outstanding dominie (Finn, 1983; Gray *et al.*, 1983; MacCrone *et al.*, 1982; MacPherson, 1983). Also, as the expression suggests, girls from such family backgrounds were not likely to be nurtured in this way (Corr, 1990; Paterson and Fewel, 1990). Indeed, some authors have argued that the Scottish education system was no more inherently egalitarian than that south of the border (Paterson, 1983).

In the first decades of this century the division between primary and secondary schooling in Scottish schools was still in flux. The leaving age was 14, with exemption from schooling permitted at 13. It is now the norm for Scottish pupils to do seven years of primary schooling followed by a minimum of four years of secondary schooling, taking pupils to a leaving age of 16. For those leaving at the minimum age at the beginning of this century, it was common for a pupil's education to take place in one school, an 'elementary' school, known to many just as 'the school'. At one time such schools could teach academic subjects to the level of certificated qualifications, although not all did so in practice. The idea that the outstanding pupil could do advanced academic work at the ordinary elementary school is an important component of the claim concerning the 'egalitarian' Scottish education system. But educational policy of the early twentieth century increasingly confined academic subjects to high schools. After 1903, pupils were required to pass a qualifying exam before they could go on to do 'certificate work', that is, academic work which was examined.

In the first decades of this century attendance at a high school was for a privileged minority. The overwhelming majority of working-class pupils left at 13 or 14 regardless of ability (Jamieson, 1990b). It was taken for granted that they would start earning and contributing to the household as soon as they could leave school. And for most rural pupils, a high school was a geographically remote option as well as a culturally and socially remote one. This was a time, then, when children of farm workers left at the minimum age and went straight into whatever work was available, while the children of wealthy farmers were often sent to be educated further in private schools.

The effective absence of working-class access to secondary education in the first half of this century did not cause obvious disdain for education itself. Education was neither blamed for the class divisions in the occupational system nor regarded as the solution. Alongside the myth of the exceptionally democratic Scottish education system, it has often been said of Scots that they particularly value education. This is perhaps half true for the first few decades of this century. Elementary education was valued, although for most it had no implications for their job prospects. The jobs for which the young were destined did not generally require certificates. Working-class jobs then, as now, were generally gender-segregated: jobs for boys and jobs for girls. But for both genders, getting on and earning some money within the constraints of the immediate class- and gender- segregated job market was more important than trying to get more out of the education system.

Farming in Scotland at the Turn of the Century

A thoughtful look at a topographical map of Scotland would be sufficient to suggest that particular regions might be distinctive in their agricultural use (see Map 1). It is conventional to identify three areas of mainland Scotland as marked out by their geographically related particular histories: 1. the Highlands and Islands; 2. the northern Lowland zone; 3. the southern Lowlands. However, within each of these categories there are marked differences between component parts. For example, the 'Lowlands' contain the largest area of readily cultivated fertile land in Scotland, but lowland hills are also more suited to sheep than to dairy or arable farming. Very large farms, at the leading edge of mechanisation, emerged first in the Lowland counties of Lothian and Berwickshire (Smout, 1986, p. 14) (see Map 2). By the mid nineteenth century these counties were already internationally renowned for their sophisticated farming techniques. The south-west, on the other hand, retained smaller and medium-sized farms much longer, and specialised in dairy farming rather than the mixed stock, grain and arable farming of the east.

THE HIGHLANDS AND ISLANDS

The Highlands and the Western Isles are not suited to large grain or arable farms. As in most of Scotland, those who owned the land and those who worked on it were not one and the same. This was a land of many tenant crofters working small amounts of land, and a few large landowners. The 'traditional' way of getting a living from a croft involved animal husbandry combined with the cultivation of small plots, supplemented by other food-generating and income-generating activities such as fishing, poaching, and waged labour on a casual or seasonal basis. This was subsistence farming: the holding was worked by household members – family labour rather than employees – and their produce was used to feed themselves.

The nineteenth century can be characterised by a bitter struggle between those wishing to live on the land and those owning the land – a struggle which continued into the present century. The extent to which 'the clearances' are responsible for the current depopulation of the Highlands is still debated (Smout, 1986, chapter 3). But there is no doubt about the extent of feeling against landowners aroused by the violent removal of people from their crofts and cottages to make way for large sheep farms. The Crofters' Act of 1886 and the Small Holding (Scotland) Act of 1911 gave security of tenure to crofters,[2] but not to those displaced to cottages with no land attached. The continued struggle for the right to be settled on a plot of land ultimately resulted in the Land Settlement (Scotland) Act of 1919. The outcome of these Acts was to make about 8,000 small holders secure tenants on their land (Leneman, 1989). However, the holding alone, even with judicious farming, was never sufficient to guarantee a reasonable living for the crofter household (Hunter, 1976, 1991).

FIGURE 1.3:   Uig, Lewis, showing the pattern of small fields typical of crofting for generations.

THE NORTHERN LOWLANDS

The northern Lowland zone is an arable, low-lying east-coast strip at its widest around the Moray Firth and further north in the eastern corner of Caithness. This was also a land of crofters, but there were important differences between crofting here and in the Highlands and Islands. The land was more fertile, and many peasant farmers had tenancy of sufficient land to make a decent living, at least in the early nineteenth century. Throughout the century peasant farmers were increasingly overshadowed by large capitalist farmers who did employ labour and were producing primarily for the market.[3] Ian Carter's gripping history of the region is the tale of the demise of subsistence agriculture as a viable way of life between the mid nineteenth and the early twentieth century. It was not being thrown off the land by ruthless landlords that was the issue but rather an inability to compete against capitalist farmers in changing economic conditions (Carter, 1979).

THE SOUTHERN LOWLANDS

The agricultural area of the southern Lowlands lies between the Scottish/English border and the line of the Forth and Clyde valleys. This area has always had the geographical advantage not only of being the largest area of land suitable for grain and arable farming, but also of enjoying proximity to the largest markets – the cities and industrial towns of the Central Belt between Glasgow and Edinburgh. This was a region of tenant farmers and large landowners, particularly in the counties of Berwickshire, Roxburghshire, Peeblesshire and Selkirkshire. According to the 1874 land census, for example, the estates of two aristocratic families accounted for over a third of the county of Roxburgh (Morris, 1989). The large farms of these Border counties were mainly leased from the big estates by capitalist farmers or, more exceptionally, owned by 'bonnet lairds' – small landowners who farmed their own land – turned capitalist farmers.

Changes in techniques of farming and the technology of farming have been particularly dramatic in the case of large-scale capitalist farms, since it is here that economies of scale permit the necessary investment in expensive agricultural equipment. Increased mechanisation has meant less work for agricultural workers. The change has been most dramatic in the twentieth century: 'in Scotland in

1840 it took 22 man-days a year to tend an acre of barley; by 1914, it was down to 12, and by 1958, to only 3' (Smout, 1986, p. 61).

NOTES
1.   It is generally believed that there were two periods of real increase in the wages of agricultural workers – the 1880s and 1890s, and the 1940s (Armstrong, 1988, pp. 120–21, 218, 246–7).
2.   Following the 1886 Act, holdings with an annual rent not exceeding £30 could be registered as a croft; following the 1911 Act, this was extended to include land with an annual rent not exceeding £50 or 'inbye' land – land occupied and worked – not exceeding 50 acres.
3.   Parts of the North-East became famous for their beef cattle, as the capitalist farmers responded to demand for meat from the urban markets of England.

CHAPTER TWO

Children in Crofting Communities

THE ECONOMIC CONTEXT

Opportunities for Making a Living

THE CONSTRAINTS AND OPPORTUNITIES for gaining a living in crofting communities were partly determined by the conditions of crofting itself – natural factors, like the amount and quality of land, the geographical position and climate, and social factors like the willingness of neighbours to lend a hand and the resources they had to lend. But crofting alone did not typically provide a decent living, and the access that crofting households had to alternative means of earning a livelihood could be even more important to their standard of living than crofting as such. Supplementary forms of self-provisioning, such as poaching, were often significant, but the range of opportunities for paid employment were of particular importance.

Our 'crofting' interviewees[1] came from two broad areas of Scotland which provided somewhat different opportunities for making a living (see Appendix Two). The first of these was the north-west Highlands and Islands, and the second was the area around Speyside (the valley of the river Spey forms the border between Morayshire and Banffshire before branching into the east of Inverness-shire) and the southern parts of Morayshire. The basic distinction between the two was the closer access to the sea and to fishing in the north-west and Western Isles. Fishing provided an important component of the diet. Many Highland households ate fish more regularly than meat. Fishing as a source of income made a substantial contribution to the crofting economy in these areas. Indeed, the Napier Commission inquiry into crofting conditions in 1883 found that crofters derived a larger annual income from the sea than from the land (Hunter, 1976, p. 109). In the 1880s, between 500 and 600 Lewis boats, with crews of six or eight, fished off this island in the Western Isles (Hunter, *ibid.*).

Mrs Gillies, born in 1899, our respondent from Lewis whose interview is reported at length at the end of this chapter, came from an exceptionally well endowed crofting household. She describes how her household had three clocks and a parlour with a sofa. Besides these visible trappings of wellbeing, the difference between her and her neighbours was reflected in the fact that she went on to high school after the school-leaving age. The prosperity of Mrs Gillies' family was most likely the result of the success and good fortune of her grandfather and father as owners and skippers of a fishing boat, coupled with their security on their croft as guaranteed by the Crofters' Act. Although she talks of herring fishing at length, and clearly her father brought home herring for the table, it was likely to have been white fish rather than herring which her father and grandfather fished commercially. By the end of the nineteenth century, coastal fishing for white fish, cod and ling was a winter activity centred on Lewis and the Western Isles.

Not all in Lewis fared as well as the Gillies household. Despite legislation to protect crofters, some, whose ancestors had been cleared from crofts, remained the tenants of cottages with little or no usable land and without the capital for a boat or fishing gear[2]. The herring industry, with its seasonal demand for extra labour, was an important source of income to such households. Commercial herring fishing required larger, more expensively equipped boats than the offshore white fish industry. Crofters from the Western Isles did not own boats or nets suited to commercial herring fishing but, as Mrs Gillies describes, were prepared to travel by boat to Stornoway for employment. In the season from May through the summer months, east-coast drifters travelled to the west of Scotland, Shetland and down the east Scottish and English coast (Buchan; Thompson, 1983). The poorer the crofter, the more reliant the household was on paid employment, and the more vulnerable they were to a slump in the demand for casual labour. By 1900 the herring fishing industry had already experienced serious reverses of fortune. Apart from fishing, there were few, if any, opportunities for wage-earning in the tiny settlements, which meant that in most cases young people were obliged to leave home to make a living. In the case of Islanders, this meant going at least as far as the mainland. Many migrated to the nearest cities, and some sought a new life in emigration. Even the relatively well-off among the fisherman/crofters were not entirely in charge of their economic context. Although boats were owned by Lewis men, they never had complete control of the white fish industry, being at the mercy of the curers to whom they sold their catch.

In comparison to Mrs Gillies, the more modest level of material well-being experienced by the other crofter whom we report at length is more typical of crofters as a whole. In Speyside, where Mr Geddes, born in 1900, was largely brought up, fishing was not important as a means of making money. The small barrel of salt herrings and the dried and salted cod he talks about would have to be bought in. In this area the railway, the large estates and particularly the shooting lodges were the most likely sources of employment. Further north in Morayshire where Mr Geddes was born on the edge of the east Lowlands, the 'muckle farmers' were a regular source of casual employment during the harvest. Mr Geddes describes his family as fortunate because his father was employed by the railways. As a young man before his father's death, he alternated periods of working away from home on neighbouring shooting lodges with periods on the croft. He also describes a variety of other forms of casual labour which he used to generate income as a young adult – carting stones for road mending, clearing dead wood for the forester, ploughing for those who did not have a horse of their own. In addition, the whole household was involved in catering for summer visitors, for which purpose they had to move out of their own house. Although never well-off, the range of strategies that he and his siblings employed kept the household going without exclusive dependence on a particular industry. This was despite the burden of a severely handicapped sister, who needed their mother's constant attention.

Much of the work Mr Geddes did would not have been regarded as work which could have been done by a young woman. Crofters' daughters who were not needed at home often had little choice but to go into domestic service. Once in service, they could continue to contribute to the household economy by sending or bringing money and goods home if they could afford to do so.

Cultivation, Animal Husbandry, Self-provisioning and Buying-in

The historian of crofting, James Hunter, has suggested a number of changes in the intensity and style of crofting in the first decades of this century. He indicates that when paid employment has been readily to hand, then crofts are less intensively cultivated. Also he suggests that once food could be bought-in, crofters shifted from producing food for consumption to rearing food for the market – for example, the rearing of calves for cash rather than growing potatoes as a staple.

Most of our interviewees were brought up before the 1930s, although there were some younger exceptions. Mrs MacDiarmid (born 1929) was brought up on South Uist in the 1930s; Mr McClelland (born in 1925) was brought up in the same period on the west coast of the mainland, and Mairia MacKay was exceptional, being born in 1951. Clearly, a small number of respondents from different locations and various decades are insufficient to judge the pattern of change, but the interviews do clearly illustrate the juggling between generating cash to buy in produce and directly providing for the household from the land. Mrs Mac-Diarmid, although one of the 'younger' interviewees, emphasised self-provisioning, although she also acknowledges that the staple food, oatmeal, was bought in.

> We depended on the cattle. We milked the cows and we made the butter and the cheese, crowdie, fed the calves. After we had taken the cream off, we gave the rest to the calves along with some [cattle] cake, and that kept them going. Had our own butter, salted in big jars, our cheese for the winter ... we never had to go to a shop for butter or cheese. And the eggs, of course. We had hens – forgot about them! Sold the eggs. Paid for the grocery bill with the eggs.
>
> *Who was in charge of the hens?*
>
> Oh, just the housewife ...
>
> *Women's work? ...*
>
> Yes.
>
> *Unless it was a bachelor?*
>
> Oh, well, if it was a bachelor he would do all that for himself.
>
> *I've heard stories about taking eggs to someone else's hen for sitting on ...*

Yes, that's right, they always used to swap their eggs. If you had a nice big cockerel, if you wanted a setting of eggs, you would have a different breed of hen.

You might take him along with you too?

I suppose you could; somebody else who didn't have a cockerel ... would let them have a whiley of the cockerel.

You would have chicken meat?

Oh, yes. Always reared the chickens and the cockerels we used to kill off when they were seven, eight weeks old, for the summer visitors, you know.

MRS MACDIARMID, BORN 1929

The experience of Mrs MacDiarmid's family was fairly representative. The produce from the croft (particularly calves and lambs) earned some cash for the rent; some (particularly eggs) was bartered for groceries, and also provided much of the basic food required for subsistence (milk, some meat, eggs, potatoes, vegetables, and sometimes meal). It should be noted, however, that her family earned extra cash by boarding summer visitors.

Cows were kept on crofts throughout the Highlands and Islands according to all our interviewees. Depending on the size of the croft and needs of the household there would be one, two or three milking cows. Mrs Gillies, an older respondent, describes how the calves were sold or kept to replace an ageing cow. Most crofts also had a few sheep, and some had their own horse for carting and ploughing. The staple food described by Mrs MacDiarmid was oatmeal, as elsewhere in the Highlands and Islands.

We used to get that in half-hundredweight bolls [61 lbs, 25.40 kg] oatmeal. Everything was bought by the half-hundredweight... We killed our own cow, we salted it for the winter. Salt herring and killed a sheep and salted that for the winter.

Did you keep pigs?

No, we didn't have pigs, no.

MRS MACDIARMID, BORN 1929

Its purchase may have been paid for by the sale of calves and it may have been a strategic decision to rear calves and not oatmeal, but even according to older respondents, most crofts were unable to provide all their own meal.

Potatoes were also an important staple and, being a higher-yield crop than grain, it is not surprising that in many crofts arable land was devoted primarily to potatoes. Mrs Gillies (born in 1899)

FIGURE 2.1: Peggi MacRae, milking outside her home, South Uist, 1920s.

remembered being kept off school to help plant potatoes. Poor crofts grew little else. Of the crops which Mr McClelland listed, only potatoes were for human consumption. The croft is only credited with keeping the household in milk and potatoes, and the animals in oats and hay.

> There was very little cash when I was young, it was all hard times for everyone.
>
> *Did you produce most of what you ate on the croft?*
>
> Oh, no! We wouldn't produce close to what we ate but we had two milking cows and we had to have them calving so that we had milk all the year round. If there was a period where there was a crofter without milk, it was quite likely that his neighbour did have milk and they would give to each other. There was no milk coming into the area except that which we produced ourselves. We were dependent on the croft for milk, and for potatoes.
>
> MR MCCLELLAND, BORN 1925

Hunter suggests that the traditional crafts like spinning, tailoring and shoemaking declined from 1900 as it became possible to buy ready-made items. While this was undoubtedly true, a considerable amount of making and mending at home persisted well into this century. A couple of our families sent the wool which they had hand-sheared to a factory for making into cloth or for spinning. Mairi, born in South Lewis in 1951, remembered wearing clothes knitted by her mother from their own sheep's wool in the 1950s and '60s.

> When we clipped the sheep in the summer time my mother used to send the wool, I think it was to Edinboro [Edinburgh] to a mill, and she would receive back wool, spun, in place of the sheep's wool. And she knitted our jerseys and our skirts and our knee socks, our hats and scarves and gloves and things for the winter time... It was rather itchy. I don't believe I would wear it today. But in those days, you had to wear it and you got used to it. Maybe you would get a vest or something to protect your back and your chest, but your arms and your legs meant nothing, you know. We got Harris Tweed because there were mills in Stornoway itself, where you could buy it pretty cheap. We had our treat, we had our Sunday skirt of tweed which you had to look after and you had your one pair of shoes ... oh, yes, no sandshoes, no nothing... Wellingtons or nothing at all.
>
> MAIRI, BORN 1951

Much was said by our interviewees about making the most of the physical environment, making ends meet and helping others to do the same. For outdoor work, crofters do not work to the clock, but to the weather, just as crofters fishing for their own families work to the tide. According to Mr McClelland, who took over the croft from his father,

> The crofter isn't working for an employer. The crofter, I think you'll find, is working to weather. If it was a good day you worked from dawn till dusk, if it was a bad day – as most of them are on the West Coast ... [laughs] ... if the weather was good for hay making, you got on with it as long as you could – we still do ... If it's good weather, we work till ten or eleven at night.
>
> MR MCCLELLAND, BORN 1925

But the indoor work of knitting, making and mending, mainly done by women, was fitted around outdoor work and could result in constant occupation. This work remained as essential for the well-being of the household as forms of economic activity undertaken outside the home.

Hunting and Gathering

The physical environment and cycle of the seasons dominated the content of outdoor economic activity, though social factors intervened. As Mrs Gillies' interview indicates, fishing was a winter activity which ended in May (by law); this was followed by spring planting, then the gathering of peat, which was followed by harvesting. Throughout the year, men, women and children would be involved in other activities designed to supplement their diet or keep them warm. There were gathering activities – for instance, collecting tangle for fertiliser,[3] blaeberries[4] on the moors (Inverness-shire), cutting peat for fuel and gathering firewood. Many respondents mentioned the hunting activities of men and boys spoken about by Mrs MacDiarmid.

> We had rabbits, of course. My father trapped them, all winter, that was the winter's work.
>
> *The boys?*
>
> Oh yes, my brother did.
>
> *Shooting, fishing?*
>
> Mmmm yes, there would be poaching [laughter]. Geese, ducks, cormorants, they used to go and kill them, eat them. Eider duck. We were never hungry. Had plenty to eat.
>
> MRS MACDIARMID, BORN 1929

Poaching appears to have been quite common, and although punishable by law, was considered an attractive and viable way of providing variety in the diet. Generations of Highlanders and Islanders, aware that their ancestors were violently deprived of land and sustenance during the Clearances, may have felt little moral obligation to 'honour' the 'rights' of alien landlords.

THE CULTURAL CONTEXT

Economic Reciprocity

It is impossible to separate the cultural and economic aspects of crofting life. Necessary activities for survival and physical well-being could also be occasions for social intercourse. Getting a house built is a good example. Until quite recently, crofters built their

FIGURE 2.2: Cutting peat, Aberdeenshire in the 1880s, as it is still cut in some parts of Scotland to the present day.

houses if one was required for a young couple about to be married (often they inherited the home after having shared it with the young man's parents). Mairi told us about her maternal grandmother's case.

> The village we lived in, everybody helped their neighbours with anything and everything that needed to be done. She had seven brothers, my granny, my mother's mother, and they helped build the house with the neighbours. And the next couple that were to get married, they were to give a hand with their house. Just a two-roomed house... When there was word of marriage, they started the house.
>
> They used to take the stone for miles around, looking for stones to build a house with. And we sowed corn, and that's where some of the thatching came from... There was heather involved too, as well as the corn. They used to make the corn stacks and dry it out and they used this for the thatching. They used the heather for dampness, I would imagine. The heather growing on each house, and sometimes, if your house was situated to the four winds – if there was no shelter to the house – it needed to be thatched every year. But there were some houses that would last for three or four years if they had a hill behind them. If they were in a glen ... my granny's house was in a kind of a glen, it wasn't exposed to the four winds, so it got done roughly once every four years.
>
> MAIRI, BORN 1951

Mr McClelland was one of our younger respondents and had served as a soldier in World War II. On being demobbed, he was employed in forestry work before taking over the croft several years later. His remarks on the nature of crofting work, the spirit of co-operation and reciprocity which appears to have been universal in similar communities, reflect his ability to make comparisons with what he had observed elsewhere.

Did you have any horses?

Yes, my father kept a horse, and a neighbouring crofter kept another horse and they teamed up for ploughing. With crofting, it was team work all along.

Would you like to elaborate on that?

Well, each crofter ... they all helped each other out, shared their duties as best they could, gathering sheep for clipping, they all combined, clipped each other's sheep, helped each other at hay making. The corn was all cut by hand and hand sheafed, so they would club together for hand sheafing. A much more friendly and more neighbourly type of existence than it is today. They're all out for themselves today ... Everyone's more independent today. In those days they were dependent on their neighbours, very dependent. There was more ... community.

A community of mutual interests?

They had mutual interests, they shared each other's joys and sorrows you might say, much more so than they do today. I mean, in a community this size [population about 500] they all know each other but they're not as involved with each other as they were at that time.

Do you think it was mainly a case of mutual need?

The basis of it all was that they were dependent on each other.

MR MCCLELLAND, BORN 1925

Mr McClelland's comments illustrate well some of the difficulties in trying to separate out different aspects of crofting life since they were interrelated to a degree not experienced in modern urban life, or even among the farming and agricultural labouring families whose lives will be described in later chapters.

The swapping of eggs and the sharing of the cockerel described by Mrs MacDairmid is another example of mutual help. Economic reciprocity took many forms, including the sharing of food. For instance, when the men of a family were away fishing during the week (or the father was a merchant seaman), households with no shortage of hands would help their families, if help was needed. When the fish or wages arrived back, the crofters who had helped would be rewarded.

Gaelic Language and Culture

For our West Coast crofters, Gaelic was their first language, including our youngest respondent, who had never uttered a word of English before going to school. Yet even for the oldest respondents Gaelic was a subordinate culture. English was essential if you 'wanted to get on'. In recognition of this some parents censored their own speech in order to encourage English in their children. Mr McClelland (born in 1925) remembered that his parents never talked anything to each other but Gaelic, but they used only English when addressing their children – with the exception of his older brother. He spoke English to his parents and Gaelic to his grandmother, who could not speak English at all. At the time our respondents were being educated, Gaelic was not taught in school at all, so many had never learned to read or write Gaelic. Moreover, at school the teacher may have known no Gaelic and the child no English. In so far as Gaelic culture was kept alive, this was largely done orally, and particularly through the telling of 'the old stories'.

It was quite common for the children from crofting communities to have a range of relatives living in the neighbourhood. This was not surprising since the extended family usually had long associations in the area. Provided that the parents' brothers and sisters had not died or emigrated, there was likely to be regular, even daily, visiting. Just as crofting people got together to help each other when necessary, economic reciprocity was paralleled socially. Many respondents commented that neighbours would frequently drop in on the long winter evenings to work at their knitting ('nobody bought socks'), spinning, to mend nets or creels and to tell stories. This was most common in the West where Gaelic was the common language and where the practice of telling 'the old stories' helped bind children into their cultural heritage. It was only when they went to school first at the age of 5 that children were obliged to speak English.

The Moral Community: Sunday Observance

One interesting feature of life in most crofting areas was the strictness with which Sunday was kept.[5] What is even more interesting is that whereas most children from crofting areas endured a Sunday in which they were obliged to follow the rigorous standards of their elders, this was not always the case. There were also differences between the Gaelic-speaking areas of the West and the predominantly English-speaking East, although more or less strict parents could be found in each case.

Mr McClelland (West), a younger interviewee brought up in the 1930s, said that the whole family went to the Free Church twice every Sunday like all other members of the congregation. When he was a boy, there used to be boatloads of people coming in from villages from miles around up the loch. The church used to be packed to capacity on Communion Sunday. After church, the visitors dined with the villagers. Since no work was allowed on Sundays, the meal had to be prepared on the previous day and heated up. Other people said how they had to polish everything, including their shoes, on a Saturday night.

Although Mr McClelland and his brothers and sisters had to attend church, he said 'we daren't go outside on a Sunday' in case they were observed. While they might have liked to play a ball game outside, these were strictly banned in the community generally. However, it seems that his parents had some sympathy with their children's needs and allowed them to read books other than the Bible while observing the strictures imposed by religion. Mrs MacDiarmid was a similar age and also from the West, but from a Catholic family which did not keep Sunday strictly in the same way. They were allowed to go outside and play but knew that other parents were much less liberal. No such accommodation to the exuberance of childhood came from Mrs Currie's parents (Morayshire), who were also members of the 'Wee Frees' when she was young in the 1920s. When she and her brothers and sisters attended church without their parents it was expected that the children would tell them the text when they returned to make sure they had been. Mr Campbell, born in 1910 (Speyside), had to be quiet, and was expected to read the Bible at night, but might be allowed to go for a walk after church. There was no visiting on Sunday in his part of Inverness-shire.

THE HOUSEHOLD

The broader economic and cultural background characteristic of crofting communities has been sketched out above. In order to understand the strategies of households, their work organisation and divisions of labour associated with gender and generation, it is necessary to know something about the fabric of the houses themselves and the comforts and facilities they offered.

Housing and Domestic Technology

The type of primitive house that Mairi grew up in in the 1950s and 1960s was the norm in the Western Isles at the beginning of the century. Her childhood home had thick stone walls, double walls 8 inches apart and lined with clay. The doors and windows were deeply recessed for protection against the winter gales. Older

versions of her house – the famous 'black house' – had the hearth
and fire in the middle of the floor in her grandmother's generation.
In Mairi's home, however, the hearth was built into the side of the
house. The co-operative building of houses like hers and her grandmother's is described above.

> We lived in a black house, in a thatched house, stone. The floor was
> never even. The hearth had a stone floor, barely raised from the
> ground. There was a contraption, called a stroughlie in Gaelic (in
> English [Scots], swey), bearing a hook and chain, which carried a
> large black cauldron with three legs.

Was it your grandmother's house you lived in as a child?

> No, I lived in my mother's house. My father was the youngest of a
> family of nine. In the olden days, the oldest son got the croft and the
> house and everything if he wasn't married. But if he was married and
> had his own home, it fell to the youngest child, why I don't know, it
> was the youngest son who fell heir to the house. That's how my father
> got his house. My father and mother when they married and moved
> into the house, my granny and grandmother [paternal grandparents]
> were still in it. It was what you would call a three bedroomed house,
> three sections, three partitions.
>   When my father's parents lived in it, there was only the one room
> and when their family got bigger, well when the family was getting
> bigger, they were puttin' more bricks to the house and making it
> longer and this was the extra bedroom ... and the extra bedroom.
> With having so many in the family they had to extend because the
> children and the parents couldn't stay in the same room. But the
> children were always in a bedroom and the parents stayed in what
> you call a lounge, but what we called a living room. The room they ate
> in, and the room the fire was in. They had their bed kinda sunk into
> the wall, and it had curtains round it for their own privacy. Ye know.

MAIRI, BORN 1951

She went on to explain that the animals were kept under the same
roof as the family and that it was possible to walk from the living
quarters straight into the byre. This was divided into two sections,
with the hens in one area and the cows in the other. The cows were
kept inside only in the winter when the weather was really rough.
At other times, they were allowed to graze where they wanted.
  The buildings reflect a form of building ideally suited to the
harsh climate, inhospitable stony land and the organisation of work
in the Western Isles. This type of dwelling, housing both people
and animals, was common in crofting areas, and was similar to that

which had housed our interviewees' ancestors for generations. On Speyside and in Morayshire, animals were housed separately. What descriptions we have indicate that domestic arrangements were not much more comfortable than in the West.

Virtually everyone used a swey for cooking and for baking the ubiquitous oatcakes. Few households had an oven. This was sometimes through choice rather than lack of the wherewithal. Mr Geddes, a Speyside crofter, talks of putting in a range for the summer visitors and taking it out again when they left. In consequence bread was rarely baked; oatcakes, pancakes and griddle scones were the norm.

Water typically had to be carried, as there was no piped water into the house. Water always required heating for personal washing and household cleaning work of all kinds. In areas where there was peat, it was used for heating and cooking.

Household Composition

Most crofting (and family farming) fathers had remained in the homes of their birth, having inherited the use of the land and house as a going concern. Some mothers had inherited the croft, and in such cases it was the father (her husband) who had moved in. While most of the crofting households of our respondents appear to have been nuclear in structure during their childhoods, a few households were three-generational at some stage of the family life-cycle, and one included other kin as well. These kin came and went according to seasonal requirements, since their services were needed on the land, or because of their special needs.

There were other types of household, suggesting that crofting communities varied greatly in respect of household composition. For example, Mairi's mother ran the croft and household effectively as a single parent family, since the father spent virtually all his time at sea in the Merchant Navy (she was not aware as a young child that she had a father). Mrs Fleming (born in 1907) was brought up in a different type of fatherless household. She was a foster child who had joined the household of a widow and her adult daughter who was sometimes away from home, working as a domestic servant. Mrs MacDiarmid's household included both parents and brothers and sisters, but also included members who were not biological kin. In this case they were a young male and a young female servant.

The average number of children in our crofting families was smaller than the mean completed family size of 7.04 listed in the 1911 Census for crofters. Our sample included two households in which there was a single child (one of them fostered). In the typical large families, some children had already left home by the time younger children were born, this being a period when the vast majority of children left school at 14 years of age and immediately started full-time work.

Divisions of Labour: Generation and Gender

In almost all our 'crofting' interviewees' family households, it was the parents who were in charge, but in Mrs Gillies' case (born 1899), it was the grandfather who was the head of the household and she knew other similar three-generation family households. It was the grandparents who got the best bed and a bought mattress. As she said, adult children 'accepted the word of the old people', just as younger ones obeyed their parents, their grandparents and, indeed, elders in general – including older siblings. At the same time, however, the male head was not typically the everyday authority as far as children and young people were concerned. Mrs Gillies' household was not atypical, in that the mother 'doled out' the jobs and was the one who had to be obeyed at once.

Children performed a variety of tasks for their parents, both on the croft and in the house. Any income earned by children was not for their personal consumption. As in working-class households of the time, urban or rural, it was a contribution to the family economy. In the most remote crofting communities there was little opportunity for children to contribute to the household by earning cash. In some areas, however, children could earn cash in the shooting season as beaters.[6] Mr Geddes explained how money from the beating was used to buy winter clothes. He also spoke of gathering and selling the wild blaeberries. Whether or not there were ways of earning cash, children typically contributed to the household economy through their labour. Mrs Gillies claimed that crofters' children did not have to do outwork, though in fact she gave several examples of jobs which she herself did, such as stacking peats, planting potatoes, going for water, driving the cattle and looking after other children. Her apparently contradictory statements are explicable because children were never expected to do the whole range of crofting work; only very particular jobs were given to children.

The jobs listed by Mrs Gillies were commonly mentioned as children's jobs by crofters. Other respondents listed collecting seaweed to use as manure (Fleming, born 1907, West Coast), clearing the pebbles from the field (McClelland, born 1925, West Coast) and taking a turn on the pounder or handle of the butter churn (Campbell, born 1910, Speyside; Firth, born 1899, West Coast). It is likely that there was considerable variation in the amount of work children did, by season (there was much less work to do in winter since it was dark so much of the time), and by their age. Certainly by early teens, all of the children were responsible for what would be regarded as adult tasks and no-one 'got off' helping to contribute to the livelihood of the family household as a whole.

In general, household membership carried with it expectations of contributing one's labour, in the same way that membership of the community created ties of economic and social reciprocity. As Mr McClelland remarked, 'the children of course were very handy for getting all those little jobs done'. Expectations of adults were met by children without much in the way of rebellion. We asked Mr Firth how the parents got their children to do all the work they did and he said, 'You just went and did it . . . you reverenced them, you reverenced the people. And when we were in school that was taught us too in school.'

Tasks typically varied by sex as well as age. Mrs Gillies, for example, remembered that the jobs she and her brothers did were not the same; boys did not drive cattle or fetch water, but they were expected to tether rogue sheep – a job which girls never did. This reflected a division of labour between adult men and women. Mrs Gillies' description of getting the peats exemplifies this. Peat is cut with a special tool in thick rectangular slices down the side of a bank. It is then thrown from the foot of the bank up on to the turf growing on the top of the bank. It lies there in little piles until it has been dried out by good weather. It is then stacked at the bank to protect it from bad weather until it can be carried home and stacked again. In Mrs Gillies' testimony, men removed the turf from the top of the bank and did the cutting. Women threw the peats and carried them home in wicker creels on their backs.

FIGURE 2.3:   Woman carrying a creel full of seaweed, Lewis.

According to a number of accounts, the stacking was often done by children.

The extent to which men and women, boys and girls had different jobs should not, however, be exaggerated. Although the division of labour Mrs Gillies describes was the general rule for peat-cutting, it seems that women cut peats when men were not readily available, just as a bachelor living alone would do 'women's work'. Moreover, a number of respondents reflecting on their past saw the crofters' divisions of labour as 'modern' because of the extent to which women were involved in a wide range of out-work tasks rather than being confined to domestic work. Also, divisions of labour between boys and girls which operated in Mrs Gillies' household did not operate with equal rigidity in many other households where boys did fetch water and herd cattle, for example. The north east poet Charles Murray also documents the existence of boy herds (see 'The Whistle', Murray, 1927). Nevertheless, there were jobs within the crofting context which were exclusively male, most notably fishing, and some domestic work was near-exclusively female. It was very rare for men or boys to do housework. For example, Mr Campbell laughed when asked if he helped his mother with her domestic work and said he had 'plenty of other work'. The work he described was also done by women and girls in some households but not, as in his case, to the exclusion of housework. He learned how to milk at the age of 12 and gradually took on the main responsibility for the cows: cleaning out the byre, putting the cattle out for the day, bringing them in at night in summer, and feeding them all winter when they did not go out to grass.

Parent-Child Relationships

It is not possible to identify a distinctive 'crofter' style of parent/child relationship on the basis of our interviews. Perhaps this is not surprising, given the diversity among our respondents in terms of place of upbringing and year of birth. However, like Paul Thompson, we believe that no such single style could be identified. There are two reasons for this which we particularly wish to emphasise.

Firstly, the economic realities of this distinctive mode of subsistence farming alone did not determine the quality of parent/child relationships. The social and moral context of a particular household has to be considered. The strict religiosity practised by Sabbatarians in some parts of the Highlands required the firm exercise of parental authority. Parents had to be sufficiently severe to contain childish exuberance on Sundays when there was no place for singing, whistling or running around. This was the case regardless of whether obedience was also required in order to ensure economic survival. However, not all crofters were strict Sabbatarians. Mrs McDiarmid, for example, whose parents were Roman Catholic and who was brought up on South Uist, said that although no work was done on Sunday, her parents were not strict: 'we could go outside and play ... we weren't kept inside the way that some people [were]'.

Secondly, the economic realities could and did vary considerably between crofting households. In some households the contribution of children was crucial to the standard of living, and hence 'doing as they were told' arguably had a particular importance. Mr Geddes tried to make this clear to us through the specific example of how earnings at 'the beating' paid for winter clothes, and in his general statement: 'When you came to any age at all, you knew you had to do it or else live very soberly indeed, and dress even more soberly.' Children did not necessarily have to be told what to do; they could see their help was needed and wanted to participate in the adult world.

It was not necessarily the case that the poorer the croft the more was demanded of children. A very small croft in an isolated area with few opportunities for casual work did not always afford a wealth of opportunities for children to participate. On the other hand, a large croft generated more work. Mrs Gillies was brought up on a prosperous croft but, like other children, she did a number of chores for the croft. Despite being interested in her education and encouraging her to stay on at school, her mother did not shelter her from crofting work, but both told her what to do and complained that she did not do enough, 'always having her nose stuck in a book'. As she states, Mrs Gillies feared rather than loved her mother. The elder Mrs Gillies' treatment of her daughter was observed by a neighbour who tried to intercede in the unfairness of her criticisms. We are not told what difference this might have made, but other parts of the interview indicate that Mrs Gillies' mother was 'a goer' [in Mrs Gillies' own words] who was prepared to be more demanding of her children than her neighbours were. Her father, on the other hand, was considered to be gentle and easy-going, and the children took advantage of his gentleness.

Mrs Gillies' interview also provides insight into the relationships between generations among adults, as well as indicating the position of elders generally. Power and authority inescapably rested on age and tradition. It bears repeating that it was her grandfather who was head of the household, and this was the case in other families in the area.

They didn't throw their old people out, ever. Usually it was the woman who came into the household, for the eldest son, but they accepted the word of the old people and if they didn't, they were the odd ones out, they were ostracised if they didn't conform to what the elders wanted ... there was this great respect for old age ...

MRS GILLIES, BORN 1899

The point is not that the aged were not thrown out, so much as it was their homes to which one son brought a wife and later established the next generation – a situation clearly very different from societies in which adult children set up homes independently of their parents and rely on their own wage-earning to get a living. When elderly parents are obliged to rely on their adult children for accommodation, and when wages provide the only basis of getting a living, the power relationships are reversed. Several respondents commented briefly on the deep respect paid to age, indicating the unthinkability of challenging their opinion or their orders for work to be done.

Considering the combined power of the church, the school and elders in general, it is not at all surprising that children did what they were told, or indeed, never thought to question that their behaviour should be helpful and that family members, like the village community, should work as a team, in co-operation – even if some members of the team were more equal than others. In Chapters Three and Four we will return to the question of parent/child relationships. In the meantime, the fully transcribed interviews of Mrs Gillies and Mr Geddes are presented.

INTERVIEWS WITH CHILDREN OF CROFTING FAMILIES

The people we have chosen to represent the range of experience of children brought up on crofts are a woman from the Western Isles and a man who was born and brought up on Speyside in Inverness-shire. Both lived their first fourteen years prior to the First World War, but Mrs Gillies' household was much better off than that of many crofters at that time. The interviews demonstrate something of the variety of lifestyles contained within crofting communities in two culturally distinct areas of Scotland. A brief introduction to each person precedes the transcription.

Mrs Gillies, born 1899, Isle of Lewis

Mrs Gillies is a widow who lives with her daughter in a large industrial Scottish town. Both pursue their interests in Scottish culture and history. Their home reflects these interests clearly in the paintings and ornaments which stand in the many nooks and crannies of the rambling building situated in a picturesque close. Mrs Gillies' account of her childhood is full of drama and anecdote, analysis and descriptive detail. This reflects her particular interest in Gaelic culture, a subject she studied at university as a young woman. Life in isolated crofting areas was dependent on co-operative labour and a very low level of technology. Mrs Gillies gives us lively descriptions of working life in particular, showing how household members, kin and neighbours co-operated in order to survive on a day-to-day basis on land and at sea.

Mrs Gillies was born in 1899, the eldest of eight children – three boys and five girls. Like several of our interviewees, she was brought up in a scattered settlement, isolated from any town, in an area in which generations of her ancestors had lived – or left. Both her mother and father had been born in the area and had grown up nearby. Indeed, the household was a three-generational one, since her paternal grandparents still lived with them in the house in which her father had been born and brought up. Although her father had had many brothers and sisters, all were dead by the time she was born. Her maternal grandfather was drowned together with his two sons in a tragic incident.

Mrs Gillies' parents had more land than most crofters and their house was more comfortably furnished than others in the community. As a child she was spared the more grinding hard work done by some crofting children, like picking stones from the field. When Mrs Gillies' father had to give up his main source of money income – fishing – they were able to buy a shop and to provide transport services for the rest of the village. They were also able to send their daughter to university. She regarded herself as atypical because of her parents' relatively favourable material and social situation in the community – a fact she establishes early in the interview.

Interview with Mrs Gillies

(Note: the words of the interviewer are shown in italics)

We had a large barn, a stable for the horse and we had an outside loo there which was actually under the same roof as the stable; there was a partition, you know. And we had a lovely garden, which was quite unusual, I can tell you.

There was a woman from India, a teacher-missionary who came back [much later] to give a talk to the Highland Society. She said, 'We always looked on your grandfather as the pet Brahmin of the district. Of course, you were all Brahmins to us' – That was because we had three clocks. Whenever someone had to go a message they sent over to find out the time, the only time that time mattered. It was nothing for people to come over, because they didn't have clocks. I would hate to put across that we were a cut above the others, but we certainly were more comfortable.

The barn was separate from the house, the loo was separate from the house but the byre was under the same roof as the kitchen.

Could you walk straight into it?

... No, there were two doors, leading outside, there was a partition, a proper wall, though they were kind of under the same roof. [The roof was thatched.] The main house had one large, and one smaller bedroom upstairs, stairs leading up to it, cupboard at the top of the stair where the cream and the butter ... we made butter in summer – were kept there in a jar, salted and put down. When our butter ran out – I hate to give you the impression that we were ... but we were better off... we sent for butter from Orkney. We did that when our butter was finished. And we worked with barter; we took eggs to the shop. It was amazing what you could get for a dozen eggs.

There was one large bedroom which had two beds in it, box beds[7] ... There was a carpet on the floor, there was a lovely grate, and a lovely mahogany table, a circular table, and a bed. It was a box bed too though. There was a walk-in cupboard at the end of the bed – instead of having two beds in that room, let's put it that way, they stored blankets up there. Now this house was not a bit typical, it was a better house. Then you came downstairs, and there was the parlour. It had a carpet on the floor and it had a sofa! A sofa! Padded chairs, you know. None of your wooden chairs. Oh, it had a bed in it too, you had to have a bed everywhere. It also had a rocking chair, the style of it, oh, you have no idea! Tile irons and the mantelpiece had a fringe, drapery, with little bobbles. Well, we had that and we had a lovely mirror, ornaments with jingle bells, you know, tassels, glass things.

Icicles?

Yes. And we also had corner cupboards, little things, for ornaments. Ornaments stuck in each one. There were pictures, ordinary ones – prints, Kitchener of Khartoum, or somebody like that, not Kitchener, Lord Roberts. That was the parlour.

There was another new bedroom, kind of built out.

Was that a later addition?

No, that was it. . . . now there was a corridor, a passageway from the parlour which took the full width of the house, to the kitchen and the kitchen was two steps down. In between in this corridor was a nice window and I remember sitting in the window. Opposite that was a bedroom. In that bedroom there was also a table and a lovely clock. The clock in the parlour was a very special French clock, had a figure stuck on it . . . You must not forget that my grandfather could tell the time from the sun, when the sun hit a certain point every Saturday, and the clocks were wound and adjusted.

This other bedroom had this big ugly clock really, but it did have a lovely panel with storks standing in the water [tries to remember]. There was a nice grate, and of course the usual bed. And a closet under the space under the stairs. And that's where we kept certain meals . . . certain meals . . . not the barley and oats which came off the croft, but flour, white flour, Canadian flour. It sat in the kitchen on the end of the bench. Golden Wheat, Canada. And that's where I learned my alphabet, the flour bag.

You made bread . . . as well as oatcakes?

Oatcakes, and barley. Don't forget the lovely barley. You made it just like oatcakes. Mother had quite a pile of medicines. [They were kept in the closet under the stair.] We had Chemical Food which was bought in a chemist, God knows what that was.[8] And nothing was ever wasted. The feathers off the chickens were kept for stuffing pillows, the tail feathers were kept and tied in bundles to clean girdles and things, or used for hands. There was nothing – but nothing – wasted.

Did you use chaff for the bed?

No, but I think we used to have a bolster and feather pillows. I think the bolster might have been made of chaff. [Discussion about other people's use of chaff, which had to be changed regularly.] The beds in the best bedrooms were real, bought mattress. Whatever was in them I couldn't tell you. But some of them had straw mattress, and that was changed quite frequently. Probably every autumn when straw was available.

Who had the best bedrooms?

My grandfather and grandmother had the bed in the sitting room, a bed with knobs on, a brass bed. The rest of us had built-in beds. Very comfortable. The built-in bed was the ordinary thing, you see, not many of them boasted a brass bed.

The kitchen had what we called a *cran*, but other people call a swey. It was a marvellous contraption. Some of these things that they've done away with, you wish you had them. There was a chain attached and you put the pot, or girdle, at whatever level you wanted it on. What mother could do with that girdle! We did all our baking on it – which was not a mean task with our squad, I can tell you that. And I've never tasted barley, or oatcakes, or pancakes like that. Nobody, like nobody made pancakes like mother! I don't know how she learned it, dear knows. She was wonderful, she had a gift, there's no doubt about it.

The croft must have been fairly large for you to have been that prosperous.

Yes, yes. I think it was ten acres, but I'm not positive about that . . . but the grazing wasn't included in the croft, so that the animals . . . [as well, the ten acres were used for arable, and the outer land for grazing].

Your father would make some money on the fishing too?

Yes, but he gave up the fishing [as employment] because something went wrong with his legs, his knee [about the time she went to secondary school]. So then we started a little shop, and father got a gig, and later on an early bus – really a van, but people travelled as well as the goods! There were a lot of ways of making the odd penny.

You were looking for the opportunity perhaps?

Well, it's strange that he did that . . . Mother was the goer, but I can't see mother doing that – I think that would be his own idea. Probably liked working with horses, perhaps didn't like the sea all that much, but he had to do it.

What about your water supply?

Water was quite a problem there. Of course, having the white house we were lucky. We had rhones [gutters] and the water was collected and it was very special. It was kept for tea and for washing hair. The rest of the water, you had great wells that you carted the water from, a bit away – it was magnificent drinking water, tea water, it was kept for special purposes. And in the summer time, you had an awful job getting it, you had to queue up ... and you had one [well] at the back of the house. It was all right for washing potatoes, fed to the animals, I think the trouble was it was too much iron in it. There was another one, a little distance away, good enough for washing clothes – but it didn't have iron in it and you couldn't drink it. You carried the water mostly, from a succession of wells.

It would be everyone in the family?

Usually ... jobs were allocated. I'll give you an example. Coming home from school, my job was – a fire and something waiting for me. We had our big meal in the evening; that wasn't for style, it was because it suited us. You could have chops – I told you we were better off – we had these things in the evenings. You were hungry coming in from school. There was usually a frying pan on the swey, potatoes or bacon or bits of anything, it didn't matter what, maybe a bit of fat or roast. Whatever it was, that had to do you till your real meal when the day's work was over. The lamps were lit – that's another thing – and occasionally when you were absolutely down on your uppers you had to eat salt herring twice a day. Now that was quite usual for other people. But occasionally we ran out of stores too. But [laughs], to eat the herring under the lamp was much nicer than mid-day. Perhaps it was just unusual for us. I didn't feel resentful of it ... the lamp was on the tilley-lamp. To begin with, just an ordinary paraffin lamp that hung on a hook.

Can you describe the ordinary working day?

Depended a lot on the season. The cutting of the peat, peat-cutting weather was always lovely. This took place around – this is guess work ... the potatoes were planted around March, that was got over, I think the next was the peat, that was May. And of course the people foregathered, you had a squad. And you paid back – if somebody came to you, you went to that fellow. There were roughly

FIGURE 2.4: Johanna MacDonald, Lewis. Both pails are attached to a metal hoop which keeps them off the carrier's legs.

three or four people to every peat knife. One cut the peats and the others flung them out to dry, and they were left till peat weather, usually the end of May – peat weather, breezy and dry and pleasant. Then when the peat were fairly dry, you put them out into small stacks, like a triangle. After that they were stacked properly into big stacks. Sometimes, they were ferried home at that stage, and a huge peat stack made at home. But more often they were stacked at peat bank and carried in creels.[9]

Who dug?

Didn't matter. First of all, of course, a strong man had to cut the turf off the top of the bank. You know, the heather and the grass. An ordinary spade. Then it was tipped down to the base of the bank, and that gave you a kind of foothole in case the place was boggy. As your cutting began you used the real tool for cutting peat, and one person – the men were the ones who cut, and the women flung. But wasn't necessarily the order. One cut and one flung ... the further down you went, the better the quality of the peat, so that the ones at the top were cut in bigger slabs and the further down you went, till you got to the very bottom, it was like coal, very good and very dark. Now sometimes when they were left at the peat bank, stacked in the ordinary peat-stacked way, they were just heaped turfs, until they were ready for creeling home. I often think of these women, their good posture – I took the children home during the war [World War Two] – I had to cut the peat myself, well of course somebody had to help me.

Did you help with peat when you were a child?

Oh, I had to help with the short stacking. Not the carrying, oh no, the women did that, and I often think that's why they had such marvellous posture. When I went home during the war, I had to do the carrying, you couldn't carry a creel without standing properly. The creel sat ... on your waist. The people were used to it – it was better than going to a ballet school – you couldn't do it properly any other way. They were all such beautiful walkers and I'm quite sure that was the training.

Did the men carry peat?

No – oh, no – don't be silly! The men did the fishing. People used to say those men were lazy! They weren't lazy. The thing was that they were kind of like the camels.

When they were at sea, they were in open sailing boats from Monday to Saturday. And on Saturday, they had to dip their nets in something or other called [cutch] to strengthen them, and put them on railings. So that when they came home they slept until Monday morning. Because they had no sleep, no beds or anything [at sea]. They went away early on Monday morning and they didn't get back until late on Saturday afternoon. On Saturday forenoon was the ... dipping the nets [she is not sure of term, only knows it in Gaelic] that had to be done, then it was hung on fences

to dry. Then the men went home to their homes and practically well
... ate reasonable meals and slept most of the time till Monday
because they had slept very little. During the week there was no
way that they could have. The accommodation on the open boats,
they were just sailing boats, no cabins. The stories around that the
Lewis men were lazy. They were not! Meals were mostly hard
biscuits, hard-tack. They lived on that and the fish they caught.
The herrings were just chucked into a pan. My uncle said you had
no idea how delicious herrings were straight out of the sea into the
pan.

When the time came for harvesting, for the crofting spring work,
my word, they weren't lazy at that because they hadn't yet gone to
sea. You see the herrings came in shoals and went around the coast.
It was until May, I think, they had their closed time. They weren't
allowed to. Then they did the croft work, as much of it as they
could, until they went off to the fishing. And often followed the
fishing round the coast. Funnily enough, they never went to Orkney – I wonder why not? They went to Shetland which was much
further away [probably following the herring].

The fishing girls – those who gutted the herring – they too went to
Shetland. And do you know how? In the fishing boats. Girls too
went in the open fishing boats, all the way through the Pentland
Firth up to Shetland.

What do you mean by girls?

Oh, no, I mean women, really, from the age of sixteen.

Young girls just left school?

Oh, yes, and older girls until they married and if not, until they
were about 40, 50.[10] They went on to Fraserburgh, Peterhead – I
don't know why that was – then they used to come home and they
did the cropping, the autumn work and then they went off to the
English fishing. I think they went by boat and train. When they
could go by train they did and they used to go to strange places like
Blythe. More often than not, they went to Yarmouth or Lowestoft.
Either. I think that depended on which fish curer they were with,
whether he had his premises in Lowestoft or Yarmouth. I can't
think of any other reason.

I think the arrangement was that they lived in some sort of
upstairs dwellings above – I don't know if it was premises belonging to the fish curers, maybe the coopers – they made the barrels,

perhaps they worked downstairs and the women lived up. The women worked in threes, two of them gutted the herring and sometimes they had to make as many as four–five selections of herring and they had to chuck them into basins at certain angles according to their size or quality. And there was the packer who stored them into the barrels – the third member of the crew – and she had to pack them properly. They used special salt, coarse salt, big crystals, and they put layers of salt over them. Then the coopers came and put the lids on the barrels, nailed them down – however they finished them off, I'm not sure.

Do you know what klondyking means? We used to get the klondykers coming to Lewis. They usually came from Russia or Germany before the war, the Baltic ports. The herring was not now gutted at all, they were put into these vast containers and salted, sort of tossed about in the salt. That was klondyking. You can still see it in Ullapool, but nowadays it's Americans. When we were children, we wouldn't eat mackerel if you paid us, they were scavenger fishes – won't eat mackerel to this day. I never eat them, isn't that strange?

The fishing girls only went in the fishing boats when there was no other way. When they went to Lowestoft and these fishing places, they went by train. If they went straight from Stornoway. But when they didn't, when they had to go to Shetland first, then it had to be the fishing boats, because there was no other way.

For a boy who had just left school, cooking was his job. Chucking the herring from the sea into the pan! The other thing I could perhaps mention. That their only way of earning a little extra money was to go into the militia. That was the Army side, or the Royal Naval Reserve. Most of them chose to go to the Navy. But quite a few of them – I think, now this is guesswork – I think they took them in the Army at an earlier age. I should have thought that naturally they would go to sea. Why? Because they got a retainer twice a year. And they went to town and usually got drunk twice a year and that was them finished. This hard drinking, later on when they went to sea properly, they really did become drunkards. I wonder sometimes if they weren't driven to it because they weren't fluent English speakers. It might have helped. But another extraordinary thing. There was hardened drinkers, once they married they gave it up completely! Not that they had joined a Church or anything but that they married.

FIGURE 2.5:   Fisher girls from Barra working in Ullapool, 1929.

Thinking about men giving up the drink on marriage. Was this something to do with local concepts of what a good family man was, the head of household?

I think you're right. It could have been.

I'm making assumptions there, maybe they weren't heads of households.

... But it could have been and I couldn't say yes or not. Probably that was why.

Did you have a head of household in your own house?

Yes, my grandfather. Not only in ours. That was another thing. They didn't throw their old people out, ever. Usually it was the woman who came into the household, for the eldest son, but they accepted the word of the old people and if they didn't, they were the odd ones out, they were ostracised if they didn't conform to what the elders wanted. It seems a peculiar society, but oh, my goodness, it made for sanity, it worked. It worked. And there was this great respect to old age. Not chucked out into homes...

I remember when my grandmother died, she died suddenly on a Sunday, getting ready for church. I just adored her. When I wanted to ask awkward questions like when your periods came – we didn't know *anything* that that was going to happen! And I remember going to my granny's... 'Something terrible has happened and I think I know why.' So I told her what happened... and I think it is that hard black sugar [she shakes with laughter] because I was eating it in bed!

You were saying earlier that women travelled with their employment ... I'm surprised that the young girls were given the freedom to travel like that ... on the boats.

[Hushed voice.] Oh, there was hardly ever ... see there's another strange thing. Their way of courting was to come in at the dead of night and spend the night with the woman, sometimes in bed– dressed.[11] And if you heard of anyone having an illegitimate child ... it was just the end, she was just ostracised – completely. Do you know – I'm not sure that until this day, but I shouldn't be surprised if the Free Church, the Wee Free Church, still holds on to this. Supposing it happened and you were having to have an illegitimate child, and supposing you were married before the child was born, that didn't matter, that child could not be baptised. It was just recorded 'shessive'. It means that you stood before, and you were slated by the Minister. I have seen it happen.

You saw it yourself?

Oh, yes. I think it still happens. It certainly happened twenty years ago.

The courting too, was that in your day?

Yes, it was in my day, but of course I was above it all, I was away to High School. The people, well for want of a better word we'll call them peasants, still went on then. That was the only way.

Can you tell me about any work you did when you were at school?

Usually there was some farm work that the older people were on. We didn't call it lunch – the midday meal, it was a kind of repast. The dishes were left and you came home from school and you dusted the kitchen and you did the floor and you took in two pailfuls of drinking water [which was about a quarter of a mile away]. You came home to do that. There were no hard feelings about that, that was your contribution. Then you got into a book and learned the English. You didn't have the English till you went to school.

Do you think that your mother was more interested in your education than getting you to help around the croft?

Oh, no child was expected to do any outwork. When you were stacking the peats, children did that. And also planting potatoes in a row – helped with that. But no child, however poor and poverty-stricken, was expected to work on the croft.

Other people worked as children?

In Lewis?

Yes.

Sometimes we were asked to drive cattle in. But they came to the gates themselves, and we led them in. But if you were scared of cows, like I was, you weren't expected to do anything you were scared of.

What would happen morning and night when cows had to be milked?

Cows were milked fairly early in the morning, and they got a titbit when they were being milked, something in a bowl. They were milked in the byre. Sometimes in summertime, they were left out all night, tethered all night. But mostly, they were milked in the byre, the milk was brought in and the cattle let loose out of the byre, and then you – shooed them out – we didn't have far to go, to let them loose and they wandered over the moorland at will. They came back on their own to the gate. You would think they had a clock.

Did you help in the dairy?

You would hardly call it a dairy, if you only had three cows like us. And usually it was two cows and a calf coming up so that when the cow was old we sold her and the calf took her place. You either reared or sold the female calves, but the bull calves were slaughtered . . . that was something about the cattle I didn't like, you knew you had them on the table. To this day, if you paid me I wouldn't eat veal. Most men, in fact, I think you would have been regarded as a softie if you didn't kill a sheep. Now, that's my surmise. I can't imagine my father willingly killing a sheep. It was because it was expected of them . . .

The children had nothing to do with sheep except when there was a rogue sheep. When they drove the sheep to the inner pastures in the summer, there was always a rogue one who escaped and came home on its own. It would be tethered, so it wouldn't get near the oats or the barley growing, the crops. There was always a lot of spare pasture on the croft and it would be your job to shift the tether, or take it to water.

Who would be telling you to do these things?

Mother, father was usually away [at the fishing] when I was very young. So that was your duties.

Would the other children have the same sort of work to do?

Yes, when they got to that age. The boys, most of the time, I shouldn't say the girls, but the boys had to do the tethering of the sheep. They didn't have to drive the cattle. You see that was the strange thing. The male and the female duties were usually delineated, the one didn't encroach on the other, 'That's not my job, I don't do that' sort of style, and I can't remember that the boys went to the well for water even, I may be wrong. Murdo going to the well, never, no.

But they went fishing at an early age on the rocks.

And girls didn't go?

Oh, no, girls didn't go. I remember one father who was very indulgent and he would take me and his daughter down to the easy rocks, you know. And he used to give us a little willow rod, but that was unusual, that was a titbit. He was an understanding father, like my father was. If his daughter, Maggie and I . . . depended on the state of the tide. If the tide was full, we got, if it was not, we didn't.

Was this unusual, a sensitive father?

Was it? [Hesitates.] I'll put it this way. I think the father's job was to earn what money he could, and the mother as a rule was to cope with the children. Except, the only exception would be that you didn't step out of line when father was around. He would come down like a ton of bricks. Not our father [indulgently]. If he said [loudly and staccato], 'Stop that girl, stop that boy!', you just laughed at him. Fancy him shooting out his neck! He was unusual.

But did you stop?

Och, no, you didn't stop for father, but if mother said [firmly], 'What's that you're doing?', you stopped then, by Jove! No, you didn't stop for father.

Did she dole out the discipline?

She doled out everything. She was really very special, my mother. I'm sure a lot of girls loved their mother more than I did when I was a child. I was afraid of her. But for all that . . .

Why were you afraid?

Because I would get into trouble, and she would never give me credit for doing anything. When I came home from school – I told you what my duty was – and the mother of my chum next door was very different. My chum did exactly what I did. And one day, it was within my hearing, she said something about Rosie had done this and that and my mother said, 'You're lucky, our one does nothing but sit and looks at books,' you see. And this woman said, I can remember her saying, 'Now look here, I don't think that's very fair of you. You said that before, and I asked Rosie and she said that, "Yes, she does what I do. I've seen for myself that she goes for the water." You just watch yourself, you'll break that child's nerve. You give her credit for nothing. There couldn't be an easier child. You never even hear her in the house.' A good job somebody notices!

And yet I had a tremendous admiration for her. I was so interested in knowledge myself, I was amazed how much she knew for the short time she had been to school. She was lucky, not many girls of her age got to school. At that time, you could please yourself. But she was the one girl in the family, there were three boys. She was somebody special, being the only girl. So she went to school ... she would leave at 13, but she would go at 6 or 7 to school. What she assimilated in that time was nobody's business!

What did she do after she left school?

I think she went once to the fishing as a fishing girl. She was once in Fraserburgh or something. If that. She was the only girl and three boys older so it's likely she was kept at home.

What you're saying is that they could afford to keep her at home because she had three brothers who could earn money?

... Yes, and her father. And I think they had their own boat, because her father was drowned entering the harbour the year after I was born, that was about 1900. And his two sons were in the boat with him, it was an open boat of course. Apparently the tide is very awkward, the Pentland tide, and a freak wave came and swept him off the ship and his two sons with him. That was quite usual, oh, yes.

Did you ever look after your younger brothers and sisters?

Yes, I took Callum, he was my younger brother. He was my concern. If I went down to the shore, I took him with me. But how they allowed a child of 6 or 7 to go to that shore. They were so used to it. Little do they know how near danger I was many a time. I didn't tell them that either. He was my concern. My responsibility. I was to keep him away from danger. But I wouldn't have been forbidden to go to the shore. I wouldn't have gone. I was too nervous a child ... Now Callum should have had Betty. I wouldn't like his job looking after her, because she was the one who roared in the morning, when we were having porridge, she didn't want porridge, she wanted bacon. And she got bacon. She didn't want bread, she wanted biscuits, wanted cake if that was around. She wanted that and she would get it.

I can't remember Callum being in charge, although according to the rules of the game he should have been. Then she would be in charge of Ned – and heaven help her. Oh! he was the wild one.

From what you've told me, your mother placed a very heavy value on education.

... Absolutely

... She had great plans for you. You were the eldest daughter, and you could well have been kept at home to help with younger children ...

Yes, she would never do that, and she would never have kept me off school. They did keep me once off school, and I was very annoyed, to put the potatoes in the rows. You see it was a great help and it wasn't too much for a child to do, when they were covering up. I hated to be off school at any time...

I'm interested in your parents' attitudes towards education.

Oh, that was what counted. It always counted. They sacrificed anything to educate you. It would be very difficult to send a child away. Well, when I went to the Nicholson [Institute, the high school], I got a bursary of I think £15 and only one person in a school of about 300 pupils qualified. When I think of the number of people who could have benefitted. I was the lucky one.

There wasn't the money for them to go?

They were dependent on the bursary. And £15 went further than you would think. Because you took eggs with you from home and they got the digs for you. But you were only working in digs from Sunday nights until Friday. You were expected to go home and you did, there was nothing else to do but walk the ten miles. I was in second year higher grade, because I was considered to be clever but my goodness, it was terrible to tackle second year geometry without having done first, second year Latin – it was very difficult. Fortunately one of our teachers – at that time teachers were not confined to their own subject. Usually teach other things too. For instance the man who taught us Latin...

At this point the tape breaks off, but we will have occasion to return to the problems faced by children from the Highlands and Islands in achieving their educational goals below. Our next interviewee, Mr Geddes, left school early like the vast majority of the people we talked with, at 14 years of age.

Mr Geddes, born 1900, Banffshire and Speyside

Mr Geddes was born in 1900 in Banffshire, and his story includes information about farm workers in the North-East as well as crofting in Inverness-shire since this was where he spent his holidays as a child in the company of his maternal grandmother.

His father was born on a farm but was brought up on a croft. The father left the croft in order to go in for banking, but an economic crisis brought him back to crofting – the same croft which Mr Geddes farms today, though much more land has been acquired during the intervening period. His mother was brought up in the heart of the North-East. Her father was a gamekeeper. His mother spent some time in Edinburgh in domestic service and later became a cook in the north of Inverness-shire. His parents met when his mother was visiting a cousin married in the area. What had been intended to be a few days' holiday resulted in her marriage. They had six children, including twins who died when Mr Geddes was very young. He had an older sister and brother and a younger sister who was a virtual invalid for thirty years. She predeceased her mother by only a year or so. His elder sister left home before he left school and is only mentioned once in the interview.

Although the croft provided some of the family's sustenance, Mr Geddes's father was employed on the railways. Their income was supplemented by letting the house to summer visitors, while they themselves moved into temporary quarters. The interview starts with an account of the vagaries of Mr Geddes's father's early career, and shows that the changing fortunes of a family could result in both downward social mobility as well as residential mobility.

Interview with Mr Geddes

How did father originally acquire his first farm?

Well, he was born in Speyside, I think, but his father died when he was quite young. And it was a man who was well-known in Speyside at that time . . . they called him Markinch after the farm where he was born. He was a banker . . . and also a solicitor. A lawyer. I don't know what the relationship was, whether he was his uncle or half-brother or what – he never spoke about him. But this man Markinch was a gambler . . . It was the times of the gold mines in Africa, òr diamond mines, I'm not sure which. He began using other people's money as well as his own to gamble with. If things had gone well with him overnight, he would have been a millionaire and all the people who had been involved with him would have been well off. But it went the other way aboot and the whole thing crashed [1906], as they do still to this day.

He had arranged for my father to get into a bank, a job in a bank. He was fairly clever I suppose. But a job turned up in New Zealand, they were opening up banks there, and he thought it would be a great opportunity for my father to go to New Zealand – the young chap thought it would be a good thing too, likely – but when it came to the bit of leaving, his mother wouldn't hear of it at all. So he stayed on, and there wasn't much to be made on the croft at that time. This farm in Glendronach turned up and Markinch put him in there, partly with his [Markinch's] money – or other people's money more likely. My father wouldn't have very much.

The times were really very bad. Late harvests and snow, grouse coming on the crops and destroying them so that he found it very hard going so that he was unable to save anything. In the middle of all that, Markinch crashed. Everybody that was involved with him crashed too. So he had to come out of that farm in 1906 and come back and start [here] again in the croft which he left nearly twenty years before. He was lucky enough to get a job in the railway as a surfaceman.[12] That and the croft kept us from starvation, but only just I think.

But how could he get the croft?

He had it before. His mother had it. He wasn't born on the croft. His father came from somewhere else, I'm not sure where. But he was born in a farm or a croft [somewhere else], but he was brought up in this croft down by the lochside [here]. He had three sisters, I think. He had stayed on there till his mother died. He wasn't making anything of it – there was nothing to be made of it. He thought this was a good chance that Markinch was giving him, putting him into this farm, but I don't know, perhaps he wasn't a very good farmer. He should have kept sheep but he didn't like sheep so he kept cows and things like that. He wasna doing very well. But he might have made out when we grew up. Before that happened, Markinch crashed altogether. Markinch poisoned himself rather than face the consequences of what he did. That's a subject he never spoke about. Anyway, we came up here in 1906 to start again.

Where was your mother from?

She was from Brig o Doun. Her father was a gamekeeper.

How did she meet your father?

She had a cousin married in [here] [indicates house]. She came up to visit when her mother had a bad bout of rheumatic fever and the wife wasn't able to . . . so she came to visit and stay with her cousin for a few days on holiday and she met him there.

So your mother would have had her own relatives in Brig o Doun?

I would go over to my granny's house at Brig o Doun for holidays. The little cottage she had is now renovated, but at that time it was just a small housie and it was in an awful bonnie place called [Gaelic] the Place of the Larches.[13] On the side of the road, and the brae went down steep to the burn.

   One morning when I was on holiday there, there was an older boy lived in the house. I had a sling, two lengths of string with a little pouch of leather on the end of it. You put a stone . . . David killed Goliath with it. I had found this thing and I was throwing stones down the brae . . . but unfortunately, one of the stones went wrong and I broke a window of the house. So my mother came out of the house and dealt with me in the old-fashioned way. My grannie came out and said, 'For God's sake, lassie, dinna kill him till ye get him hame' [laughs].

What would mother and grandmother have done before they were married?

My mither was a cook, a pretty good cook and she was a good long while in a big farm up in Ross-shire, [a castle] way north of Inverness. She was quite a while there. She was in Edinboro [Edinburgh] when she was younger. That was the only thing open to young folks if they werena educated.

You don't know about your grandmother?

Pretty much the same. She taught school for a time, not academic subjects, but she taught girls to sew and knit and crochet. One of her dearest possessions was a little stick, a crochet stick, made out of the bone of an eagle's leg. I often wonder what became of it.

How did you get a living? I don't mean earning money but living off the farm – when you came it was a croft, but it's a farm now. What's the difference between a croft and a farm?

In Laggan, we had a farm, large size and here we had a croft, about twenty acres which did not provide a livelihood without some other . . . as I said my father was fortunate enough to get on to the railway.

So he would earn his money from a full-time job on the railway?

[Mr Geddes nods.]

What did you keep on the croft?

Three or four cows and maybe a few sheep, whiles. Probably a pig now and again. That's about all.

You bought the animals you could afford to feed off it?

Yes, yes.

Family size changed over time, so that as children grew bigger, the croft would have to feed more people. What would happen then?

That's right. Well, it provided us with our own meal, really all the time, and potatoes, and if you had energy, you would go after a rabbit, or a hare, or even a roe deer, whiley. But it was a pretty poor living for everybody. We really had no money of our own at all, we had just to do without lots of things, that you would much like to have had.

But somehow, by being thrifty – my mother was very thrify – we would manage to waffle through. With children going to school and other children's clothes and that, they changed them about till they were really worn. That had to be done.

That would be fairly general, I suppose?

Yes, I think . . . yes, indeed. Lived very soberly indeed. Porridge twice a day, perhaps soup made out of a rabbit or a hare, or a sheep's head. At the weekend, perhaps a shilling's-worth o' boiling beef or something like that. Mother made mostly oatcakes and scones, pancakes. We never bought any teabread or cakes or things like that. If we had it at all, it was home made.

You did have four cows, a lot of milk . . .

We tried to get four cows. Sometimes we had plenty and sometimes not. When it was plentiful, she made butter, cream, crowdie. It was very good, new oatcakes made of new meal with farm butter on them. This crowdie's a soft cheese, before the cheese is properly made. It was very good indeed.

What did you keep in the garden?

A few curly greens and cabbages.

Kail?

Carrots and things like that. I don't think there was an awful lot of time lavished on the garden. We would have that. Mostly curly kale. You don't see a lot of it at all now, it was very common, we made it into broth, brose if ye know what brose is. It's a concoction of oatmeal with boiling water poured on to it, salt, stirred round about and it's very good indeed. If you had a hard day's work to do, you needed it. But they sometimes put kail bree into it to make it nice.

The broth? To flavour it and get the goodness into it too?

Yes. Sometimes bree of turnips or butter, a big lump of butter. Butter in your brose.

That sounds to me to be a good diet...

It seemed to be sufficient ... all that was necessary. I don't remember anyone taking pills in my young time. I scarcely know anybody today that doesn't take them.

At this time of year ... they used to shoot the hinds and my father was able to buy a whole hind for a pound.

Now, where on earth did you keep it?

It was cut up and put into a tub and salted.

So that would keep you going all winter?

A good while, anyway. But it wasna so nice towards the end of the time...

It seems to be true of those times that you ate what was in season, and you didn't get other things?

... And then probably, a small barrel of salt herrings, that too, and dried codfish, they were split up the centre and they were just like a piece of board – as hard as a board – ridged with salt.

Did that not make you feel very thirsty?

Well, I think so, but they had to be steeped and boiled and steeped and boiled, then used with milk. Milk came into almost every diet. Potatoes. It wasn't too bad ... It usually had a very good sauce to go along with it.

Mebbe to disguise the salty flavour?

Hunger! A good healthy appetite anyway. Very occasionally, some people were known to be so misguided as to cause an accident to happen to a hen or something like that ... [laughs]. You had a nice meal out of a hen, or a duck.

A treat?

Yes.

How did you contribute to the getting of this living?

Well, as long as my father was alive – well, he did retire before he died, I used to work for other people with horses and at shooting lodges. My first job was at a shooting lodge along here. I left the school on Friday and I started at the lodge on Monday, I think the day the World War started . . . I was 14.

I was offered two jobs. My father would have liked me to stay at home on the croft and do the work there but nothing for it, so I had to make a start. I had the offer of a job at Aviemore, I think 10s. a week as a clerk, and a job in the stables at the shooting lodge looking after ponies at 18s. a week. So when I went along and saw the ponies, it didn't take me long to make up my mind which job to start. And I worked there for three months and the job was finished then. The season finished. I got no wages during that time.

Why not?

Just the custom . . . till it was finished.

So you got your wages after you had done [the three months'] work?

I had ten golden sovereigns and some silver. My feet were barely touching the ground coming home.

What did you do with the money?

It didn't take long. My mother was waiting [laughs].

She was expecting it?

I mebbe got the silver to myself, I'm not sure.

Did you expect to have to give her the money?

Oh, yes, oh yes. She would probably have bought whatever clothes I needed. Even at that age, whatever I needed, boots. Before that, years before that, every boy that could, was able, went driving flags . . . driving the grouse into the shooters.

Beating?

That's it. They gained enough from that to get winter clothes on theirselves. And at that time, the moors were covered with berries called blaeberries. It's a small red berry that grew on the moors at that time. Heather needed to be fairly short where it grew. It was in great demand for jam or jellies, particularly to eat with game and that sort of thing. The local shopkeepers gave a fairly good price for it. We gathered it and we had to clean it up in the wind to drive the leaves and all the dirt out of it. If you presented them in a clean and nice manner, you got a fair price for them. I can't just remember what it was, but it was quite a bit of money to be made for it.

This was a way you could make money before you left school?

Yes, yes.

Did you have other jobs like that?

... Not a lot, the only half crown you would get would be carting a load of coal to somebody or taking home a load of wood or something like that. In the springtime of the year, we made some money ploughing and putting down crops for other folks that had no horses of their own.

What age were you when you were doing the ploughing?

Fifteen or sixteen.

What about before you left school?

At that stage, there was really nothing to be done except the beating, and people would want you to do a bit of hoeing for them or maybe a bit of gardening – odd jobs like that. But it didn't amount to very much.

On other crofts?

Other people, yes.

Did your sister contribute to the croft?

Oh, yes, very much. She worked for other people for the high reward of sixpence an hour, I can remember, when she started. I think she was supposed to earn a minimum of four hours or something like that, but it was usually more like five before she got ... she didn't add greatly to her fortune. But it was a little money.

For hoeing?

I don't think she ever went to hoeing ... it was more housework. She certainly went to the berries, she was very good at them. She could pick much more than most people could.

Your mother made a whole lot of things on the farm. Did she also work on the farm?

Not outside, she was too handicapped with my younger sister to take part in any outside. She had more than enough to do inside.

What happened there?

FIGURE 2.6:   Young woman picking raspberries, Perthshire, 1916.

Well, she just nursed her that way. She died when she was over 30 years of age.

This was the sister who had meningitis?

That's right.

She was younger than you?

Oh, aye, she was the youngest of the family.

She got meningitis when she was just a baby?

Something like that, yes.

So your mother had to look after her all her life?

It would have been much much better if she had died because she was really nothing at all in her latter years.

That would have been a terrible strain on a family like your own, you would need the labour resources . . . must have affected you all.

More or less, yes. Mother was really never free at all. She got to be, she could hardly take a day's holidays, for thinking about what might happen at home. She only lived for jist about a year, after this daughter died. She just didn't know what to do with herself.

Your mother wouldn't get much time for leisure?

None at all really, very little.

What about your father?

He was quite a busy man too, in his own way.

He had a full-time job, and he would have to work on the croft too. What about the garden?

No, he wasna a very hearty gardener. He wielded the scythe in the garden, if he was put in to do work.

I was thinking about these cabbages and things.

I suppose he would work at that too. He used to sow cabbages and carrots and things in the fields until the rabbits and the neighbours got to know about it.

Did your father have any outside leisure at all?

Very little. People in their situation in life didn't expect to have much leisure. They would go to visit each other of an evening, perhaps to a show, or things like that. He didna go to the pub or anything like that at night. For one thing you had no money, and I don't think you had any inclination to go. In the daylight, there was something to do outside and in the winter nights, he liked to work in his workshop. He was a fairly good joiner. So he would work at that sort of thing at night at making furniture or wooden implements for use on the farm.

I get the impression that you didn't have much leisure at all in summer, but maybe in winter when you had to be sitting indoors. What was it like with the family around?

I played the fiddle when I was young, not very well perhaps, but I played. People would come in of an evening from this house here, or neighbours. They didn't knock at the door, they just cam' in. The door was never locked, night or day. I don't suppose we had anything that was really worth stealing, but it was very rare you heard of anything being stolen. Tools you could leave lying about, they would still be there in the morning.

They didn't have terribly hard work such as they did on the bigger farms or that. We went at our own pace more or less, but fairly constant at it. We didn't get up so early in the morning as the larger farms or dairy farms or things like that. Oh, we had quite a pretty busy, hard life.

[*Wife* interjects: These weren't statutory wages then, you just paid them what you could. *He*: Not what they were worth, they took what they could get and had to leave it at that.]

The first money that ever I really made was carting stones off the field. Goodness knows, we had plenty of those, and still have. We carted them down to the lochside there and a crusher came in and crushed the stones for use on the road. They were just gravel roads at that time and we were paid half-a-crown a yard. It was very hard and unpleasant work. What haunds we used to have on wet days with stones! But we made a fairish bit of money on that.

What age were you when you were gathering the stones?

About 23 or 4... It was cartloads... Some still do, it's a very necessary job but a most uninteresting and unrewarding job. But it's got to be done.

Sometimes you think the farm is growing stones.

Mm-huh. I used to have an arrangement with the forester to keep part of his forest tidy, clear the dead wood. I was allowed for a small sum to take it out and tie it up and sell it as firewood. Made a little money that way, just to keep me from starvation.

When you were a wee bit older again?

Yes, over 20.

You wouldn't see much of your father away during working day. Who told you what to do next?

He did. In the morning before he went out, he left a list as long as your arm. Any human being couldn't have accomplished in one day. He made sure I was never out of a job. And at night he was there . . . got a reprimand for not having done . . . but that's just the way it went. And my mother, she wanted something different done. On her side, there was cut sticks or work in the garden or get vegetables in and that. But we just went on that way.

You might have had conflicting demands sometimes?

I suppose that's it.

What about your brother?

When he became 14 he . . . when we left Laggan and came over . . . on a horsecart to come to Aviemore, that's the first time we saw railway engines. He said when he saw the engine, I'm going to be an engine driver when I grow up. He never lost that notion, he did become . . . I'm not sure what he did between [the ages of] 14 and 16. He worked on farms round about Aviemore and here. He thought at one time he might be a joiner, but he never continued with that job. He did whatever he could find to do. But when he was 16 he joined the railways as a railway cleaner, cleaning the engines at Aviemore.

He eventually got to do what he wanted to do?

Yes . . .

Father had the croft . . . I guess you would be a likely one to inherit the use of that croft . . . Is that what happened?

That's right.

But did you want that?

I'm not sure that I particularly did, but at that time, I was too old to maybe learn anything else. I would have gone on, but my eyes precluded me from doing that [he had trouble with his sight] . . . It was awkward hours. When he started [his brother] he went on at six o'clock at night, didn't come home till about six in the morning. I can weel remember when he came back [after] the first night . . . my mother had got him a rig-out of dungarees, new things to put on, and when he came back in the morning, she hardly knew him. They had a habit . . . when a young lad joined the cleaning shed, they tarred him all over with grease and feathers if they had any . . . His new clothes were all torn [laughs].

How did your mother react?

She was very wild. That's the way they did. No use being up getting upset. He would be doing the same thing shortly afterwards for some other boy. Mm-huh.

I should have thought that they would have been sensitive to the fact that somebody else was paying for it?

Well . . . they were a tough lot . . . they a' had to go through the same thing. In his case, the hard work and the hard upbringing on the croft fitted him for the work he did. He would have been one of the best workers at his job, and he got on much better than most of his kind did.

That tarring and feathering, that's like an initiation rite. It would make him one of the boys.

. . . Mm-huh.

When do you think children became adults then? When you were growing up?

Rather later on in life than the day. Oh, yes.

Do you know at what point?

In some ways, maybe as soon as they do now, maybe sometimes sooner. Because ye had to fight for yerself then in order to live. Ye didna get any handouts, no Saturday penny or Government grants or anything at a' like that. You had to jolly well strike out for yourself.

You also had to strike out for your very food.

Oh, yes, indeed. There was nothing for nothing then.

Well, were you a child then?

[Wife says the children worked.] Oh, yes, as soon as they could do anything. [Wife says her husband's father died when he was quite young: father was seventy-three and R was twenty-two.]

Do you feel you were regarded as an adult by then?

Yes. Moneywise, I don't suppose it meant an awful lot. He would have had a pension by that time, the old aged pension. As I remember it, it was long years after that before we came to be anything like well off. Anything more than the bare necessities of life.

Looks to me like a good farm now, not a croft.

It's a very untidy farm, not a good farm, too fragmented. Three or four miles between the two ends of it. It's a collection of small crofts. There used to be people in every croft. Our people were the best off.

They didn't have very big wages but much more than crofters had. And steady, there was no broken time. Masons, and people of that kind, when the winter time came, I don't know how they lived because they couldn't build houses, they had no income at all, no dole of any kind.

They must have had to save during the good times ...

They would have had to, or else starve.

You wouldn't ... [starve] because of the croft.

Just about. Just about kept us alive. Some of them were even worse than us. The people who were here before us, great big folks they were, one of the sons was ill one winter – their mother had died when they were young – his sister was terrified that he would die because there was no money to bury him! He hasna died yet, he's 95 [laughter].

The children today do so little by comparison ... How did parents manage to keep children working so hard?

Well, the children did what they were told, they accepted that their father and mither was tellin' them what to do. When you came to any age at all, you knew you'd to do it or else live very very soberly indeed, and dress even more soberly. In fact, some of them in this house – there was one young woman – one month she wasna able to go anywhere because she had no clothes or shoes. We were never just quite that bad, but not much more. We used to buy the shoes a size too big so that we would grow into them.

Then in the summer time, summer visitors began to come about and we began to let our house ... for as many weeks as we could get.

What did you do yourself?

My father made a house out of the barn and we went out and lived there. My brother and I slept in the stable or the henhouse or the byre, whatever.

Wouldn't worry you too much?

Not at all, I've slept in the Banff Springs Hotel in Canada and in the Green Thorn Tree in Nairobi and I think I slept just as well in the henhouse [laughter]. [His wife says that then the father bought the little house.] After that ... just a little wooden shack, but it was new and quite nice, wasna luxurious by any means, but better than living in the barn with the rats.

To what degree did people build their own houses still when you were a boy?

Oh, they did. Wooden houses, anyway, perhaps not many of them but ... oh, yes.

These would be quite strong?

It's up yet, after all those years.

It would be a lot cheaper than trying to build a house these days.

Oh, they couldna ha done it. Things have just changed.

Standards have changed too – you wouldn't have water laid on, water would have had to be brought in in pails, and you would have had a fire/range?

Yes, the system we worked was that we had an open fire all winter and in the summer time, the first of June or thereabouts, we took in a range for the 10 summer visitors to cook properly on and by this time of year [October] it was taken out again and [we used] the open fire.

Because you liked the open fire?

Oh yes. We cut the sticks, that length.

I notice you said sticks, not peats?

No, the peats [went out] about the turn of the century here. I've seen them on the top of the hill, set out to dry as they left them, but a flood came and washed away the lot ... but I do remember my brother worked all night on the railway, even in 1914. He was home sleeping in the loft, the barn. There was a terrific thunderstorm came on in June, I think. It washed a railway bridge at Carrbridge, washed away the train, people were drowned ... it happened twice, just a mile about Carrbridge, just torrential rain. He was sitting up in bed with an umbrella ... The roof was leaking.

How did you get on with your parents?

Just average ... I would think ... I got on better with my mother than with my father ... From her I learned most of the old stories and things.

NOTES

1. The information on which this chapter is based was drawn from a number of interviews including eleven interviews with people who said that their fathers had had a croft. The overwhelming majority of crofter fathers also had another form of income generating work, either self-employment, typically as blacksmiths or fishermen, or as employees. The

interviewees are listed under Crofters in Appendix Two and their additional occupations are specified there. A twelfth respondent, also listed there, became a crofter in her own right as a young woman. We have also drawn on information from two children of blacksmiths and one of a gamekeeper who lived in cottages with large gardens which were almost crofts, a farm-owner living in a crofting area, and a Highland laird. In three cases, information about crofting life was given by the children of farm servants. The problem of overlap between the categories crofter, farm servant and farmer is discussed in Appendix One.

2.   Lewis was a 'main storm centre' (Smout, 1986, p. 70; see also Hunter, 1976) in the Highland Land Wars in which crofters and dispossessed crofters illegally occupied sheep and deer farms in a campaign of direct action for land redistribution. The targets were farms which had once been crofts before the landowners cleared the crofters to make way for commercial farming. In Lewis there had been no clearances since 1844, but land was seized which had been cleared before that date. The Land Settlement (Scotland) Bill of 1919 extended the powers and responsibilities of the Board of Agriculture in order to make them more able to purchase and redistribute land (Leneman, 1989). Land seizures continued until the Board of Agriculture was seen to be effective. Farms which had been subject to raids in early periods of acute discontent were reoccupied in Lewis in 1920. This was the last time such direct action was exercised there.

3.   *Kelp* – a type of seaweed. This was once a money-making activity as it was used in the alginate industry for cosmetics.

4.   Blaeberries are a wild fruit related to cranberries. The everyday activity of gathering blaeberries features in a popular Highland lullaby with a Gaelic chorus. The English lyrics are: 'I left my dearie lying here, lying here, lying here. I left my dearie lying here and went to gather blaeberries.'

5.   Only one of our respondents grew up in one of the predominantly Catholic pockets of the Highlands and Islands. Most came from areas where strict Presbyterian protestantism predominated.

6.   Their job was to scare grouse and other game birds out from their camouflaged position on the ground into the air and into the sights of the gun-bearing gentry.

7.   Box-beds were wooden cupboard-like structures, usually free-standing. They were standard pieces of furniture and afforded occupants greater privacy in shared rooms than the conventional beds of the present, as well as providing some protection from draughts. The recessed bed (described earlier by Mrs MacDiarmid), with three sides and a roof provided by a rectangular recess in the wall, had similar advantages and was also common. Both could be referred to as 'built-in' beds. Mrs Gillies suggests that beds as we know them now were regarded as higher-status than box beds or recessed beds.

8. This was a standard 'pick-me-up'.

9. For some discussion of regional differences in peat-cutting techniques, see Fenton, 1987.

10. For oral testimony of 'fishing girls', see Buchan, 1983. See also Thompson, 1983.

11. This is a reference to a rather dramatised and exaggerated version of the practice known as 'bundling'. Although the courting couple were placed in the box-bed together, they were prevented from embracing by being wrapped separately in bed clothes and/or separated by a bolster. This did not happen in the middle of the night, but rather was a supervised business.

12. Also called a linesman: a person who walked the track to check whether it was in need of repair.

13. Details of place names such as this have been changed slightly in order to preserve the anonymity of the interviewees.

CHAPTER THREE

Farm Servants' Children

THE INTERVIEWEES who speak in this chapter are the children of the
core of agricultural workers – the farm servants. The term 'farm
servant' was used to describe the all-year-round male farm workers
who, like domestic servants, were tied to their employer by their
accommodation.[1] They were hired for six months or a year,
depending on the region, and given a tied cottage and perquisites as
part of their conditions of employment.

In 1900 there were a number of ways of being employed as a farm
worker in lowland Scotland. The most important distinctions were
between the full-time regular employees and the casual labourers
and between the men and the women. Throughout the nineteenth
and into the early twentieth century, considerably larger numbers
of women were employed on Scottish farms than south of the
border. Devine (1984) accounts for this difference by arguing that
the dominant types of farming in Scotland were particularly suited
to the use of women as a reserve army of cheap labour.

Devine identifies four types of women agricultural workers: full-
time regular workers who were either dairy-maids or 'out-workers',
that is general labourers; women working on family farms; 'in and
out' workers who combined some domestic service with some
out-work; and casual labourers. Even when working as regular
full-time 'out workers' doing general farm labouring, women's
wages were always less than that of men's.

Women out-workers were most common in the south-east counties of Fife, Lothians, Berwickshire and Roxburghshire which were
associated with large arable farms and a rotation system which
included very labour-intensive green crops such as turnips. The

FIGURE 3.1:   Alice Hall, servant, Ramrig, Swinton, Berwickshire, going to milk the cows, hiding the pail behind her back.

1921 Agricultural Census recorded women as forming 20 per cent of the regular labour force. This percentage ranged from 32 per cent of the regular labour force in the dairying county of Ayrshire and 30 per cent in arable East Lothian to only 6 per cent in Forfar.

Women 'in and out' workers were rare in districts where large farms were the norm, but common in districts of medium or small holdings where 'no single task could absorb labour on a continuous basis in a fashion characteristic of the regime in the Lothians' (Devine, 1984). Single women, if not the daughter of a male farm worker and hence already living at home, were also dependent on the farmer for their accommodation. They might occasionally be given their own cottage, but were more likely to lodge in the farm house.

Five types of male farm servant are commonly identified. Anthony describes them as follows: '"shepherds" who had direct responsibility for the flock, effectively worked on their own, and reported directly to the farmer; "grieves" who consulted with the farmer on immediate farm activities and who supervised the rest of the workforce; and "ploughmen", "cattlemen" and "orramen" who were responsible to the grieve for particular production sectors' (1992, p. 7). Shepherds could be further divided into 'in bye' shepherds who lived in the farm cottages alongside the other workers and the 'out bye' or hill shepherds who lived in isolated cottages near their flocks. Of the last three types of worker, only the 'orramen' needs explanation. A typical farm employed young men as general farm labourers, referred to as 'orramen', 'orraymen', 'orraladdies' or 'orraloons' (as they were called in the North-East), that is, odd job men or odd job boys. Mrs Doughtie described the Berwickshire farm on which her father was cattleman in the 1920s as having three ploughmen, an odd boy and two women. Mr Linton described his first job as one of three orraladdies at a Berwickshire farm when he left school, and his shortened apprenticeship and rapid promotion to hind during the First World War. As an orraman he was in charge of one horse, unlike the hind who was in charge of two, and his main job was to do any carting that was needed on the farm.

> The men had double horses. We had one. We did all the odd jobs. Carting turnips to the sheep in the fields, anything that had to be carted wi' one horse. . . . The war came and the young men were called up. Although the other two and me were still orraloons,[2] the farmer

had no option but to promote us to full two horses before our time. So I went from 10s. to 14s. when they went away. Then every year we got a rise because prices were going up.

MR LINTON, BORN 1898

In addition to these regular workers, large numbers of casual labourers were also required at particular times of the year. Tasks such as planting potatoes, weeding potatoes, thinning turnips, grain harvesting, potato lifting and turnip pulling needed extra labour and on a sizeable farm at the end of the nineteenth century could involve temporary employment for as many as sixty people. Adoption of reaper binders in 1890s did reduce demand with respect to grain harvesting, but other tasks were to remain labour-intensive into the twentieth century. The need for seasonal work arguably increased between 1880 and 1914 and was met by women dependents of male farm workers; male and female Irish labourers (see O'Dowd, 1991); Highlanders; and migrant labourers, such as crofters and workers from towns and villages, which included the wives and daughters of miners and other industrial workers. Migrant workers lived in specially-built separate (sex-segregated) quarters where they cooked for themselves. These were called barracks or bothies. Alternatively they ate and were allowed to sit in the farm kitchen and slept in the chaumer (sleeping accommodation somewhere on the steading, usually above the stables). More regularly employed single men might also be accommodated in a bothy or the chaumer.

Whether or not a farmer employed the full range of types of workers depended on the size and nature of the farm. The dominant form of lowland farm was mixed, that is, it included stock, grain crops and green crops. On small farms specialisation of tasks was less possible; a ploughman was often also the cattleman who had to feed the cows, and he might oversee the work of the orralman. On large farms, ploughmen and cattlemen as well as a grieve or steward were employed (Carter, 1979, p. 138; Robertson, 1973, p. 74). Mr Duncan told us of a 10,000-acre farm with twenty-five workers, at least seven of whom would have been ploughmen. But Mrs Doughtie's experience of a farm with three ploughmen was probably more common, in that smaller farms numerically exceeded such large farms.[3] The average regular workforce of a south-west dairy farm of typical size of 140 acres was one ploughman, one odd man, and four women workers – two girls, one for the

FIGURE 3.2: Tattie liftin' (potato picking), Fife, c. 1900.

house and one for the dairy and byre, plus two milkers (Campbell, 1984, p. 62). Opportunities for farm work diminished over the 1880–1930 period for both men and women, but it seems that the supply of agricultural workers also diminished.[4] By the early twentieth century, farmers were complaining about the problems in getting regular farm labourers, and women in particular were difficult to recruit (Devine, 1984).

We interviewed fifteen elderly people who were the sons or daughters of farm servant fathers. The majority of the fifteen farm servant families lived in the Borders or just to the north, in the Lothians. Four of our respondents were from the north-east Lowlands (Caithness, east Inverness-shire, Easter Ross and Aberdeenshire) (see Appendix Two). In some cases, both parents and siblings of our interviewees were, had been, or would become agricultural workers at some time in their lives. There was a limited overlap between agricultural workers, crofters and farmers among our interviewees. Only Davy Renton made a shift from agricultural worker to working farmer after his father acquired a small holding. But in the North-East, there were often family connections between crofters and agricultural workers. Visits to crofter relatives made children of agricultural workers knowledgeable about their lifestyle. For instance, the interview with Mrs West (below) includes some particularly interesting descriptions of 'crofting' life in Aberdeenshire. Before the formal interview, Mr Geddes (see the interview in Chapter Two) told us about life on farms in the Tomintoul area (east of the Spey) where he had spent his holidays with his maternal grandmother. He reported that both men and women worked on farms in the Tomintoul area. Some of the women were out-workers, some worked both in the farmhouse and in the fields; sometimes, he added, they were unmarried mothers, glad of a day's work hoeing or harvesting.

These examples represent something of a transition between crofting and the families of agricultural workers. In the full interviews at the end of this chapter, we show this overlap.

THE ECONOMIC CONTEXT

The conditions of getting a living were more standardised among farm servants than among crofters, whose households depended on a wide range of money-earning strategies and whose living from the land varied with size of croft and local conditions. Because of security of tenure, members of the crofter's household had more opportunity to exploit any locally-based ways of getting a living. The yearly or half-yearly agreement of employment[5] and the standard perquisites of the farm worker necessarily imposed more uniformity. The pace and content of farm work was dictated by the farm servant's employer as well as by the weather, and by the necessity of doing a range of jobs appropriate to the crops being produced and animals being raised. The crofter's relationship to the land was a direct one, but the farm servant's was mediated by an employer and necessarily involved less control of the work.

Although the agricultural worker was defined by his or her relationship to an employer, this relationship was not expressed purely in money terms, and in one case not at all (see Mr Collins's interview at the end of this chapter). The full-time regular agricultural worker 'started' with a fixed-term job with known wages and hours of work, and a range of perquisites which might include access to means of self-provisioning, such as the right to keep a cow, to use land or to grow food.

The common circumstance of making use of small amounts of land resulted in some overlap in the strategies for getting a living adopted by members of the households of crofters and agricultural workers. Some of the self-provisioning strategies to be found among highland crofters were also features of the lives of lowland agricultural labourers. Their situation was nevertheless very different. The crofters 'started' with the croft and then looked for other ways of making money in order to have a reasonable living; this included casual and migratory work as agricultural workers.

Unlike crofters, farm servants typically moved a great deal. The protected tenancy and 'fair rent' afforded by the Crofters' Acts made it possible for crofters to remain in one area. For the farm servant, the annual or half-yearly contract coupled with many frequent sources of dissatisfaction – low wages, inadequate housing for growing families, dissatisfaction with the farmer and problematic access to schools – encouraged regular moves, at least for those at the lower end of the farming hierarchy. In the period 1911–39, ploughmen, cattlemen and orramen had an average stay on any one farm of just under three years, while shepherds and grieves, the better-paid and highest-status workers, had average stays of over six years (Anthony, 1992).

Opportunities for Earning Money

Wages and conditions of service varied with the category of job. The households of farm servants often contained several workers bringing in contributions according to their specific occupations. The fathers generally had the best paid jobs. Shepherds were generally the best earners, with the possible exception of grieves. But unlike a grieve, a shepherd was not necessarily receiving a fixed amount as a wage, but rather might be earning by the sale of lambs from sheep he was allowed to keep as his own. While Anthony places the 'orramen', the odd job man, on the same rank as the cattleman and ploughman, several interviewees suggest that this job was less prestigious, less well paid and done only by young single men. The ploughman's management of a pair or team of horses and the cattleman's skills were regarded as specialised jobs worthy of a higher wage than that of other farm workers. Being a ploughman was exclusively a man's job, and both ploughmen and cattlemen were often, but not always, married men. The jobs of shepherd, cattleman and ploughman all involved perquisites, including a tied house.

It was traditionally a condition or 'bond' of employment that each ploughman, commonly called a 'hind', was responsible for supplying a female farm servant as needed by the farmer throughout the year and always at harvest time. A hind without a wife or daughter who could do this work was at a disadvantage as he had to employ such a 'bondager', a living-in servant who was always available for farm work. The farmer paid the hind for each day's work received from the bondager (over and above work during the harvest, which was often in lieu of rent for the hind's cottage) (Devine, 1984; Robson, 1984; Robertson, 1973, 1990). As a contractual requirement, the bondager system had virtually disappeared by the 1900s. A family system of hiring persisted well into the twentieth century, however, and women workers who were members of the hind's family, and hired as part of a deal made with the hind, continued to be referred to as bondagers as late as the 1930s (Robertson, 1990).

A few of our interviewees talked of their mothers or even their sisters working as bondagers. Mr Walker was born in 1899, and as a young lad had worked on the farm in which his father was employed. There were seven men, seven pairs of horses and seven bondagers working together in the fields, among them his sisters – like their mother before them. All of these people actually lived in the farm cottages.

> My sisters both worked on the farm, two o' them, bondagers. They were younger is me. It meant that the men rode the horses and the ploughs and things but the wimmen shawed all the turnips and the swedes by hand, pulled them, knocked the roots off, ye see. They did the stookin'. The binders cut the grain and they forked the sheaves into the cairt to drive them into the stockyaird... Bondagers were nice lassies, just the same as what they are now... But the bondagers got done away wi'.
>
> MR WALKER, BORN 1899

Mr Collins remembered that there were bondagers around in his youth too, not in the hill farms where he and his father worked, but on the arable farms of the Merse (see Map 1). In his full interview (below), he commented that they were expected to do all the jobs nobody else wanted. He also pointed out that where the hinds had no daughter who would turn out to work on the farm they had to engage someone else, otherwise they themselves would not get a job. The only woman employed in his area was the wife of the other shepherd working there.

According to Devine, the best paid of the women workers was the dairymaid. One of our respondents had herself been employed as a dairymaid immediately after leaving school at 13 (a special exemption was required). She describes her working conditions:

> ... we had three milkings a day ... and then we made the butter... We were up at five o'clock in the morning. We had the cows' udders for tae wash, ye ken wi the water and then we had to milk again at one o'clock and the last milking, it was a five o'clock at night. Nine shillings a week! Oo had a Sunday every third Sunday.
>
> *You had to work two Sundays out of three?*
>
> Aye, two Sundays out of three. One Sunday oot o' three weeks ... [repeats]
>
> MRS ALLISON, BORN 1900

Mr Ritchie's mother worked full-time as a dairy maid when her youngest child was still at school and the rest of her children were working. Mrs Aikman's mother supplied the milk, cream and

a

b

FIGURES 3.3a and b: Bondagers, Lothians, 1875 and c. 1900.

butter to the 'big hoose' when the gentry were in residence. One of her two cows actually belonged to her employer; the other was her own.

Farm servants were generally poorly paid. Several of our respondents said that they had moved again and again to get another sixpence a week in wages![6] They also had large families on aver-

FIGURE 3.4: Cow herd and milk maid, Tail Farm, Perthshire, c. 1900.

age.[7] Difficulty in making ends meet financially probably varied with the life cycle stage and the ability of the particular family to generate extra money in the form of wages from older children or the mother. A young person who left school and went to work on the same farm as his agricultural labourer father would not be paid directly. Rather, their wage would be 'in with' their fathers, a practice reflecting the kind of conditions experienced by the bondagers who were paid by the hind for whom they worked. As already noted, a system of family hiring persisted into this century; the farmer struck a single deal for the labour of male and female members of the household with the male head (see also Devine, 1984).

The opportunities for casual earning by children were probably greater on the farm than on the croft, but varied according to size and type of farm and its hinterland. School-age children did odd jobs on the farm like cutting down thistles. Mrs Alison Allison (born in 1900) told us that she used to take milk to the customers for 1s. 6d. a week morning and afternoon: 'Oor fingers used to be a' sore wi the pitchers.'

Sometimes too, children contributed to seasonal work like 'the tattie lifting' (harvesting potatoes). Indeed, well into the twentieth century children's school holidays were organised so that they got two weeks' holidays at the time of the 'tattie' lifting to make sure the crop was harvested. In the summer holidays, some of our respondents living near market gardens spent the time berry picking. For instance, when Mr Pearson was around the age of 10, he went to some gardens about two miles away to pick berries at 10d. a day, working from seven in the morning till five at night.

Perquisites

There were variations in the kinds of perquisites which went with a job, though every married man was provided with a tied house. Housing is discussed in a later section. It is our impression that the older respondents got more in the form of payment in kind, and less in the form of cash payment, but there were also differences according to the kind of job the father did. Mr Renton believed his shepherd[8] father's wages in Peebles-shire in 1917–18 was 30s. a week, and included an allowance of coal, oatmeal and potatoes. Such allowances were common and often sufficient to keep the household for the whole year in these items. In some areas flour was provided instead of or in addition to oatmeal.

The dominance of oatmeal reflects its continued importance in the diet. In the north oatcakes were more of a staple than bread, and everywhere porridge was eaten daily. Porridge was also the main food of sheepdogs. In addition to these allowances of food and fuel, Mr Renton's household could keep a cow and, as was customary, the tied house had an associated garden. Keeping a cow or pig in this period was common but not universal. By the 1930s Mrs West's household in Aberdeenshire did not keep a cow, but her cattleman father's perquisites included milk as well as coal, oatmeal and potatoes. Anthony (1989) found no significant decline in perquisites in eastern Scotland for the period 1914–39.

Self-Provisioning: Animal Husbandry and Cultivation

One of the most important perquisites was the provision of some land for grazing cows and for the keeping of other animals such as pigs and hens. Caring for these animals was included in the work of most of our interviewees' mothers and their sisters when they grew old enough to feed the animals and milk the cow, separate the milk, and make butter. Sometimes the housewife was able to sell her produce to neighbours, to the farmer or to the people in the 'big hoose' when they were in residence. If there was a nearby village or if a grocery van called, she might be able to exchange the produce for groceries of some kind.

The provision of land on which to grow potatoes could result in enough to feed more than the family. An allowance of potatoes from the farm was also sometimes in excess of human needs. Mr Duncan's father's potato allowance was 1,600 yards of potatoes. He said,

> Well, we couldna eat 1600 yairds, so we fed pigs wi them, ye see. I can remember we killed three pigs every year ... oo never had a lot o' money but oo never went hungry.

In households like Mr Duncan's, bacon was an important part of diet. This was also the case in Mrs Aikman's household, where her father took the responsibility of curing the bacon.

> They had one pig, fattened it in the summer time till about maybe November when the weather was colder and then it was slaughtered and they had to make it up into hams. To cure. Father did the slaughtering and butchering and some of the neighbouring shepherds used to come. That was a big day. The whisky bottle had to come out. The old boy who was at Heriot, he used to declare the hams wouldn't keep unless the whisky bottle was opened [laughs]. My father used to mix up this brine in the copper and let it cook. Put the hams in this wooden tub, pour the liquid on top and leave it for about six weeks in the brine. Then take them out and let them dry – hung on hooks from the ceiling.
>
> MRS AIKMAN, BORN 1918

The garden was a seasonal source and often the sole source of vegetables – besides potatoes and turnips from the farm. Getting the garden planted was a high priority, so when agricultural labourers were moving to a new farm (new contracts being made in March) they would sometimes plant the garden in advance of 'the flitting' (in May). If this were not possible it would be the first job after the move. The vegetables which Mrs Doughtie remembered included cabbages, chives, peas, onions and carrots. However, the size of the garden and the quality of soil were not always sufficient for a good crop.

The diet of farm servants and their families was supplemented by buying food they could not produce themselves from vans selling groceries, butcher meat, salted and fresh fish (sometimes this was sold by an itinerant fisherwoman carrying a creel of fish). Doubtless, their diets would be somewhat monotonous by today's standards, but what was grown was eaten, and choice was dictated by season and availability rather than impulse. As many people said, you ate what was put down in front of you, and you ate it quickly because you were hungry and not inclined to be picky. Indeed, our questions about what happened to pernickety eaters were greeted with scorn.

A useful supplement to the diet came through the hunting and gathering activities generally of boys and young men. Among the Border families, this was not as extensive as in the Highlands or among crofting families. Mr Collins, who lived on a remote sheep farm in the Borders, comments in his interview that rabbits were always there and you could always get something to eat. He had learned to catch rabbits when he was quite young. These rabbits were consumed by the household. However, some of the young men sold the skins in order to earn extra money for the household. Mr Linton (born 1898) used to run around the farm at night chasing rabbits. There were no objections to this from the farmer because rabbits destroyed the crops and farmers were glad to have them kept down. Poaching was not a common supplement to the diet, as it seems to have been in the Highlands and Islands.

THE CULTURAL CONTEXT

People living on farms at this period seem more distant from neighbours than those living in crofting communities. There are several reasons for this, including the physical layout of the farms themselves, the residential mobility which resulted from the practice of annual contracts (feeing), poor pay and working conditions, large families, and the social relationships involved in employment. All of these would vary considerably from farm to farm and from family to family.

In the early twentieth century a sizeable farm was like a little scattered village with the farm steading forming a nucleus. In some areas, they were called 'ferm touns'. Away from the farmhouse and farm buildings were the rows of workers' cottages – three or four dwellings with their gardens, to which the workers would return for meals. During harvest time, a mid-day meal would be brought to the workers in the fields by members of their families. Hill shepherds' cottages were a long way from the steading, sometimes in very isolated situations.

While we have little direct evidence of this, it is likely that on large and prosperous farms where the farmer did not dirty his hands with manual work, and where there were many gradations in types of farm labourers, there would also be a social hierarchy among the workers themselves. On smaller farms[9] where the farmer, his wife and their children laboured on the farm and dairy, social distance between employer and workers would have been minimal.

High residential mobility among some kinds of agricultural labourers could result in considerable change in personnel from one year to the next.[10] Mobility was often very local, however, with little likelihood of the newcomer ever feeling like a stranger, especially when the similarities of interest, values and life experience are considered. There were cases among our interviewees where other kin were present either on the farm on which the father was working, or nearby – at least at some stage during the life-cycle. It should be pointed out that not all families moved. They were less likely to do so where the father was a shepherd, steward or grieve in a secure and relatively privileged economic situation. It may well also have been the case that after the youngest child was born and the eldest ones were bringing some money into the household, the pressures for moving were reduced.

Although social life on the farms may not have been as close-knit as that in crofting communities where families had resided over generations, physical proximity, economic hardship and mutual interests necessarily brought opportunities for conversation and a high level of awareness of other people's business. Like the men, the women working in adjacent cottages certainly had opportunities for interaction on a daily basis. In some cases, respondents said that they had helped each other during childbirth. In general, our interviewees often commented on how helpful neighbours had been when they were young.[11] Children living on the farm and walking the (usually) long way to school, chatted and played together.

To a much higher degree than in the crofting situation, the spheres of activity of people involved in agricultural labouring were differentiated. The fact of employment created greater constraints on what people could do, and at what time. Most employees were

FIGURE 3.5:   Children posing outside farm cottages, Charleston, Angus.

expected to work hours set by season and tradition. The fixed meal times of farm labourers also structured the day of the domestic worker at home. The long hours of employment meant that there was little time left in the evenings for leisure or visiting.

Leisure in Homes and on the Farm

Leisure as a distinct type of time for particular activities was arguably an alien concept in the childhood of may of our intervie-wees. A few mentioned some form of music, such as singing or playing a fiddle or accordion. A couple spoke of playing cards or dominoes. Reading the paper was quite common, though news-papers might have come only once a week. Mrs Alison Allison (born in 1900) said how much she had looked forward to the evening the newspaper came, for her mother used to read them stories from it. If the paper was bought at all, it was usually the father who read it, and usually to himself. In general, however, there was little to say about leisure because there was limited free time and little sense that it should be filled with special pleasurable activities.

The evenings were used by women for mending, sewing and knitting – necessary activity if household members were to remain reasonably well clad. Most of the mothers made all the children's and most of the adults' clothes, and they also refashioned garments and mended constantly to try and save money. A few also men-tioned home-made rag rugs.[12] Many people mentioned wearing hand-me-downs, and emphasised the importance to the household budget of their mothers' thrifty domestic activities. The mothers' priorities are nicely summed up by Mrs Doughtie's mother, one of the two mothers who had bought a sewing machine rather than have false teeth fitted – much to their husbands' annoyance. As she said, however, 'it was a better friend to her in later years than her teeth'. For married women with children, it seemed there was little or no leisure as we conceive it. As Mr Collins said, his mother would wash them in the tub in front of the fire on a Saturday night, and that was all the leisure she had, beyond going to church and putting on a clean blouse for the occasion.

Times for adults and children to go to bed varied with age and with the season. During the normal school week, children tended to go to bed very early indeed. Mrs Alison Allison (born in 1900) said that she was ready for bed at six o'clock because she had so far (three miles) to walk to school. Other children, however, tended to go later than this. Even when Mrs Allison was grown up, however, she was usually in bed by nine o'clock, because of the early rising required of her job as a dairy-maid. In general, all farm servants had to be up very early in the morning. While finishing times varied with the season, starting times remained early throughout the year. For example, ploughmen fed their horses and started work before returning home for their own breakfast, winter and summer.

Some farm workers did enjoy regular visiting with neighbours and kin living within walking distance. Sometimes the families would walk many miles in bad weather to enjoy conversation and music. Mrs Aikman, a shepherd's daughter, said that their family had had great times in the slack season visiting neighbours, including in turn, all the five shepherds who lived on the farm. (She was one of two children; it is unlikely that larger families of young children could have gone visiting other homes so far from their own.)

> We used to visit neighbouring shepherds in the winter time. We used to have musical nights. My father used to play the fiddle. We had sing-songs and what not.
>
> *How far?*
>
> The nearest was Heriot, about a mile down the road. An old couple lived there. The others were approximately two to three miles away. We used to go on a Friday night because there was no school the following day, come home elevenish at night, I suppose. Dark, winter nights [laughs].
>
> MRS AIKMAN, BORN 1918

Speaking of his experience in the North-East, Mr Ritchie remembered that there was more fun to be had when the farmer was away:

> On the farms we had the bothy. Always one or two ploughmen, single fellows, living in the bothy. We would all meet in the bothy and we would have ceilidhs in the bothy. And dances. Och we had a great time . . . Any night the chap would be away. They didn't go away very often then.
>
> MR RITCHIE, BORN 1905

Several people remembered happy times spent in the bothy. A couple of interviewees also mentioned the annual social evening arranged by the farmer to celebrate the successful completion of the harvest.

> Efter that, the farmer gave ee a kirn – we had a dance in the granary to celebrate the in-gathering of the harvest. The farmer supplied the drink and whatnot, and the wives aboot the farm supplied the eatables. Ye danced to a couple of men wi fiddles tae aboot six o'clock in the morning. So ye changed into yer breeches and nicky tams for workin'.
>
> MR WALKER, BORN 1899

Miss Fraser, the daughter of a rural worker who had spent several years of her childhood on a farm in Midlothian, told us about how her mother as a young maid employed in the 'big hoose', enjoyed the occasional 'fling' when the gentry went off on holiday. This comfortable country residence with farm attached provided employment for a range of house servants, grooms and farm workers as well as casual workers employed for the shooting season, a very busy time for the staff. However,

> when the lady and gentleman went away from home, they would just have a party. If they had a good cook . . . a lot depended on the cook . . . The gamekeeper would bring in a rabbit, make rabbit pie. Oh, sometimes they had a whale of a time. There would be dancing all night, just the people on the estate.
>
> MRS FRASER, BORN 1913

Mrs Fraser is the cousin of Mrs Aikman, whose father was also employed on the farm belonging to this big house.[13]

Not all of the sociable activities enjoyed by our respondents' family members took place at home or on the farm. Some men were able to get to the pub to enjoy a convivial drink with other farm workers, at least occasionally. Mr Duncan's father was one of only two men who appear to have played any sport at all. His father had played quoits once a week at the village. The men on the farm would practise in the fields at night. When asked about curling he said, 'Ye had to be a bigger wig tae be among the curlers. The fermers and the gentry.' *They* did not play quoits.

Mr Renton described the leisure time of his mother and father as follows:

> Well my mother did nothing else for pleasure [except] shopping down to the town. My faither he did whilst go on a Saturday night and have a drink whilst, especially sale day, when they were selling sheep he always had a wee bittie [to drink]. I've never seen him really drunk

FIGURE 3.6:   Farm servants with quoits and fiddles, Fife, *c.* 1900.

coming home. He was always sober enough. He always met other shepherds. That's what they did then on a Saturday night.

MR RENTON, BORN 1912

For farm servants, hiring fairs also appear to have been important annual and biannual social gatherings. The only outings married women seem to have had were in connection with going to town to shop, which was unusual, regular attendance at church, perhaps a little visiting with neighbours, and sometimes annual Sunday School or school trips when they accompanied their children to the seaside or some park.

Going to Church

Although all of our farm servant respondents went to church or Sunday School regularly as children with one exception,[14] there were differences in the strictness with which the Sabbath was observed. In the North-East Mr Ritchie's labouring parents were members of the United Free Church. Like many of the crofting children, they were not allowed out unaccompanied, and the whole household went to church twice a day and was read the Bible by his

— 87 —

father also twice a day. Children who were brought up in the Borders had to go to church or Sunday School on a regular basis, but that was the only form of Sunday observance spontaneously mentioned by them, apart from the fact that some of them had special clothes to wear on Sunday.

Children carried out their religious duties with varying degrees of enthusiasm. Mrs Alison Allison obviously enjoyed her Sunday jaunt. Unlike other children who frequently had to walk several miles, her Sunday School was held at a church on the farm itself.

> We went to the church at night because our parents were great... you know they liked to go. My mother was a great singer. She used to be in the choir ... years and years ago ... when she was very young ... All the families joined in the church. Every Friday night for six weeks to join the church. It was the ... church up there that we joined. Then we had wir first communion there. We was a' in a row in the front of the pew, ye know, the communicants. The whole lot o' us. Young girls and young boys, we all went thegither to join the Church. I think I was sixteen.
>
> MRS ALLISON, BORN 1900

Few of the agricultural workers' children said much about church or Sunday School, apart from commenting on the distances they had to walk to get there. However, the socially observant Mr Duncan did note, drily, that in the church his family attended, status was observed in the seating arrangements, reflecting the same sort of practices observed in sporting activities. Quoits was played only by the workers, curling by the gentry, whereas in church, 'Gentry and farmers were up aboon the others at the Kirk in their rented pews.'

THE HOUSEHOLD
Housing and Domestic Technology

Invariably, married farm labourers were provided with a tied house. In most cases, these would be one in a row of farm cottages housing similar workers and their families. Despite the large sizes of families, interviewees complained little about the houses, which varied between two and four rooms. Most of them had a bed in the kitchen/living room usually occupied by the parents, while the children bedded down in the other room. As was the case in many working-class households in this period, urban and rural, there was little privacy and much sharing of beds. Mrs Alison Allison came from a family of five. She remarked that:

> Sometimes the farm houses werena very big. In fact, I've seen mebbe two beds in the kitchen and then there would be two in the rooms, ye know. The toilet would be outside and ye had a wee kitchenette. Farm houses were nothing in these days.
>
> MRS ALLISON, BORN 1900

Even small families had trouble accommodating their members (see the Report of the Royal Commission on Housing). Mrs Aitken (born in 1916) had only one sister. In their house, there was a living room in which the parents slept and one bedroom for the girls. When their grandmother died, they could not provide accommodation for the grandfather who had to use the bothy on the other side of the road where a groom, the gamekeepers and gardeners lived.

Facilities were generally quite primitive. In the newer houses, concrete floors replaced the hard-packed clay, and a range with an oven replaced the open fire of earlier times. Outside toilets were still the norm. Only one of our younger respondents (born in 1922) said that there was running water in the house. Usually there was a shared outside tap. Water for all purposes had to be heated on the coal range, which was also used for cooking and baking. The range was invariably situated in the living room/kitchen. Some of the houses had a back kitchen which was used for washing dishes and for personal washing. The kitchen would also be used for preparing food for animals, such as the hens, pigs and the working dogs of shepherd families.

Mr Duncan described the domestic facilities very clearly:

> ... mostly ranges in the ferm cottages ... awthing was done on the fire, ye had the swee, ye hung yer pots and things on there, ye, aye.
>
> *Back kitchen?*
>
> Yes, but there were nae bathrooms in thae days, mind ye. Ootside toilets.
>
> *And you'd wash in the back kitchen, have to heat up the water?*
>
> Yes, aye. Ye had what ye ca'ed the washin' pot, hung on the swey, just the same, boilt the claes in there, and ye had a tub and a board for scrubbin'. There was nae water in the hooses then, ye had to gang to the well for't. In later years they got pumps in but just a well at one

time [they had to draw water by hand]. Sometimes the well was just
. . . ye just dippit the pails in.

Was it safe to drink?

Guid spring water in them days.

MR DUNCAN, BORN 1900

Household Composition

Most of our agricultural labourer respondents were brought up in
households that consisted solely of their parents and siblings, but
there were exceptions. In some cases grandparents who had also
been agricultural labourers came because they needed a place to
stay after their own days as farm employees were finished and they
were obliged to vacate their tied house. This might have required a
change in employment to a farm with a larger tied cottage – or
accommodation might be found for a grandfather, as it was in two
cases, in the bothy with the single men. Mrs Doughtie explains the
situation with reference to her father's parents (see the full interview at the end of this chapter).

Division of Labour by Age and Sex

The classification of work into inside and outside was also a division of work into women's and men's, except that women also did
out-work. However, men never did inside work. Boys might do a
restricted range of 'inside' tasks, but men did not. This classification was the backdrop to the organisation of agricultural work as
well as the division of labour in the household. When our male
respondents told us about who did the housework, they tended to
mention their sisters when explaining why they themselves did no
domestic chores – 'Well, no, because we had a lot o' sisters and . . .'
(Mr Linton, born 1898).

What was labelled 'inside' and 'outside' were not simply jobs
done in and out of the house. Men were not involved in the care of
the household cow, for example; that was classified as inside work,
as Mr Doughtie's response made clear when asked about this: 'Oh
no, they werenae supposed to do anything but work out.' It is not
clear whether milking the cow was 'inside' because it was the
household rather than the farm cow, or if 'inside' took in the byre as
well as the house. On some farms most byre work was women's

work, but this varied with the number of hands and the degree of specialisation. The working of the classification was a matter of customary expression of gender, rather than a logically derived division of labour.

As in poor households elsewhere at this time, farm labourers' children accepted that their contribution was needed, and rarely complained about working whether the work in question was paid or not. Most of the girls routinely helped their mothers when they were not at school. For instance, Mrs Aikman as a young child used to clean the brasses on a Saturday, and clean the cutlery and the cutlery drawer. She also used to dry dishes occasionally as required and make her own bed. She never liked cleaning the brasses on a Saturday, but it was just one of the necessary evils that you had to get on with, she said. During the week she had to wash up the dishes on her return from school at half past four in the afternoon. Later on, when she was older, she also trimmed the paraffin lamps and fed the dogs for her father – the working sheep dogs.

Mrs Aikman was the elder of only two children, an unusually small family. Housework was a bone of contention because her sister used to be out playing on the Saturday while she herself had to stay in and do these chores. Complaints would fall on deaf ears. In terms of the contribution of other girls, Mrs Aikman was not overburdened as a young child. Much worse was to come. When she was 13 her mother was taken seriously ill, and Mrs Aikman had to assume much heavier domestic responsibilities. When her mother died a year later, she did almost everything her mother had done, keeping house for her father and sister. Fortunately for her, however, she had never learned to milk the cow.

> Aye well, my Dad had to milk the cow because I had never done that job before. But I had to use the separator for the milk, wash the milk dishes, the various jobs.
>
> MRS AIKMAN, BORN 1918

Her father was able to milk, but when her mother was there, it was a job she did, a job specifically done by the mothers – and by daughters when they got old enough to do it.

Changes in family circumstances could always result in a daughter having to shoulder a heavy burden of domestic work and responsibility. Elder daughters were most likely to have a lot to do. Mr Linton (born 1898) told us about his eldest sister who was kept from employment in the fields on leaving school in order to work full-time at home assisting her mother. There were other cases like this (see Mrs Doughtie's interview, for example).

> My mother was getting on in years and she kept my oldest sister, instead of working in the fields, to do work in the house, to save her. It was the idea of all of us and my mother, then she [the mother] had it easier. Then my oldest sister Jessie [she was ten years older than him] didn't engage on the 28th, she came to work in the house.
>
> MR LINTON, BORN 1898

Not all mothers in our sample required work from their children as with Mrs Aikman's younger sister. Mr Humphries (born in 1901) said that his mother didn't get children to work for her. He felt that she had made a mistake in this. 'She didnae teach ye to dae that kind o work.' When asked why not, he said that, 'We wasnae inclined to that work . . . we were aye outside playing with bairns.' It was not clear whether he was talking about boys only, since many of our male respondents had rather hazy ideas about what their mothers and sisters were doing in the house.

Mr Humphries' family was a small one compared with other farm servants', consisting of the two boys and one girl. Perhaps his mother did indeed expect little of them. Mr Humphries did in fact do some outside work. Earlier in the interview he said that he had gathered wood and chopped it up for the fire, a chore that was shared with other working-class boys who had access to woodland. He did not say so, but in cases where this was expected of boys in villages or at the outskirts of towns where wood could be gathered, it was the father – not the mother – who saw to it that the boys did this work.[15]

Several of our respondents recall doing paid work, either around the farm, in the dairy or in the vicinity. This was less usual for girls than for boys. As we noted before, Mrs Alison Allison had her paid job as a child, delivering milk for 1s. 6d. per week. Her younger sister, who was present at the interview, did no work of this kind. But if Mrs Allison felt resentment, she only indicated it indirectly. Indeed, there seems to have been little rebellion felt at having to do either household chores or paid ones. Mr Pearson (born in 1898), who was brought up on a farm in the Lothians, put it like this when asked how he felt about spending his summer holidays berry picking:

Well you needed to do it. In these days they didn't have big wages. They got a lot off the farm such as potatoes and all the rest of it. Otherwise you'd more or less to do it.

ALEC PEARSON, BORN 1898

Mr Pearson was typical of children from households with low incomes, in that he had no *right* to retain what he earned berry picking or doing anything else as a child. But by his last year at school, as one of the youngest ones in the family, he was allowed to keep his Saturday earnings since there were already multiple earners in his household. Mr Ritchie was also one of the few lucky ones who got to keep some of his earnings. His father was an agricultural labourer in the North-East near Invergordon, and by the time he was 12 his mother was working as a dairy maid and three older siblings were also bringing money home. At this time the farm grieve paid him 1s. 3d. for a full Saturday's work bruising oats – that is grinding them to make them suitable feed for the cows. He was able to take himself to the pictures with the proceeds – a measure of his new-found but limited autonomy. Poverty, and heavy demands on able-bodied children, were a family-household life-cycle phenomenon which particularly afflicted large families in which the older children were too young to leave school and earn money on a full-time basis. At a later period, when the older children were working, the more fortunate younger ones might be allowed to keep their Saturday earnings or even get a Saturday penny.

There are other reasons for variability in the amount of work which children did. In some households housework was kept to a minimum, as it was not necessarily the mother's priority where she was also engaged in farm work. In general, the range of tasks that farm servants' children were expected to do without pay was not as extensive as on a croft, although there was some overlap – gathering and chopping wood, gathering eggs, turning the butter churn, helping with milking. The direct contribution of children to the household economy through self-provisioning tasks, earning money for the common purse, and, in the case of girls, domestic labour, typically continued beyond school age into their twenties in cases where children remained at home.

Relationships between Parents and Children

If we consider relationships between parents and children among
the farm servants' children alone, we could conclude that there was
no clear style of parenting which emerged as 'different' from that of
crofters, just as there was no single style of parenting among the
crofters. There are some subtle differences between crofters and
farm servants which are associated with their relationship to the
means of production and to the social context within which they
lived, as well as many similarities. Let us start with some of the
similarities between crofters' and farm servants' children.

Taking into consideration how much time they seem to have
spent in contributing to the household, all these children lacked the
freedom to develop individual interests as children do today, just as
their parents were unlikely to be able to buy them toys, and just as
the communities in which they lived afforded little in the way of
entertainments of any kind designed specifically for children. None
of the children whose lives we have investigated up to this point
appeared to have much in the way of toys of any kind. They played
while they worked, when they were coming home from school and,
in the case of children who lived on farms, they played in the fields
around their homes. They took part in home leisure activities and
in visiting with parents, they went to church and Sunday School,
and in some areas sometimes went on Sunday School picnics or
took part in school sports.

Furthermore, these children did not have easy access to parents
in the sense of being able to talk to them about their fears or
problems. Several of the women, for instance, said that their first
period had come as a great shock to them (this was also true of Mrs
Gillies as can be seen from her interview). None of our respondents
claimed to know about sex[16] until they were almost grown up.
Other forms of behaviour exemplifying the ways in which parents
distanced themselves from their children were at mealtimes, when
children were usually expected to hold their tongues, at least while
adults were talking. Some children were expected to be silent
during meals.

There is little evidence that parents showed any great degree of
sensitivity to the needs of children in the ways that are expected
today. Indeed, what evidence there is suggests that some of the
children suffered from teasing and other indignities, not so much by

FIGURE 3.7: Sunday School picnic outing, Scone, Perthshire, c. 1900.

parents, but by older children and other adults. In brief, it can be said that all these children were seen and treated more like small adults than children are today. At the same time, some aspects of adult life were absolutely closed to them.

It is widely believed that children were often punished on a regular basis in the past. Like other researchers using oral histories, we have not found this to be the case, either among crofters or farm workers. Parents may have been strict, but it was not usual for children to be regularly smacked among either the crofting or the farm servant families. Serious offences *were* likely to cause a great row, and sometimes a beating. A good example is the case of Mr Renton (born in 1912), who had been talked into truanting by his brother. After about a week, someone reported them. Double retribution was to follow.

> The headmaster ta'en us through all the classes, two bright sparks. I mind he put me up on the top of a blackboard. I was pretty frightened because when you put your feet on it, it birled round about. But he made a spectacle of [us]. A pretty sad time . . . we got a doing up frae my father . . . He lifted the skin from below my eye wi' a dog leash. So that's what I had to pay for it . . . We ran about among the woods and these places but we'd been spotted. Maybe it would have been better if they had found oot [before] and then we wouldnae have had such a doing up at the school probably.
>
> MR RENTON, BORN 1912

Mr Humphries (born in 1901) was an exception because he did not have to commit a serious offence to get a beating. He got an 'awfu' lickin'' from his father when he was young, 'just for very little. Made ee feared you know.' But fear of parents was more common than these exceptional circumstances. Many of the interviewees said something to the effect that they were afraid to talk back, to sound cheeky, to avoid doing their chores or to do them badly, mentioning various forms of punishment they feared they might get.

Given their circumstances, parents must have been sorely tried at times by the behaviour of their children. Some parents reacted with restraint, even though the child's behaviour must have caused them considerable anxiety. For instance, Mrs Allison was once bought a pair of long-legged boots which she hated, so she cut them down to make shoes of them. Her mother said that she would now have to go barefoot, having ruined them, that she would never get another pair of shoes or boots from her! 'She was only saying that of course.' This family seemed to operate on the basis of threats as did many others:

> One look from my father and that was enough. He never once lifted his hand to any of us. Cos, I mean to say, we never done anything really. We were aa country and we all just played on the land, in the fields and things like that. My mother never had any bother wi' us . . . She used to say, 'I'm no very big, but ye'll never get the better o' me!' [laughter]. But she wasna bad. She was a grand wee soul really. Naw, we never done anything really. I mean, we thought a lot o' our mother and fathers in these days. They worked very hard, ye know, they didnae have much money. And they worked hard fir to keep us a' goin.
>
> MRS ALLISON, BORN 1900

It should be pointed out that the children themselves had a great appreciation of the problems their parents faced.

> Sometimes oo thought we were maybe hard done by but in the sense that they had to keep order among a big family it was possibly the only way they could manage, ye see. Oo sometimes thought that oo werenae fairly treated, but looking back, I don't think that that was the case at aa. Sometimes you would get punished for something you thought shouldnae have been and so forth. But there was no abuse.
>
> MR COLLINS, BORN 1906

If the children felt resentment, there was little they could do about it. Parents in those days had traditional authority on their side and this was reinforced by other children, by neighbours, by the school and by the church. Parental expectations were known, as were the obligations of children towards them. There was little in the way of physical punishment because everyone knew what was expected – and did it.

There were, however, some subtle differences between crofters' and agricultural workers' children. Some of these were associated with the families' economic situation and some were to do with the social context, or a combination of the two. Crofters' children usually spent their childhood more among kin and neighbours who had lived there for generations, or where, at least, the family was well known and respected in the community. The basis of their economic life was subsistence farming, which depended on co-operation with each other. It was essential that children would grow up having learned the basic principles of reciprocity in social life – of sharing work and leisure activities which blended into each other, and respect for the elders, especially parents and grand-parents. It was among these crofting communities that children were more likely to do chores without having to be told what to do. They learned by doing.

None of our crofters' children told us about being beaten for serious offences. Although parents were strict in general, especially about religious matters, the strictest of parents in crofting com-munities appear to have been those who were dissatisfied with their position or were marginal to the community in some way, like Mr Geddes' father who had to return to the croft when his farm failed.

In the case of farm servants' children, it tended to be fathers who dispensed punishment for serious offences. Living and working on the employer's farm fostered sensitivity among farm labourers to their own children's behaviour, since any misdemeanours would have reflected on them as heads of household. Parents who were socially aspiring or struggling against some exceptional difficulty were particularly strict. Mrs West's father had had a very difficult youth as a result of the struggles of his crofting family, and had been obliged to return to the croft on his father's death. His very firm, even harsh control of the income of his eldest daughter could be attributed to anxieties about 'siller' occasioned by early struggle. Mr Renton's father's social mobility depended on the labour of his son. He exploited his son by commandeering his earnings beyond boyhood, having him work for him without payment on the small farm the father managed to acquire until he, the father, died. Mr Humphries' father was suffering from rheumatics, yet carried on in an all-weather job which aggravated the condition.

Relationships between parents and children reflected the social controls present in their living situation. Neighbours had to be considered. There were not many of them in most cases, but crofters in particular could not afford to quarrel with them for both social and economic reasons, since they depended on each other. For the children of both crofters and farm workers there were also outside influences in the form of the school and the church, where the same sort of values and ideologies would be promulgated in respect of work and duty towards employers and parents alike. In general the church loomed less large in the lives of farm servants' families than among crofters living in areas dominated by strictly Sabbatarian churches. On the other hand, being judged a 'good worker' by current and potential employers was necessarily more important to the farm worker than to the crofter – although recent work suggests that farmers had to be as careful of their reputations as farm workers (Anthony, 1992).

INTERVIEWS WITH CHILDREN OF FARM SERVANTS

We have selected three people to talk about their childhoods in different parts of rural Scotland. Two of them come from the Borders and the third from the North-East. Between them, they provide a vivid picture of farming and social life in a range of situations. Mr Collins's family lived in an isolated region of the Borders having strong economic and social connections with England. A rather different sort of life was experienced by Mrs Doughtie, whose large family moved from farm to farm in a much more populous area. Her childhood is representative of many of the children of farm servants. Mrs West, whose testimony is presented first, lived in north-east Aberdeenshire in an area in which crofters were also present. Her childhood experience spanned both crofting and life on a large farm, so that the content of the interview overlaps somewhat with the interviews of crofting children.

Mrs West, born 1921, Aberdeenshire

This is an interview which expresses tensions between parents and children in more than one generation – tensions created by their economic situation, and cultural differences created by disruptive social change in the locality in which the extended family lived. We see this first in the situation of Mrs West's mother, who as a young woman had not wanted to follow the expected course of remaining on the farm or croft. She had wanted to become a dressmaker. However, as the eldest of a large family she was forced to give up her miserably-paid apprenticeship when her mother demanded her return to the family to help out on the larger farm they had acquired. Instead, she fled to work with her aunt in the kitchens of an employer, presumably gaining her desired independence and freedom from field work. As we shall see, Mrs West's own experience was not dissimilar to that of her own mother.

Readers may well find this a difficult transcript to read, but we urge them to persevere since it is one of the richest in terms of language and social content. Mrs West is an acute social observer. As such, she is able to provide valuable commentary on the links between crofting and farming people and to tell us something of what it meant to be caught up in the rapid change taking place in her area as a result of the later stages of the transition to capitalism.

The interview starts with an account of the moves made by this family as a result of the father's employment. On the family's fourth move, Mrs. West started school. From time to time she reverts to the dialect of her childhood.

Interview with Mrs West

Did you move because of your father's job?

Yes. He was a dairy cattleman. He was working for PP. He was a Tory MP I think for Aberdeenshire or somewhere roond about Aberdeenshire.

He had a big farm?

He had big farms. He had a lot o' farms.

Who lived in the household with you when you were a child? How many brothers and sisters had you?

There was a family o' one brother [corrected to 'one sister']. That was all. There was just the two of us there. Two girls.

That was quite a small family. Was that usual?

It was beginning then, to have a small family.

Was your father born in the Huntley Hall area?

No, he come from Maryculter. That's jist – what side o' Aberdeen? – different side from the Huntley Hall side.

Was he a cattleman then?

Yes, he was; he went in to help his father. And his father was a cattleman; a dairy cattleman. He was working for somebody else.

What about your mother?

Well Mother . . . she was the oldest of the family. And she wanted to be a dressmaker and she used to have to cycle into Old Meldrum to get her training and she got sixpence a day. And that was from eight o'clock in the morning till six at night.

What happened?

No she couldnae afford to. They had to stop her and then she took a bigger farm and they wanted her to come home you see and she wouldn't do it and she went to work in the kitchens wi' her aunt. She just wouldn't do it because she didn't want to work outside. She didn't like the outside work. It was only the housework that she liked.

A lot of girls would have done that at that stage?

Quite a few, there was quite a few did it. But mainly where there was a lot of girls at home that they couldn't afford to keep. If you was kept at home you had to work on the croft as needed and if they werena needed they used to have to go and find a job somewhere else.

They mightn't have liked them getting married?

Oh no, a lot o' them never – in fact I know of two people never were married. Because they were working on the croft and their father and mother just wouldna let them go.

But they would be big enough to go.

They were that.

Why didn't they go?

Well, it was just the way that . . . they were wee bairns . . . they never had any inclination to leave home. No, they would nae think about it. There was nothing to think aboot.

Obey thy father and thy mother?

That was all.

Did you do jobs in the house yourself when you were little?

Oh, aye we had our little jobs to . . . we would never have got away . . . we had to have something [laughs]. My good job . . . not so much at home, in my own home, but at my grandmother's . . . I fed the hens and fed the calves and did . . . trampit the blankets[17] . . . when you washed them you had to get in and tramp them . . . in a tub, a big tub [much laughter].

It would be a job getting them dried?

There was no wringers in thir days. Ye just wrung them in your hauns. Ootside the door.

You said your grandmother was a crofter. She made cheese?

I used to get the milk and they never took the milk until it had been on the grass for so long ... and after it had ... they[18] had ... been on the grass you collected your milk and we did it wi' rennet and there was a big stane ootside the door and you screwed yer cheeses into it – it was just ootside the hoose door, aside the barrel wi' the rainwater. They made different kinds. She changed cheese. For a bit o' variety. The top shelf o' the milk-hoose was aye full,[19] for the winter.

That was your grandmother ... What about your mother?

No, she never did that ... well, she did if anyone came doon to see us. She made small ones. But my grandmother made the great big ones.

What about other things you grew?

Aw well, ye grew all your own berries, ye had your strawberries and your rasps, gooseberries ... and made all your own jam ... there was aye the two hundred punds o' jam in the season.

You spent a lot of money on sugar?

Well, she used to collect the sugar throughout the year. Ye wasna allowed nae mair as what eggs ye sell or what butter ye sell. That was for your provisions. Your buy-in provisions. There was no money to make your ... but just eggs. The more eggs you had to sell the more you had for your budget [?] ... and the butter was the same. That was what you had to keep the house.

Your grandmother's black leghorns?

We used to visit so many crofters at the Spring holiday. We took off in the afternoon for maybe a fortnight when I was on holiday[20] and ye set off to Mrs So-and-so this day and Mrs Watt another day and we gaed to the Smiddy and swapped eggs there.

This was not for eating?

Oh no, this was for a clecking. You had a clocker set when it was aboot a week before you went away on this expedition and you had your clocker so she was going to sit on her eggs and you had to have them ready for to take them when you got them.

This was only women?

It was just the women who did this.

The men never did this?

We never took the men at a'. Oh no. We had a beig.[21] [There were five places her granny used to go to.] That was a day's gossiping. Just neighbours. Oh, they were an awfa friendly lot o' neighbours . . .

Did the neighbours help each other out?

They did. When the threshing mill came in, they used to a' come in and dae the [hesitates] well, the squirl[22] . . . no it a' . . . but we used to a' do so much. And then had a mell o' oor ain, a sma' mill and they got fresh caff[23] for their cattle when they cam to the thrashin' mill when it came in. They used to come in and do the scones? No it all, they all yist to dae sae much. And they had a mill o' their ain, a small mill and they did mebbes their [?] to get fresh straw for their cattle.

Did they grind their own grain?

Grind their own grain.

For oatmeal?

No for oatmeal. They just did it for to feed the cattle. Ye took your grain to the miller's. A special miller. Normally, at that time it was just oats up in Aberdeenshire. You took your oats you see and you ran back and when you gaed back for your oats you got different oatmeal. Oatmeal for to make porridge and oatmeal for to bake oatcakes wi'. And then we had the seds;[24] and that ye'd gie to your hens. And we used to make sowans.[25] [Interviewer utterly baffled!] I cannae tell you how you spell sowans, but that was what we used to have. It was made . . . ye soakit them for a week the seds that came back from the mill-rink. You soakit them for a week and then you took off the brew and ye boiled it and pit a spuneful o' syrup on the top o' it and a wee drop o' cream and that was eaten . . . that was a treat! It was just a porridge done wi' a floury meal but it was sowans.

What else did you produce? Did they have a pig?

Aye, but there was nae pig-killing up in Aberdeenshire. They kept a pig just for to sell or just to help to buy [hesitates] – another piece of land.

What kind of meat did you eat?

Beef. Aa beef. I never can mind o' having mutton. Or pork. At my grandmother's. But beef was bought on a Friday and it did all week. It was boilt for soup. They made the broth wi't on the Friday and we didnae get beef on Saturday. That was kept ... but ye got it on Sunday. We had a grocer's meal wi' mealie puddings. Ye had your beef and your cabbage and your soup and she aye used to make a dumpling on Friday afternoons. That was a big occasion. A sweet dumpling, and that was poppit into the pan, among the broth, boilt in the broth, because ye see at that time we had a peat fire and that was – there was no fire up or doon. The peat fire at nights when you brought your peats wi' a hearth on the floor. There were slab-stones on the fire.

How many rooms did the house have?

[Hesitates.] The parlour ... what we term the sitting-room was the parlour. That was where you went on a Sunday night to read your bit oot o' the Bible or ... and then they had a bedroom doonstairs for them, and there was two bedrooms up the stair. Kitchen/livingroom, the peat fire and a swey. It just held one pot and off that pot was three legs and when you took them doon you just laid them on the hearth.

Did they have a box-bed?

They had a box-bed in the room doon the stair and the twae[26] rooms up the stair. There was [counts] two box-beds and one bed and the best bedroom they took oot the box-bed and pit in an ordinary bed. That was the room for the visitors coming. The box-beds were filled with caff[27], off the corn when it's threshed. They were filled with caff every year. Ye needit a chair to get intae bed [laughs].

They'd have no inside toilet?

No, they had a toilet made in the garden. But it was just a bucket. It was emptied every week.

Who emptied it?

Oh, my granny I think would have emptied it.

That wouldn't have been men's work?

Oh no they didn't help. Because they never used it. The back o' the byre! [Laughter.]

What did the men do? They would work of course?

My uncle he drave the horse and my grandfather did the cattle on the croft and at that time they had, you see, quite a big place. And the

a   b

FIGURES 3.8a and b: A box bed.

cattle was a' tied by the heid. And they had so many feeding cattle
and so many milking cows. They fattened them up for the market.

Would they fatten them up for other farmers?

No, just for theirselves. They were independent.

Did they ever earn wages?

No, not at all. Well, if there was anything, a new mell or something
like that, that was the ...

*You must have noticed a big difference between your grandmother's and your
mother's place?*

Oh, a big difference. The mother used to milk cows where they
were. She used to work in the dairy. After she was married and my
father did the cattle, then she made the butter for them and did the
hens and brought oot the chickens. She had two children and was
expecting the third. There were three sisters.

I didnae dae much in the house, because I helped my father
ootside. I had to get up a five o'clock in the morning [laughs] and go
round and help him to feed the cattle, and well there were the
cake[28] and turnip and straw before I went to school in the morning
so he gave us a bike so I could get to stop later wi'him and be hame
as quick as possible to help him at night. Lousing-time[29] was never

till six o'clock. Then ye went home and ye had maybes a plate o' porridge, maybes a boiled egg. Of course there were breid but that was a quarter[30]. It was oatcakes. Us being north country my mother made oatcakes right up until she died. The oatcakes came a long way ... they've come doon to the Borders.[31]

Who did the housework?

Well mother ... what work there was done. There was very little done. The floors was covered wi' linoleum. Ye made your own rugs, the clootie rugs. The cooking. Ma mother never likit cooking, and there wasnae muckle attention paid to it. It was maybe mince and tatties, or stew and tatties and a wee dumpling [laughs] and boiled beef ... we never had roast. She made jam. She saved up the sugar.

Where did she get the money for the sugar?

It was just what wages was come in. [My sisters did not help on the farm.] They were luckier than I was. I was the eldest and I had tae ... at the time I didnae think nothing aboot it but later as years went past I did. I did begin to think it was a shame. Because I never got what they got, but I had to work for't. They got a better schooling than I ever got. My ambition to begin with was dress-making. Or child-nursing. That was the two things that I wanted to do. But I never was allowed because I couldnae ... they couldn't afford to let me into that. [I suggested it to them] many a time but my mother used to say they couldn't do without me bringing in a wage. They depended on you. When I started to work I got ten shillings a week. That was my wage. They got it, all o' t. When I was seeing the others, the other yins[32] getting oot – I never got oot – then they started to give us a shilling a week. A shilling didn't go a' that far. A' ma clothes was second-hand clothes. It was some maybe friend that was getting something new I got the old; but I was proud of it, I tell you.

I was 14, 15 then. I got fed up wi' that and I went away to service, thinking that I would get masel the money but I didnae, I had to send it home. They used to come and get it! [Laughter.] My father used to come if I wasn't home when it was pay-day and pick it up. The other one was working by this time, but the youngest one was away to school and of course she got a better education. She took shorthaund and typewriting and she's still in the same job the day. The other one she's retired now. They're both married.

Maybe if you had been a younger child, you would have got that too.

If I'd been a younger child, I'd have got that opportunity too. My mother, aye. My father, no. Education meant nothing. As long as ye could work for forty years for siller, that was money.

Was siller land?

No, money money money. He never had that ... [desire to own land].

What about your grandfather?

Oh, he was a hard man. He was a working man; he eggit to get up. He wanted to move up. I think it would be in his upbringing. You see ma grannie come of crofting people. Ma grandfather came off the railway. They were in the railway. He did [want to be more secure].

No welfare state then?

Nothing, ye was just down and out.[33]

With a croft you can always feed yourself.

We aye did that.

But on wages you might be put off.

There's jist nothing. Ye had nothing. My mother used to say we were better off ... that was in the 1920s ... they had very little coming in and at that time my father was paid by the six month and ye had your six month wages and ye had to work it oot ... we yins, well they got oatmeal, they got milk, they got potatoes, and they got coal. And then the free house. The rest ye had to find. Well they had a garden and ye were allowed to keep maybe about a dozen hens. We had some eggs and you maybe have a hen or something like that you could put into a pot.

A big change?

Oh, a big change. They're well off now to what we were.

How did you get on with your parents? Did you talk with them?

To my mother, yes. My mother was a very understanding woman. My father, well he never seemed to take much interest in what ye was doing; he was just different. A different upbringing. There was fourteen and he was in the middle of them. There's some o' them made something o' their life. He never had education. Had had no interest in education but, yes, he was a hard working man at manly work ... and work to anybody and do anything for anybody. But education was oot. There wasnae much for ye to go to.

What about teaching?

Well ye had to go into Aberdeen. They had to leave the area.

They wouldn't have liked their children leaving?

Oh no.

Did he play games with you?

Oh no. My mother played the games but he did make rugs, he made the rugs. My grandfather played the Jew's harp when they came in at night in the winter nights. A lot o' fun there! And then I had a younger uncle. He was at home and he played the mooth organ and a melodeon and oh I had a lot o' fun.

Did you sing?

We tried ... bothy ballads ... my grannie was a good singer. She was a singer. We did a lot o' singing. We used to sit at nights and have a sing-song roond the fire, mother, sister and me.

Did your father do anything around the house?

He was a keen gardener. That was what he wanted to do when he left school. He wanted to go into gardening. And he did a wee while of it and then his father was killed and he had to come home to keep[34] the house [for the mother]. He was [very dutiful]. I'll give him credit for that. He did what the rest wouldn't do. There was two other brothers and they didnae want to come home. But my father was quite prepared.

Did you all sit round the table at mealtimes?

At home, yes, but when we went to grannie's we had to stand at the dresser. Because the table was always full. We got the dresser.

Were you allowed to talk?

Yes – oh aye. No' the bairns. The bairns was aye telt that they were to be quiet because the were 'seen and not heard' [she 'quotes' it with no trace of dialect]. Ye kept quiet.

What would happen if somebody didn't eat their dinner?

Well, ye had to eat it [laughter]. If ye didnae eat it, ye didnae get any more.

Did you have to eat it at the next meal?

Oh no, the hens got it then. At home there were no hens, you would have to eat it.

Would you be punished?

Oh I think my mother would but I was aye wanting what I got.

Do you remember getting smacked?

No. I dinnae ... some o' them did. They were gey hard on them. Farm servants' families were not well treated; the bairns used to go to someone else's gairden to get something to eat.

Did other children?

Some of them did. Some were gey hard on them.

Crofting families?

Farm servants.

Were farm servants not well treated?

No, they werenae ... children from big families ... for as little as they got to keep them ... and I think that many a time, well the bairns would take oot of somebody else's gairden to get something to eat because they were hungry. There was a lot of that at that time. Eating berries off the roadside. Wages were sixteen shilling and some of them were paid by the six month. If ye wasn't a good manager ye was in trouble. Your neighbour might help oot a wee bit. If they could. Maybe something from the garden or some potatoes.

The parish?

Well there was [hesitates] nothing.

Who managed the money in the house?

She managed the money.

Was there pocket money for father?

Oh no, there was nae money for pocket money. She used to get him his cigarettes, well it wisnae cigarettes at that time, it was an ounce of tobacco and that had to do a week. That was it [laughs].

No beer money or anything like that?

Nothing like that.

Whisky?

No.

What about hobbies?

Ma mother had her knitting, sewing, all the things that was to be of use. Nothing ootside that would take money away because you couldn't afford to take money away.

Sports?

Oh, there was nae sport. We used to have weight lifting. The weights off the fields. There were shoving matches and plouin' matches.

Shoving?

Hoeing. All their skills – just men. Up north; no, in the Borders. It's a different life. When we came doon here it's entirely different.

Did your mother go shopping?

Yes, oh aye, she did all the shopping. Vans came to the door but it depended on where ye was. There used to be what they termed the six-monthly, when they got their wages every six month, that was when they went and bought their underwear for the winter or summer and she often bought material and wool and she made it up. She was a good sewer.

Were there neighbours to chat to when shopping?

Oh, we knew all the neighbours.

What about a trade union?

Yes, in later years, he was no' in the earlier years. 1940, 1939, I think. We were beginning the farm servants' union. [Although this was no doubt true locally, the reader will see from Robertson's article, 1978, that the union began much earlier.]

What was a 'good father' in those days? A good earner?

He'd have to be.

Good husband today helps in the house.

Never in our day, never. He might rock the cradle at night but that would be all.

And what about a good mother?

Well I would say a good mother has just to be able to do anything. Everything. She's expected to do everything. No mother earned wages after she was married.

What about your own leisure activities growing up?

No, never. Working on farm. [While in service] ye never got oot till your wark was finished and that was gey often ten o'clock at night and ye got to a dance.

FIGURE 3.9:   Ploughing match, Perthshire, February 1921 or 1922.

How did you get married?

Well my husband and I lived on the same farm. That was how we met. I was in the army. I came home wi' a sore back. And that was how we met. [I was] 25. [She couldn't afford to marry any earlier.] Ye had nothing. And if I hadn't had a husband that saved when he was in his youth I couldna hae done it as I had nothing. My money went back.

Did the girls your way not have a glory box? A bottom drawer?

Oh aye they did. Nothing to put in it. Ye made when ye were getting married covers cases and pillow. I had nae wages at the time – just sewed odds and ends that came my way.

What about the unmarried?

Well they were never oot, ye see, to get married. Never got oot to anything. No courting. The only place that they used to meet was the smiddy.

Why the smiddy?

I dinnae ken. That was just the . . . And on Sunday night we used to meet at the end of the road and have dances. I've seen us dancing the eightsome reel on a Sunday night on the road. Nae music. We just chirmed[35]. I was 18 at the time. And we used to have a walk on the Sunday night and have an eightsome reel and a dance on the road. The time I was coorting I cycled to dances. I got a bike.

Did the boys get bikes?

Aye, efter they worked for them. It depended of course on how their people might take their money off them and give them one. [It would depend] on the parents. When my husband went to work his mother had been afore him.

Mrs Doughtie, born 1912, Mid-Borders

This interview is much easier to read, though it too is quite well laden with the dialect of the area from which Mrs Doughtie came. She now lives in a bright new block of tastefully designed flats with modern facilities, a sharp contrast to her situation in childhood where all the water had to be boiled on the black-leaded range, though, as she says, the house which she remembers best was one of the better ones. It was also relatively large, something which the family appreciated since there were seven boys and two girls in the family. Accommodation was stretched to the limit when her maternal grandparents came to stay with them when they grew too old to work and stay in their tied cottage.

As a younger child, she was 'ower keen on history' and would have liked to stay on at school and become a teacher. But this was a vain hope in those days as she stoically points out. Indeed, on leaving school, she stayed at home for a year to help her mother and was subsequently sent to someone living nearby as a servant for three months. She was then employed as an agricultural worker herself in the fields as her mother had been when she was young.

Interview with Mrs Doughtie

The house was on the farm. It was a very nice house about twelve year old, quite a nice new-built house, four nice rooms in it. We had pigs, and my mother had a cow, things like that.

I suppose your father would work to the farmer?

Yes, he done the cattle. And my brothers wiz ploughmen. They were the ploughmen. The oldest one would be eleven year older than me anyway, then that one up at Earlston ... he would be ten year older than me.

You had a large family . . . How did you organise your accommodation?

The place we took oor meals in, there was a bed. My father and mother laid in there. My sister and I lay down the stair in the bottom bedroom and the boys were up the stair in the top bedrooms.

What about a kitchen?

The kitchen was at the back. We used to talk about the back kitchen in these days. The living room was the kitchen. And the back kitchen. It always got the name of the kitchen and the back kitchen.

Was there a parlour?

No, no, we just sat in this room where we had oor meals and everything. Coal fire and everything.

Did you have one of those large black-leaded grates?

Yes, where the kettles wiz boiling. There wiz no cookers in those days, y'know. All the cookin' was done on the kitchen fire. The back kitchen was used for washing oorselves. We had to wash oorselves ben there with a basin on the table.

Where did the water come from?

At the side of the house was the sprigot[36], that's where we got the water from [the tap].

So it was proper piped water, you didn't have to go to the spring?

Yes, it was joined on to our house. If you wanted hot water you boiled the kettle. Mother had a big washin' pot she put on the fire. A big washing pot, a black pot, and she boilt the clothes in this and then she had her tubs and her wringer, ye see. And my word, she had some washin's.

Did she have a special day for washing?

Well, I think my mother mostly washed on a Thursday. [Chat about this, other people seemed to prefer Mondays.]

You were far out in the country. What did you do for shopping?

Vans came so many days a week. The grocer and the baker. We hadnae many vans in those days. And I think a fishman and a butcher. Donaldson the butcher, at the beginning. [Chat about itinerant butchers. Interviewer's grandfather was one and Mrs Doughtie wants to know his name since she went to the same school as interviewer's mother and wishes to identify the family.]

You must have had to buy most of your food.

Except vegetables, what we grew in the garden.

Who kept the vegetable garden going?

Ma Dad and my brothers. Well, in the season, like. And then the potatoes you got in the field. When they were ready you got them out the field. We were provided with the amount we were supposed to get, part of the wages. I think my father got flour as part of his wages there.

Would that be oatmeal?

No, I think it was flour, for baking.

What about meat?

Well, we had oor own pigs, ye see. We would kill so many, maybe two a year and ma mother made her own butter, with the cow. In the autumn, I think, that's when they started to kill the pigs, the cooler weather.

You would have had to cure it too. Who did that?

My brothers and my father did it sometimes, and later on, a

shepherd used to do it. The shepherd killed the pigs and put your hams right for you. At W . . . Mains, my father and my brothers did it on their own.

You would have an awful lot of meat to keep?

Well, you had to put it into the tubs, you see, wi' salt and things like that, and ye left it for two or three weeks, and ye brought them out and hung them in the ceiling to dry, ye see. That's where they used to hang the hams, ye see, up in the ceiling.

Who milked the cow?

My mother milked the cow, and sometimes I did it. When I got bigger, I learned to milk and my sister and I took a turn.

And the men?

Oh, no, they werenae supposed to do anything, but work out.

So they would work in the fields maybe and the women would work in the house and the dairy?

No . . . well my sister was in a wee while in aside my mother, but we both worked out in the fields . . . at the beginning and then away to domestic service later on. [See below.]

What sort of vegetables did you have?

Well, cabbages and chivies and peas, maybe, and onions, ye know, these kinda things.

Carrots?

Yes . . .

And beans?

No . . .

Celery?

No, no, nothing like that.

Fruit?

No fruit, no fruit.

I didn't ask you much about the farm itself. Was it a big farm?

Well, I don't know what acreage it would be, but – mind you this would be aboot sixty year back what I'm telling ye about, there were three ploughmen, anyway, my father was cattleman and one o' my brothers would be odd boy. And there was always two wimmen on it. I would be one of them and mebbe a next door neighbour might be another yin. In fact my sister-in-laws was both there at the time. They worked. In fact, that one I was tellin' you about, his wife used to work along wi'me. She was older than me.

Were there other people working on the farm?

Yes, there were a maid there. They kept a maid.

Just the one?

Yes. It wasna a big house. They were very nice people to work with.

Where would all the men live?

All the men were married, except the young men who were still with their families [i.e. in the farm cottages].

You were telling me that you went to school at Stow . . .

That was my first school. I would go for a year to Leadhill. You know, country people used to flit about a lot.

Why was that?

That was just for bigger pays. Just for the matter of a sixpence they would flit. As my mother used tae say, it didna pay flittin', but however, that was whit they done.

How did they carry furniture?

At first they had the carts, and later on they got the lorries, big lorries to flit ye . . . if ye were goin' to a farmer, that farmer provided his carts to come an flit . . . they talked aboot flitten' ye.

What jobs did you do round the house?

I mind doin' the fireside for my mother on a Saturday. We always helped her. Uh-huh. Had tae.

Who made the bed?

Well, my mother mostly made the beds. My mother done the bakin' and the cookin' . . . till oo got a bit older, and we had a bit o' cookin' at the school. A wee bit. We did learn a bit from my mother, but we got cookin' at school . . .

Since you were the eldest daughter, I suppose your mother did not get much help before you came along?

No, but they had to stick in. They [her brothers] were quite good in the house, washing dishes and things. They had tae, before I was born. And one had to look after the wee ones, hurl them in their pram, things like that. In fact that brother that's up at Earlston, he'll tell you aboot hurling me in the pram [he would have been 11].

Do you remember doing any paid work while still at school?

No.

What about your brothers?

Well, they might be at the tattie picking and things like that, I can't remember. I once went but I had to come back that morning, I never got there. I didna see where they were . . . couldn't and I came back.

You did quite a lot as you grew older helping your mother with the children . . .

My younger brother, mostly. My sister was only two years younger. But the younger brothers, I used to help them with their lessons, and things like that at night.

Did your parents help with lessons?

Oh, yes, my father did sometimes. And my older brothers helped me.

Were they keen on education?

They were, the older ones.

I wonder if that was quite common around the Borders?

Aye, they were, uh-huh. But of course, in those days, there werena the grants and we hadnae the money. Y'know. They could hae went far enough, some of them, if they had had the money. But we hadnae the money.

What about organising the work? Did your mother tell you what to do?

Yes . . .

Was she fussy about getting things properly done?

She was, but my mother was more on for sewing and knittin'. She had a sewing machine. I can always remember her tellin' me that she saved up for tae get her teeth in. And she says, the man came round selling sewing machines, and she says, she bought the sewing machine, much to ma Dad's annoyance. But however, she says it was a better friend to her in later years than her teeth – the sewing machine, I can remember her tellin' me that . . . she was a grand sewer and a good knitter. They werena sae well off in those days.

What did your mother do before her marriage?

Well, she worked in the fields.

Did she ever go into domestic service?

No' her.

After she married, did she do any paid work?

No, no, she had plenty in the house. No, she never done anything.

What do you think in those days, they wouldn't have thought it right for a married woman to work?

No, no, to work and leave their bairns. They had plenty work at home. They attended to the cow and the pigs.

What would a widow have done?

I don't know... I never was near a widow for to see how they managed ... they would have some hard times I think.

You wouldn't say your mother was particularly demanding ...?

No, she was a good mother. We had good parents, we had a very happy family.

You would learn to do things in your own time?

Uh-huh. And we made our own amusements. My brothers was fiddlers and I had a fiddle but I never, I only learned with the ear ... which I can't do now... I never kept it up. We had our own amusements.

Did your parents take part too?

Parents took an interest in ye.

So you actually spent time together as a family?

Uh-huh. A very happy family, we had, happy life, we'd a good father and mother.

What were your neighbours like? Did you have good neighbours?

Oh yes. Happy times. Good neighbours. Ye always had good neighbours in the country.

Would you say you knew each other quite well?

Very well. Uh-huh.

Would they be living in cottages next door?

Just next door, or maybe neighbouring farms, they would come in, and ...

What if somebody got ill?

Well, my mother was always very good wi' neighbours that was ill.
She was.

She would go in and help?

She would go and help . . . deliver babies, or anybody . . . things that
needed . . .

Would you say others were like that?

Yes, they were . . . a good lot of them like that, in these days.
Uh-huh. They had to.

Can you tell me about your father's job?

Well, he was up very early. I would think about five o'clock or half
past five in the winter time, he would go oot to his cattle, to get them
fed.

They would be in the byre?

They were in the sheds in the winter. He'd maybe have an occasional one outside, but maistly inside in the winter.

What about the summer?

There was a lot in the fields then, and sometimes he'd maybe help
in the big hoose garden. Just do odd work till his time came for the
cattle in the winter, ye see.

Would he work with farm manager or farmer himself?

Mostly the farmer.

Your father would be fairly tired when he came back?

They were tired, right enough, in these days. Plenty hard work in
these days. But they never thought anything aboot it. They were
happy. Finished at five o'clock at night. They got two hours at the
dinner time, 11–1 p.m. I think that would really be to give the
horses a break, ye know. It's a different thing with a tractor
nowadays, but they would have to stop to give the horses a bit
break, a rest. The men came in for their dinner. The mother had it
ready for them. [They didn't eat in the farmhouse, except during
the clipping or other similar busy times.] Before the combines the
steam traction machine used to come. It was a grand time when the
thrashing mill came in. When we was bairns we used to run doon
the road and meet it coming in [laughs].

Didn't you have to help in the harvest?

Yes, in these days they had the binder. But we had the stookin', then the leadin' in, we had the forkin'.

Was that women's work?

That was women's work, doin' the forkin' oot in the fields.

It would be hot work?

Yes, but I liked the forkin', it was a nice job.

What did your father do around the house?

He chopped the sticks, and my brithers and them would saw sticks. He would dae the choppin'. And in these days, you would have to bring the water in at night. He always had the buckets in ready for my mother, put them in the table in the back place, that was his job.

How did you dispose of garbage?

Well, there was what ye called the middens in these days. Just flung them on and then they would come roond wi' a cart and spread it out on the fields.

Did your father have anything to do with the way you children spent your time? If he thought you were sitting around doing nothing?

No, he wasna bad that way, no, no. We just hid oor things we done, and he was quite happy.

What about your father's leisure?

He used to like sitting reading. He was a great reader.

Did your children read too?

Uh-huh.

What about your mother?

Well, when she had time, but her hands were always busy, knitting or sewing, that's what she ... right up to the end, she always had her knitting. She had to be doin' something.

Can you describe mealtimes?

I can remember. I can see us all sittin' round the table. I knew our places. Sittin' yet.

All sit down at one time?

The ones that wiz working. Sometimes, the wee boys, they were sometimes later getting their meals. But I can remember how we

FIGURE 3.10: Binders cutting the crop while a worker forks sheaves into stooks, Angus, early 1900s.

used to sit, them that was workin' at the time. The boys on the sofae at the back, and my father at the top, and then my mother and my sister and I. I can jist see them sittin'. Uh-huh.

What sort of food did you usually eat?

Ye had yer breakfast in the mornin'. There was always plenty bacon, plenty ham. And then you could get yer eggs up at the farm. Quite reasonable in these days. Then ye had yer dinner-times. You would have yer soup and yer potatoes, and mashed turnips and things like that. No fancy feedin', but it was wholesome.

And plenty of it.

Yes, then she had thon wheaten scones baked ... and then wi' some bacon they were quite good. No cakes, nor nothing like that, jist ... Yer home-made butter when she had it.

Night?

A big bowl o' milk on the table, and ye had your cups each, butter and jam at night. Whatever ye wanted. No meat at night.

Not much sheep meat?

No' unless ye got it frae the butcher.

What about fruit?

No, no ... unless ye was out getting some rasps [raspberries] frae the roadside. No, maybe a tomato or something, but we werena very fond o' tomatoes at the time. We got to like them. But till she got a bit more money in among her fingers and then we got more, as the years went on she was able to ...

What about gathering berries from the hedgerows?

I've seen us pullin' the berries for my mither to make jam or something like that.

And fishing?

Oh, my brothers. One o' them specially was a keen fisher, but I canna remember him bringing much in. They used to get some trout ye know.

Rabbits?

Plenty rabbits durin' the cuttin' time, ye know. Harvest time, plenty rabbits. Rabbit stew, ma mither used to make rabbit paste, ye know. Just like the paste you buy in jars, she used to make it, she used to put it through a mincer. It was right nice, the rabbits.

Were there other things your mother did that they don't do today?

We bought the bread. She baked scones. I'd seen her make seven girdlefu' of scones on a Saturday. The four big scones.

Soap, candles?

No, nothing like that. She made jam.

No chutney?

They werenae so much o' that in those days, chutnies and things. Course ye got your porridge, plenty milk. Cream and butter. No separators at the beginning. They had to let the milk settle at the top and she had what they called a reemer, it took the cream off the milk. And she put it in a bowl.

What about table manners?

We werenae allowed to make too much noise. We would hae got a tellin' off.

Were you allowed to chat?

I had a brother, a wee bit jokey ... but Dad didnae like nonsense when you were eating.

What happened to fussy eaters?

Brothers werena fussy, all quite happy with what they got.

Were your brothers working when they were still at school?

One ... especially used to go round with the farmer, but just a hobby, helping.

Not paid.

No, just for the ... In fact, he wasna very keen on the school, him. And when he got my sister and I out of the way, that's where he went.

Truanting?

Yes, but my mither got wise o' that! My mither sent him back to the school.

Did he get a smacking?

Oh no, no.

Did your parents smack you?

No' much. A tellin' off was plenty. If we got a tellin' off that's all that we needit.

Not all that much smacking?

No, no we didna need it unless we done something terrible. No, a word from our Dad and that was enough.

Mother?

Oh, my mother could keep us right. I think she had more to do with us. Sometimes we was frightened for her ... though we had two grand parents. Aye, they were.

Did you have any relatives living close?

Mother's father and mother stayed wi' us a while, five years.

Why with you?

In these days, there werena sae many houses. They had to look after them, they had tae. We shifted to another place and we hadnae room for them. Later they got into a house on their own and that's where they finished their years ...

Did your father get a wage packet?

No, in those days I think they just got loose money, uh-huh. The money was handed to my mother. My mother kept the money. She dished the money out. In later years my brothers would pay their board and lodgings, ye know. Once they got a certain age. Ma Dad would have to hand over their wages, to the boys, what they were entitled to, and they would give it to my mother, so much back, for keeping them, their board.

Some people paid their whole wages ... How much went to the household when you grew up?

When I worked in the field, every penny I gave to my mother and she bought oor clothes and things. But when I went intae service, domestic service, I got my own money. That's when I started to have my own money.

What age were you leaving school?

I was 14. The first year I was in the house wi'my mother. I stayed in wi' her. But I can remember before I started to work, I went down and I helped the head gamekeeper's wife at Kirkstain Castle for a wee while and I got 5s. a week there. I done the cookin' for her ... she was a wee bit mental ye know. But a nice old lady. And I scrubbed the house, and kept the house for her. And she was there to keep me right with the cookin'.

Were a lot of young girls doing that sort of thing?

Well, I don't think they would be doing that. It was just that my mother and them was kinda friendly, and it was just to help this old lady. She used to come back to my mother for the milk, ye see.

What did you think about it?

Well, she was inclined to be a bit keen on the bottle, and I wisna just too happy, ye see [laughs]. But, however, I stayed there for two or three months, just to help her till they got another housekeeper. Then I went to the fields at the May term.

Like to have done something else?

Well, I was always very fond of history, I would like to have been, ye know, a history teacher or something like that. But we never thought on any ... we couldna do nothing. But I was very fond o' history when I was at the school.

Would your parents have liked that for you?

Aye, they would fine ... but no, the wages just didnae ... No grants in these days, there would be bursaries right enough, but more clever people got the bursaries. But I was more keen on history.

What about jobs for the younger ones?

Well, one of my younger brothers joined up in First World War and died of pneumonia. He was only in his twenty-first year. Another went on to the farm and done his time there. The younger one, he came off the farm, he was a lorry driver wi' a building firm and things like that, and when he was made redundant he got this job [in town]. The oldest brother – he would go out fencing, put up the fences, cut the hedges, did the lambing, etc. Worked at his own hand in later years. The one at Hoose o' Mair worked on the farm all his days. Another worked at various jobs working in the forestry till he died. He had twae or three ither jobs too, but it was the farm at the start.

Was there no choice because of the money?

That's right; the money was just not there.

What about church on Sundays?

Oh, yes, sister and I were very good. We used to go to the Sunday School at Earlston. My parents and older brothers used to go too. We used to have some grand times in Earlston with the Christmas

tree and things like that. The Sunday School [trip] was always to
Portobello, it was the start of the trips away. We went in the bus,
but in my sister's day it was the trains. I can remember my sister's
white panama hat was black when she come back [laughs]. Before
the [bus] trips, they used to visit the Leader Haugh, the castle
grounds and have their day there. Mother accompanied them. No
fathers went. Oor mothers went to the Christmas celebrations too.

Mr Collins, born 1906, Eastern Borders

Mr Collins's father was a shepherd in the Lammermuirs, the hills
of Berwickshire and East Lothian. There are some familiar themes
in this interview and some new ones. There is the struggle to make a
living through a range of means. However, in the case of Mr
Collins's family, no wages were coming in during the years of his
childhood. His father had grazing rights on the farm on which he
worked, and the money he earned came from the production of his
own lambs. The 'out-bye' farm's isolation, the absence of the
tenant farmer, and his father's ability to run the farm well, choose
his stock and get a good price at market allowed a degree of
autonomy which was unusual for other kinds of agricultural
workers.

When the children were older, the father obtained a manager's
job elsewhere and they moved. More often than not, our interviewees were residentially mobile within rather small geographical
areas. The family were unusual in that the mother was of English
extraction. We can only surmise that she, at least, must have
experienced a considerable break in her social relationships as a
result of moving to Scotland.

Finally, Mr Collins's parents seem to have been rather more
ambitious than others in their situation. His father would have
liked to own his own land but was never able to save enough. Mr
Collins himself achieved what was not possible for his parents.
When we met him, it was in his own house, a pleasant stone villa in
a small Border town. This was his choice in retirement after a long
career as a small farmer.

Interview with Mr Collins

The house was an old farmhouse ... Stone floors downstairs and
the only floor covering I remember at the time was rag rugs on
floor. There was no carpets or linoleum. Wooden floors of course

FIGURE 3.11:   Shepherd, sheep dog and flock, *c.* 1900.

upstairs, only the odd rug. When your clothes got past wearing ye made them intae rugs by hand using scraps of material. They had to be made down because there was very little money at that time.

My father . . . had no money wage at all. He had grazing for a certain number of sheep and one or two cows. He had no actual money wage at all. That was fairly general for shepherds at that time, they didnae have a money wage.

None at all?

No money wage. They had grazing for a certain number of sheep and one or two cows. You only got money once a year when the lambs were sold and the wool was sold and so forth. The farmer didn't stay at the place.

What about groceries? Flour?

There was an allowance of oatmeal, it was part of the income. That came once a year, delivered from mill. The flour came at the same time. That had to be kept in wooden ark[37] so that it kept the whole year, ye see. [He doesn't know if the flour was part of income; they got it with the oatmeal.] It was white flour, seemed to keep well enough.

Your mother would have had to make bread ...

She did. In winter time, there wasnae a baker came. So she made bread. The grocer came once a fortnight from Duns. They had poultry ... the grocer took the eggs and butter that they made. That would in part pay for the groceries ... there was nothing coming monthly. [Mother kept hens and made butter, helped by the children.]

Oo had tae help wi' lots of things when there was sae many running aboot ... gathering firewood, eggs, turning the churn tae make the butter, a miserable sort of job. It took a long time in the winter time to make it into butter. [The boys helped in the dairy, but not much in the house.] The girls would help in the house when they were at school, but they left home as soon as they left school. I never thought much about the money, but I suppose they needed the money – the girls left school at 14. The only way that the youngsters could get any money was to leave home. There was no jobs. They did go to the shooting in the grouse time – beating – the grouse season, but that only lasted ... We used to get paid 5s. and thought that was a fortune [for a day]. That was a lot. Because I remember there were other two other men employed on the place. I can remember away back, them speakin' aboot the wage these people got. One was married and had this cow as part of his wage, and the other was single and stayed in the house. The married man got 13s., and the unmarried man who had no cow got 14s. That was their weekly wage. How they managed I don't know. These people left, and they took a small farm eventually ... How they managed I don't know ...

Did you keep the 5s?

[Tries to remember.] No, it would be to hand over to mother to buy clothing. Up there, there would be nothing to spend it on. We didna go to the corner shop and get sweeties, because there was no shop.

Did your mother make sweeties sometimes?

Oh yes, they used to make this tablet or something like that. But there wasna much of this sweetie business.

You would need to buy the sugar.

Yes, of course.

Did she do any preserving?

Aye, fruit. There was a certain amount of fruit in the garden, blackcurrants – made jam with that.

Where did she get the money?

I don't know ... [possibly eggs and butter]. The money for the lambs only cam' in once a year and that would be used for the clothes.

Who looked after the garden?

My father did the garden mostly. Of course, us boys had to help in the garden.

Just the boys?

No, no, I don't think the girls did much in the garden.

You would learn to garden.

Well, he ... the same as myself wasna much of a gardener, he would plant potatoes, cabbage and so forth and that was aboot it. Didna go in for flowers much. There was a flower border which mother used to look after. The potatoes – they had a bit of land on the farm to grow potatoes, ootside the garden, enough ground to grow as many potatoes as you needed. The rabbits were always there. You could always get something to eat. You learned to catch rabbits when you werena very old. My father used to catch them and I learned from that. [This was for themselves to eat, and sometimes they sold the skins. They also caught moles; later, immediately after the First World War, they were quite valuable, and they got a shilling or two for the skins. They might get to keep the money initially, but it wasn't used to put in their pockets – it was spent on clothes or boots.]

What did you have for meals?

We got this oatmeal. We had porridge for breakfast ... I don't remember if we had anything else or no'. Then we took jam and bread or whatever and some tea to school – the only way to get anything in the middle of the day. Dinnertime at home – rabbits, there was a sheep killed at the end of the year, salted it lasted a while, sometimes a sheep had an accident and was killed. Pigs were fed till they were big brutes and killed – that lasted the whole year [two of them]. They were salted and hung up on rafters. Ham and an egg for breakfast on weekends maybe. When we were at home there would be a pudding in the middle of the day. We got tea when we came home at night. Maybe some scrambled eggs or something, not meat – more [like] high tea. If they were having soup, there would be potatoes and any meat available. Two courses only. There used to be plenty rabbits. And there was this mutton, and rabbits.

Were you all round the table at once?

Yes, all round the table.

Were there any particular rules?

You had to be reasonably quiet at the table. Don't think we were taught very much; any table manners we had, they were picked up from father and mother. There wasna a variety of spoons and things to use in any case.

What about a tablecloth?

There was a tablecloth on special occasions. The table covered with oil cloth.

Who would do the washing up?

I can't remember doing much washing up; I think it must have been the girls that did the washing up.

Did you have time to play when you were at school?

Oh yes. But there was only oorselves and ... the other families moved occasionally – sometimes there were other children, sometimes mebbe no. The nearest neighbours was about a mile. They would turn up on a Saturday.

Did you ever play with your parents?

They would never have time to play.

What about games at night? You would have long winter nights. Did anyone sing?

There wasnae a musical instrument in the house when we were very young. Latterly, one o' my sisters got this little organ thing and she used to play that. What we did on the long winter nights was made these bloomin' rugs. We hated that. We got three or four of them roond about this rug, this bag – it took a long time.

Did you tell stories to while away the time?

I suppose there would be. My father used to read sometimes at night. But the main thing was getting the old rug finished.

Whose idea was this?

We would be told to do it. Certainly none of the youngsters' ideas.

You could have said no.

... but ye would have got a clout on the lug.

Was this Mum or Dad?

Either!

Did you get smacked much?

No, no, but ye had to do what ye were told. Never anything severe.
But I don't think it did any of us any harm.

What about your Mum? Did she get any recreation?

Well, she didnae get very much. I remember after the youngest of
the brothers and sisters were able to manage, she started up this
Women's Guild, there was nothing of the kind before. She used to
attend that. She never got very far away from the place at that time.
There were no cars. It was an event getting to Duns, a day's jaunt.
[He supposes the Women's Guild would be attached to the
church.]

We were members of the church up there of course. We went
regularly. At that time – it's going back a long time of course – in
that part of the country, at least, anybody that didnae go to the
church, there was something strange about them. Now anyone that
goes to the church is! Everybody went, practically ... we used to go
aboot every Sunday. Sunday School as well. [He can't remember
any Sunday School picnics because of lack of transport and isolation. If there were any, it would be locally.] There were school
sports, the only sports that I remember were school sports ...

What age were you when you left the school?

Fourteen. Started shepherding, round aboot. They employed boys
when they left school and we gradually got on to get in charge of a
flock of sheep on your own, when you were older a bit. There was no
work at home; the place that I was born and brought up in there
was about three employees and there was no work for anybody else.
It was a hill farm which employed a shepherd mainly and these
other two people did odd jobs. There was a bit of cultivation, no'
much. I went to the hill farms round aboot where it was usual to
employ a youngster to assist the shepherd if he had no family of his
own, for mebbe a couple of years. Then they started off again when

they wanted a bit more money. There didn't seem to be any difficulty getting a job.

Was there any choice of job?

Never thought about anything else really. Worked at that for aboot thirty or forty years: oo got a small holding at first and then a farm. [He retired out of that when he came to retiring age].

So it was possible to acquire a small holding. How did you do it?

Not very easy. Didn't have much money but were able to borrow some. Got started and clear of that very shortly afterwards. Worked away from there and never needed to borrow money after that. We were lucky, plenty of ... [wouldn't have been possible without the loan].

Did your wife and children help on the small holding?

Yes, well they werena very old when we went to the small holding first but they used to help right enough. Started with a dairy there. It was a lot of hard work, but there was always money coming in, every month. [He was about 40 at this time. They managed fine after they got started. A lot of people could never get started because they could never raise the money to get a start.]

What happened to your income when you were working away from home?

Yes, after we started working away from home, we kept it. It didn't take a big pocket to hold it. [It was the same with brothers and sisters; they kept it.] I don't know if that was general. But anything we needed we had to buy of course.

How did you feel leaving home for the first time when you were only 14?

Well, I went for a start to an uncle who was a shepherd. We had known them since ever we were nippers. Didna feel very lost at all. It was mebbe five or six miles away from home. But you could get home occasionally, ye see. Depended on the work that was goin' on. During the lambing season ... we didn't get away at all. After that ye would go home for a night or so. There were no holidays, ye see. At that time there were no holidays on the farm, none. I suppose I was lucky that I was with this uncle, and maybe there were a wee bit relaxation of the rules ... able to get home occasionally, no very often.

Was it important for you to see your mother and father?

Yes, quite important. We like ... were anxious to get home but it wasna ... but at that time the job was the thing, ye had to attend to the job and that was it. [His uncle was his father's brother.]

Did you have other relatives nearby that you kept up with?

There was a few in the district. One or two of my father's brothers were in the district, and my mother's family as well ... They used to visit occasionally in the slack time o' the year, possibly after the sales and everything were finished, we had a wee bit slack time. The shepherds, I suppose, were different from the other people that worked on the farms because they made their own time for having a day off, if it was possible to have a day off or a half-day off. They didnae apply to anybody. They went off. That was fairly general in the high district anyway. [They had discretion over the odd holidays – others had no holidays apart from New Year and the Hiring Fairs, and that was about it.] Never seemed to think anything aboot it then, would never do now.

We never wanted for anything. Oor wants then, I suppose they had to be set against what oo were able to get ... we had always plenty to eat, and always clothes. Some o' them getting pretty threadbare maybe, but we had always clothes.

What about entertainment, when your day's work was finished?

After ... when we got up a bit ... we used to, well there was a hall in the district which oo used to go to in the winter time at night. Dances and entertainments of one kind and another and that was jist aboot it.

How often was that? Once a week?

Wasna as often as that. Eventually, we moved to a place, over above Braeburn there, there was a hall there. They used to have a bowling club and so forth. That would be about once a week. In the summer time, ye didnae go anywhere because this work was always there. Didnae go far in the summertime at all.

Did you not manage conversation with folk your own age?

Oh, aye. We used to visit more then than is general now, I think. We had neighbours. We would go at night to a neighbour's house and have a night there, but the only conversation was mostly local. Local events and so forth. After ... nowadays ... it's different. There's everything in the way of entertainment at home.

What was important to local people then?

I suppose the most important thing was . . . To be able to get as much . . . to live on. Because . . . there was very little money, and any money that they could save had to be spent on gettin' what they just couldna do without.

What would you think of a good mother, wife, in those days?

In those days she was expected to be able to provide for whatever . . . our family was exceptional of course. There werenae many families as big as that. But she was expected to be able to provide for them, keep them tidy and so forth. And that was a general thing out in the country. In the towns maybe it didn't apply so generally. Even in [the town], you would get families where the mother maybe didnae provide very well, or the father either. But it was exceptional . . . that there was ever anybody that didna provide quite reasonably for their families, although there was no' much money.

The same for a good father?

Yes, I think so. Well, it was a small community up there, of course. There was really nobody in it that didnae seem able to provide and keep their families reasonably well.

Were parents generally quite strict? Were some excessively hard?

Well, no' in the community where I was brought up. No' to my knowledge . . . there was none any the worse o' having their parents. The odd family that wasnae sae well provided for as others. But at the same time, there was no' abuse as we know it now, in that small community, just a small corner.

Were you close to your parents?

Yes, I think so.

I have the impression that strictness was pretty general, and parents had no time to play with children? Not such a close relationship as today?

Sometimes we thought we were maybe hard done by, but in the sense that they had to keep order among a big family, it was possibly the only way they could manage, ye see. We sometimes thought that we werenae fairly treated, but looking back, I don't think that that was the case at a'. Sometimes you would get punished for something you thought shouldnae have been and so forth. But there was no' abuse.

Was there a boss in the household?

My father was the ultimate boss, mother kept order in the house right enough, but any bigger decision was always left to him. But it didnae really show through to us. Anything that had to be decided was spoken over and it was his decision at the finish, I think, that would be taken.

Were decisions discussed with children?

No, it wasna discussed with the children at a'. If it was something that affected the children, yes. When they came to be looking for jobs and so forth, that would be discussed with them. Whether a suitable place to go or something like that. But any decision about the household was entirely the father and mother.

Did your parents find your first job for you?

... Well, I suppose, he [the uncle] would need somebody to help. The position was that he and anybody else in the same position, if they needed somebody to help, they would employ them on their own. Whoever was the employer would then have to pay the wages. I suppose he would have a limited amount of money to work with, but it was he who employed whoever he wanted to help. He would know that I was available, and that was just what happened. I don't know that I was consulted very much about it... I would probably be sent there.

What happened after your two years there?

The previous boy was unwell, and I was there for a while till he came back. Then I had to find another job. I went and helped during the lambing season at different places to get a wee bit more money. Went and helped during the shearing season. Ye get more that way than the weekly wage. After the first year or two, I got a job as a shepherd for the full year.

When you were going to help in the lambing and shearing seasons, where were you staying?

Yes, we just went home and stayed there. I was never out of work for any length of time. During lambing or shearing we stayed with the shepherd in his house. I found generally the accommodation was much the same as we had at home. Quite well treated... The shepherd was yer boss, the real boss was somebody away in the distance... I was paid cash for that. I saved it, but of course we had to use it for oor own needs and there wasna verra much left to save. Saved up a bit to get a bike, I got an auld one before I left school

FIGURE 3.12: Sheep shearing and rolling fleece, Dunbeath, Caithness, c. 1900.

[free], but I was working two/three years before I got a proper bike. [The old bike was given to him, no-one else wanted that wreck, but it moved along the road a bit anyway.]

Did you pay board when between jobs?

No, ye didna have tae pay anything. Might take something home. Stayed there for a week or so. By the time that I was working away from home things were getting better. After the First War finished there was, there was more money about. Lambs when they cam' to be sold were worth more . . .

When you were a shepherd did you still keep in touch with your parents?

Sometimes went home for a visit, oh yes.

[First tape breaks off here.]

There was a wee bit more freedom after the War, we were able to get oot a bit more. Although they had to do their job just the same, they werenae just expected to stay on the place all the time a' the time as they had been before. It got, I suppose, after the War, that folk just werena willing to do that. To be tied in the way that they had been before.

Why?

I think possibly a lot of the boys that were in the War werena willing to go back to what they had been used to when they were nippers. That would have been the start . . . a bit more freedom.

Were any of your brothers in the War?

My oldest brother was the only one who was old enough. And that was jist when the War finished. He never wis away. He was in the process of enlisting about the time when the First War finished, none of them were ever in the War. No.

Did you keep up with your brothers and sisters . . . Or did you just go your separate ways?

We always kept in touch, but well, at that time they didna move very far oot o' the district, ye see. We were able to keep in touch. Later on, of course, we got spread about the country a bit more, but we was always able to keep in touch.

You wouldn't be able to visit your parents at the same time and keep together in that way?

No, it was very seldom that they were if ever all back at home at the same time. Mebbe just as well ... the place would be bursting at the seams!

In the days before the Welfare State, what happened when there was a family crisis? For instance, with your family living in the country?

I suppose we just had to cope wi' it. In what way a crisis? An illness, just had to cope with that ... The doctor was to pay when he was called out up here. He came from Duns. He wasna called oot unless it was absolutely necessary. But he came. What he would be paid, mind, I just don't know. I think that he would be paid more or less on the ability of the people to pay.

I believe some country doctors did take eggs and ham and that sort of thing. I think they would do that, but I think that he would charge according to what he thought was their ability to pay mebbe.

Would neighbours help if your mother was sick?

Oh, yes, that was usual. There's somebody would come in and help if it was absolutely necessary. There would be somebody sent for and they would come.

If your father was ill ...

Well, he wasna gettin paid in any case ... I never remember him being off work but if he were off for two or three days, but somebody else would have to turn in and do what was necessary. But it wouldna make any difference to the actual pays – because his pay was actually this amount for a year. If he was off, well that jist couldna be helped. In our case, well there was these two men on the farm and they could be sent to do what was really necessary. But he was very seldom off as far as I remember.

Do you remember home remedies?

... Can remember gettin' castor oil.

Poultices?

They used to use poultices ... I don't know whether there was very much of that done except on ... I canna remember. There was the usual epidemics at that time – measles, whooping cough and so forth ... well there wasna very much that could be done about them ... just have tae pit up wi' them till they got better.

What about a union?

No, there was nobody in a union at that time[38]. On the farms ... it was after the war before there was any union. I never was a member o' it . . . A lot of the farm workers was never in it. They seemed to prefer to make their own bargain, so forth. They might have been better if they had been in a union, but there wasnae a union.

What would they do if they weren't being treated fairly?

They would just leave.

So a farmer with a bad reputation might have difficulty hiring staff?

Aye, that was so, they wouldna stay there, if they werenae pleased with the employer. They might be better and they might no'. A different set of . . .

At the hirings did you need a reference of recommendation?

There wasnae a lot of that. Ye did have to have . . . ye was more or less employed locally, and ye were generally known in the district. It didnae . . . I dinnae mind having much in the way of a reference at a'. They would refer to yer last employer mebbe. Certainly, if ye was lookin for a job withoot the district ye would have to have a reference . . . in that district up where we were, there were very few farmers lived up there.

The farmer lived away doon near Hexham [Northumberland], he never was there. I can only remember once o' seeing him on the farm, all the time I was there. We used to meet at the sales, they would meet with their shepherds. The rest of the people on the farms, well, where we were, my father employed the other people that were on the farms here. He never referred to the man that had the farm at a'.

Was he a farm owner or tenant farmer?

He wasna a landowner, he was a tenant. He didna come. [He doesn't know who owned the land: someone in East Lothian.] There were two or three places up there in the same sort of position. Mebbe the only one where the farmer didnae appear occasionally. I can remember only seeing him once on the farm . . . only once. [Repetition.] I think he would go to a wee bit of trouble to get somebody who he thought was right for the job and he was left to it.

Someone else was talking about hinds and bondagers.

There was no bondagers up there at a'. If ye came doun into the Merse, there was bondagers.

Did any of your sisters become bondagers?

No, they didnae. But it was a poor life really. They werena paid very much, and they were expected to do a' the jobs that nobody else would do hardly. There's nothing o' that now of course. But I remember perfectly well the bondagers. The hinds, in some places, if they didn't have a daughter who would turn out and work on the farm, they had to engage somebody, or they wouldna get a job, you see. I never had anything to do with that...

Perhaps that was associated with arable farming?

Yes, the arable part, no women employed at all in that district where I was brought up. There was one woman, a shepherd up there, and it was very unusual... There are women shepherds now, but then it was very unusual. [There were two shepherds' places, and she and her husband worked the two places together.]

When you were a young man did you smoke?

I did smoke, yes. No' when I was very young. Very brave to smoke when ye were at the school, but I didna start smokin' until I was older. Gave it up many years ago when I was smokin' far too much. Course, cigarettes at that time, used to get a packet and a box of matches for a shillin', which is five pence nowadays... Ye bought cigarettes in town on Saturday night and bought them then. The grocer's van came roond.

What about your leisure as a young man?

You would go to the pictures on Saturday night. Pub, yes, a drink there. The neighbours gathered in there.

Was it just men?

Men only. No women came into the pubs then.

What age would you be then?

I suppose 17 or 18. But it wasna a thing we did very much of, didn't make a thing of it.

How could you meet young women?

... Seemed to manage! They came to the dances and so forth in local halls, but no women came into the pubs, no' in the like of Duns here.

How did the dances operate? Was there a band?

Generally, somebody local had an accordion, and somebody else had a fiddle and that was it. They were paid a trifle, no' very much. That was the music.

Did you go in groups or take a partner?

Ye went and took a partner up. Wasna formally introduced to them or anything . . . just go up and ask somebody to dance and that was it. Ask somebody else.

Were they shy of each other?

I don't think so.

Would you know everybody?

Yes, you'd know them, most of them.

So you would know who you were asking to dance?

Generally speaking. It was later on that there used to be more folk possibly coming from the town to a dance in the country, you wouldna know them. Earlier on it was mostly local people, girls mostly employed in mansion houses [as maids]. They employed no end o' girls there. Houses in Duns here employed two or three servants whereas now of course there's none at a'.

My father's father and mother lived in the district and we knew where they had come from, from the Yarrow Valley, when they were young. My grandfather's parents . . . My mother's people came from Northumberland.

Did your parents tell you stories about their youth?

No' very much, as far as I remember. I've heard stories about what they did when they were young. My father for instance, he used to go to school in the winter . . . he worked during the summer and went to school in the winter, for a year or two before he left school. I don't know what age he would be when he left school, possibly younger than I was.

Were parents pleased for you to be longer than they were at school?

. . . They were quite interested in us gettin' a better education than they had had. I left home and stayed for two years at Duns where I attended the public school. My parents wanted that. I had a brother working in the district, I stayed with him. I used to get this old bike and pedalled home at the weekends, but not often.

Was your brother married?

No, but he had a housekeeper. Never was married. A bachelor. My oldest brother, quite a bit older.

Was it a better school?

Yes, I think so. And they were pleased tae have us go there.

Was there any possibility of you staying on even longer at the school?

Well, they wanted us tae stay longer at the school and a left but possibly I should have done.

What did they want you to do?

They wanted iz tae be a vet, and I thought . . . I was at the age then, it was possible to think about things . . . and it would have been difficult for them to keep me on at school and college for the time that it would have taken and I decided against it. They werenae very pleased. But I just left and started to work.

Were you quite good at school?

Well, yes, I think I was quite good at school, I got well up in . . . [He tells of the head teacher of the public school, a very good teacher, and strict. He spoke to his parents, anxious for him to stay on at school. His brothers all left and started shepherding, and they all eventually became farmers.]

Was the main reason you didn't want to go on because you thought it would be difficult for your parents?

I didna fancy the idea of continuin' at the school, I did think about this money business as well, although by that time things were easier. But it was still going to be a consideration. I think that they were keener to see us getting on than a lot of other parents were, anxious for us to try to get a right job.

How did they have that much more imagination? A lot of parents never gave that a thought, they just took it for granted that you would leave.

I don't know but they were always anxious for their children to get as much education as they could, and look for something a bit better than they had had, although eventually . . . my father came to have quite a good job at the finish, but he never got a place of his own because, well, the money just wasnae there for a start. Never came off.

Eventually he got on for manager on a place, and then he could do what he wanted. Quite reasonably well paid . . . he had been trying to get a place of his own when I was young, how he was going to do it I just didn't know because they managed to gather some money in their time but it must have been difficult. When he died he left a bit money, but they must have done without a lot of things that we think necessary nowadays.

Did he ever talk about emigrating?

My father didn't. I used to think about emigrating, I was quite keen to emigrate at one time, but ... I had an uncle in New Zealand, two uncles, brothers of my mother. They got on quite well in New Zealand, but I never just got that length. My daughter who's at home now was in New Zealand for a year or two. She got in contact with her families, when she was there ...

NOTES

1. Taken together, these conditions for agricultural workers seem to match a degree of dependence on the employer found only among domestic servants in large towns, although the nature of agricultural work never required the degree of deference that service demanded. However, a number of social historians have argued that the power relationship between farmer and farm servant was far from reducing farm servants to 'deferential workers'. The short supply of farm servants kept their bargaining position reasonably strong, and the conditions of work were to mutual benefit to a large degree (Robertson, 1978; Devine, 1984).

2. It is not clear why he used the North-East dialect term for boy, 'loon', rather than the more common 'lad' or 'laddie'.

3. According to agricultural censuses in lowland Scotland in the period 1908–13, 15 per cent of all holdings were 1–5 acres, 37 per cent were 5–50 acres, 43 per cent were 50–300 acres, and only 5 per cent were over 300 acres. Again, the distribution varied by geographical area. To take some contrasting examples, in the North-East, in Banff with its tradition of small holding, 18 per cent were 1–5 acres, 50 per cent were 5–50 acres, 31 per cent were 50–300 acres, and only 1 per cent were over 300 acres. The distribution of holdings under 50 acres was very similar in arable Berwickshire to that of Ayr, but here 31 per cent of holdings were 50–300 acres and 27 per cent were over 300 acres. Only in Berwickshire and East Lothian were over 30 per cent of holdings larger than 300 acres. We are indebted to Richard Anthony of the Economic and Social History Department at Edinburgh University for these figures.

4. As noted in Chapter One, the age profile of the labour force in rural areas suggested out-migration in age groups from the mid-twenties upwards.

5. See the Report to the Board of Agriculture for Scotland by Sir James Wilson, 1921, Appendix II and the more recent Report of the Committee on Farm Workers, 1936.

6. Families also moved for other reasons. See Anthony for farm servants of the east Borders (Anthony, 1989, pp. 18–20, 22–23; 1992).

7. The average size of our farm servants' families was 6.3 children. Indeed, 60 per cent of our interviewees had five or more siblings. This is in line with the mean fertility given in the 1911 Census of 6.42. On the other hand, more of the crofters and farmers we interviewed seem to have come from smaller than average families. The average size of crofting and farmer families (4.4 and 4.3 children respectively) among our interviewees was considerably lower than the mean fertility of 7.04 and 6.20 given in the 1911 Census. Some discrepancies are inevitable when dealing with small samples and it may be that some of our respondents have forgotten, were unaware of or failed to report siblings who died in childhood.

8. Shepherds tended to get a higher percentage of their wages as perquisites (Anthony, 1989).

9. The next chapter suggests that 'smaller' farms were in the majority.

10. Genealogists whose research is concerned with late-nineteenth-century Scotland may well find that successive children are sometimes born on completely different farms, while sometimes a family will return to the same area later. Claire Toynbee's research on her own family indicates this quite clearly.

11. For an urban comparison see Roberts, 1984, Chapter 5 and Ross, 1983.

12. This was not a happy memory for Mr Collins, as his father required that he and his siblings sat making rag rugs on winter evenings.

13. Claire Toynbee is related to both of them through her grandmother, who originally awakened her interest in the oral tradition by telling her stories about life on a variety of farms on which her relatives had worked even before the beginning of the present century. Genealogical research on the family supports all they said, and indicates how a substantial number of related families moved from farm to farm, sometimes working on the same one at least for a few years. Claire Toynbee also spent several holidays as a child in the 1940s with relatives who were farm servants. Butter was still made then for household use, and bacon hung in the kitchen in which the families lived. Times had changed, however. There was a tractor on at least one farm, although shearing was still done by hand. The fiddle gathered dust in the loft, having been replaced by a shiny accordion.

14. The family lived six miles from the nearest church.

15. The pattern emerging from analysis of the interviews accords with Claire Toynbee's findings in the New Zealand setting. There, boys on farms and those with access to bush and woodland were almost always responsible for this task, and it was their fathers who saw to it that the job was properly done. Like their Scottish rural counterparts, New Zealand boys were unlikely to be involved in domestic labour of any kind. Exceptions to this were found in small, usually middle-class families. But even in some of them, boys did chop wood, whether it was brought or gathered, and sometimes they made their own beds and kept their rooms tidy. In

very few New Zealand households were girls exempt from household chores.

16. Questions about these topics were not necessarily asked on a routine basis, but were frequently mentioned during the interview.

17. Her speech is basically standard Scottish English with a north-east intonation and some residual north-east vowel sounds. But she must have spoken full north-east dialect in her younger days. It is noteworthy that in recounting past scenes and activities, she frequently reverts to her earlier speech. Contrast 'trampit' with the standard form 'married' (not 'marriet').

18. I.e. the cows.

19. Pronounced to rhyme with 'dull', not with 'bull'.

20. I.e. during the April school holidays.

21. *Beig*, an Aberdeen dialect word meaning 'friendly, intimate'. A *beig* was an intimate get-together.

22. She gropes for the word and then decides to use the dialect term *squirl*. It must mean some kind of rotary action. Loading sheaves on to the conveyor belt of the mill?

23. Chaff.

24. *Seds* (also *sids*), particles of oat bran. Mixed with a fine meal, steeped in water for a week, and fermented it made a mildly alcoholic drink (*swats*), while the solid residue (*sowans*) was eaten as a delicacy.

25. See note 24.

26. Her normal form is *two*, but she had relapsed to the dialect form *twae*.

27. Chaff.

28. I.e. cattle-cake.

29. The time when a worker was 'loused' or free from work.

30. North-east Scots term for quarter-segment of a large circular oat-cake.

31. At the time of the interview she was temporarily living with her daughter in the Borders.

32. In controlled speech she uses the standard *one*. Under stress she relapses to the dialect *yin*.

33. Note the 'standard' vowels. When she was a girl she would have said 'doon and oot'.

34. *Keep* here means 'retain the right' to live in the house.

35. *Chirm*: to hum.

36. *Sprigot*, usual spelling 'sprigget', an outside tap.

37. *Ark*, a large chest for storing grain (*Concise Scots Dictionary*).

38. For an account of the history of the Farm Servants Union, see Robertson, 1978.

CHAPTER FOUR

Farmers' Children

THE ECONOMIC AND CULTURAL CONTEXT
Types of Farming and Farmer

UNLIKE CROFTERS, farmers were not farming for personal consumption but in order to profit from selling produce. Farmers were oriented to capitalist markets. While crofting is associated with the Highlands and Islands, it is the Lowland areas which are normally associated with capitalist farming. However, the large sheep farms and shooting estates of the Highlands were also attempts to maximise profit from the land. But these forms of land use did not involve the intensive and increasingly mechanised working of large land holdings which is the hallmark of capitalist arable farming. The south-east Lowlands have been most characterised by large land holdings worked intensively for profit by hired farm servants and casual labourers, whose declining numbers were clearly linked to mechanisation.[1]

But at the turn of the century, even in the south-east Lowlands, there were some small farmers who used mainly if not exclusively family labour. The 'working-family farmer' whose holding is larger than a croft yet not large enough to sustain a labour force on anything other than a casual basis was obviously a different type of farmer from the farmer who housed six or more farm servants and their families.

These distinctions should not be overstated. Some aspects of most farmers' lives were shared, despite variations in standards of living and differential abilities to employ labour. In the Scotland of the turn of the century, the farmer with employees was not always a class apart in all respects from either the smaller farmer or even from his own workers. The majority were what might be called 'working farmers'. The farmer and his sons, and sometimes also his wife and daughters, worked alongside the farm servants. Often farmers' children attended the local school with the farm servants' children, at least for their elementary education. Moreover, some upward and downward mobility between the position of farmer and farm servant was a feature of the system (Campbell and Devine, 1990, pp. 59–60). The division was often greater between the landowner and the tenant farmer, than between a farmer and his workers. The closer the farmer approximated the position of the landowner, the greater the distance between himself and his farm servants. Hence, 'gentleman farmers' – who did not dirty their hands but employed a manager, a grieve or steward, and had life-styles more akin to either the gentry or the urban manager– were the most distanced from their employees.

Owner-occupation was not the norm among farmers until well into the present century. In the first decades of the twentieth century the majority of farmers in all areas of Scotland were ten-ants. Moreover, many tenancies had low rents, suggesting that the typical farmer was not so very grand.[2] There was one landowner and thirteen sons or daughters of farmers in our sample.[3] The families of farmers had at least one important thing in common – the control, if not actual ownership, of the means of production in farming; while they were tenant farmers rather than landowners, they owned all the necessary implements for producing food and livestock for themselves and for selling on the market.

Five of the interviewees were the children of 'working-family farmers'; their fathers used exclusively their own family labour for substantial periods of the family life-cycle. In the case of the farms relying most exclusively on family labour, such as those on which the Mathews and Mr MacPherson were brought up, the day-to-day life and standard of living was in many respects similar to that of crofters.[4] Unlike crofters, they did not have to rely on supple-mentary employment for getting a living. These respondents were brought up in the north-east Lowlands. In the case of the other two working-family farms, hired help was dispensed with when our respondent left school. In the case of the Marshalls' 100-acre Ayrshire dairy farm, 'the married man' was 'let go' when Mr

Marshall reached 15 and could replace him.[5] Mrs Haslitt and her sister were also used to replace paid help on their 200-acre Borders dairy farm when they left school.[6]

The remaining respondents grew up on farms which always had employees, although not all were larger than farms on which only family labour was employed. For example, Mr Henderson's father had a 210-acre Ayrshire dairy farm on which there were two unmarried men, a married man and a young woman for the house and dairy. Dairy and arable farms were generally labour-intensive. Mr McManus talked of three single men, three single women and a married man on a 320-acre dairy farm. Mr Veitch talked of three ploughmen, a cattleman and an orraman on a 300-acre north-east Lowland farm.[7] These respondents' families all had middle-class connections, with professional, commercial and business occupations represented in their family networks. Nevertheless, in five cases their fathers were 'working farmers'.

On the three largest and most prosperous farms there were considerable numbers of employees both on the farm itself, and in the households, where several servants were kept. These interviewees were all from substantial farms in the Lothians or Borders,[8] that is, the south-east Lowlands. Along with the son of a Highland laird, Mr Gilanders, these four respondents were as close as we got to the upper-class elite of landowners and gentleman farmers. For example, Mrs Tanner described her father's supervision of his 640 acres.

> He had three farms. One was four miles away, the other six/seven miles off. He used to go to the nearer one once every day and the other every second day perhaps. . . He had a grieve in each farm. [He was] a gentleman farmer.

To all intents and purposes, farming families gained their living[9] from their tenanted farm. In some cases they had held the land for centuries, usually for a couple of generations at least. In a couple of others, the family had farmed for generations, but had changed their tenancies. For instance, Mr McManus (born in 1895) told us that his father had leased the 320-acre dairy farm only in 1893. His father and forefathers had been situated on another farm since 1709. He explained that the tenancy was likely to be transferred from father to son if the son was capable of farming.

> If the son was capable of farming, it followed on, withoot any trouble.

In they days there wiz a very friendly atmosphere between tenants and landlords. When he took that farm the factor said whit rent he wanted and [his father] said he would take it and they never had a signature of a pen or a lease drawn up. Word of mouth. He had it twenty years.

... Then there was another farm called Pleasantoun. The second year my father was there ... the factor asked him if he would take it ... He says you can half it and let it. And he halved it and let it to two miners. I went to the school with the miners' sons ... The rents then were 30s. an acre, the men's wages were a pound ...

[My mother] was brought up on the farm. She worked on ma father's farm, and learned to make cheese. My grandmother made cheese, and she learnt with a neighbour. No' at the dairy school. She won [a cup] three years in succession. At Kilmarnock. My grand-mother won the cup ... We made cheese on this farm ...

MR MCMANUS, BORN 1895

A man might make the arrangements with the landowner or his factor to enter into a tenancy agreement on his own behalf, but sometimes a lease was organised by a father in respect of his son(s). This need not have involved a great deal of capital, and providing the father planned well in advance, it would be possible to settle sons on nearby farms – at least in some cases.

At that time, there wasn't such a big lot of money about. A man, when he thought his son was getting up would ... eh ... would get at the landlord and he would prepare him for a year or two and hive off so many cows and so on, stock, to the son. They wouldna need such a big lot of money. Then they would build up again.

MRS MARSHALL, BORN 1900

In three cases where substantial farms were involved, the father had had some other occupation and had married an heiress or had inherited the land from a relative other than his own father. Never-theless, all of the fathers in the sample came from farming families, and like Mr McManus's mother, most of the wives had learned domestic and dairying skills as children from their own mothers, aunts and grandmothers. Farming was very much a family affair.

Self-Provisioning and the Household Economy

Farming families took advantage of what the woods, hedgerows and rivers had to offer in the way of natural resources, and supple-

mented their diet by catching rabbits and by other forms of hunting, but these kinds of activities were less important in keeping the
families fed than were the resources produced on the farm itself. In
the case of the wealthiest farms, both a gardener and a gamekeeper
were employed. Unlike crofters, who could never make a living
from their crofts, farm families were sustained by their farms. Farm
family households lived off the farm, both directly by eating its
produce, and indirectly through income generated by the farm.
How much could be spared for comfort and enjoyment depended
on the general wealth of the farm and the style of life sought. But in
general there was a cautiousness about taking money out of the
farm.

Our farming families from the North had a similar if sometimes
more plentiful diet to that of the crofters. More of their food was
produced on the farm itself, and wild game might have been killed
on their own land rather than poached. The son of a landowner, a
sub-chieftain from the Highlands, emphasised how frugal their
lives were, despite their social status.

> We were brought up on a very frugal, and I think, healthy diet on the
> traditional oatmeal. We had porridge every morning. In those days,
> most of our neighbours and everyone else did. It made a great
> difference to people's health, porridge and milk. We had lots of
> produce off the estate and garden. Fish, game, especially venison. I
> remember we had to eat a lot of pike, more than we wanted because
> we netted the pike in [the] Loch ... On the whole, we had a very
> simple and healthy diet.
>
> MR GILANDERS, BORN 1915

Farming respondents often talked about having porridge every
morning, and many of them kept pigs and cured their own bacon.
Sometimes they killed a sheep for household consumption. A
garden supplied vegetables for broth. Many people mentioned the
hens, so that presumably eggs were available most of the year and
hens available from time to time for the pot. Everyone kept at least
one cow for milk and other dairy products. In dairying areas, of
course, there was always butter and cream and sometimes cheese
produced on the farm. Most mothers made scones, pancakes and
other home-baked products. In the Highlands, oatcakes were made
daily. As among the households of agricultural labourers in the
Borders, some groceries, fish, meat and other goods might be
obtained from an itinerant trader. These goods were not necess-

arily bought, but may have been exchanged for farm-produced goods.

It was customary not to take money out of the farm where at all possible. Sons and daughters contributed their labour without payment, except in the elite families where this was not expected. At least among our 'working' farmers, there was little evidence of spending money on goods which could be produced at home, and little to show that the cash economy was important to them on a day-to-day basis. This did not mean that the lives of farmers and their families were not distinctive from those of other rural workers. Most of the farmers had a much more varied social life than their other rural contemporaries. Most had some form of transport, and most spent some money on goods which displayed their status, such as clothing appropriate to social gatherings.

Social Relations on the Farm

When farm servants were employed, the social relations of work contrasted quite sharply with crofting; there were class divisions between employers and employees in the working environment of the farm itself. Although few of the farmers' children spoke about social class directly, it was clear that some of their fathers kept a degree of social distance from their employees. For instance, where there were single young maids and farmhands, they ate in the kitchen separate from the family.

On the other hand, farmers also used techniques to bridge social distance. Mrs Roberts, the daughter of a gentleman farmer, whose interview appears at the end of this chapter, was amazed as a child to hear her 'cultured' father speaking to his workers using broad Scots dialect. But speaking the same language as the workers assisted the farmer in his management of them. This is illustrated by Mr Isbister's father's constant frustration with his workers' use of Gaelic.

> My mother spoke Gaelic but my father didn't. She never spoke Gaelic in the house. It was after we went to school. All the men on the farm spoke Gaelic, nothing spoken but the Gaelic. When father came about the place, he wanted such and such a thing done and of course, there was two or three men about and we started discussing this in the Gaelic. One day he got so angry with this, he said he had got thirty-five men under him [in the distillery] and had never got treated like this.
>
> MR ISBISTER, BORN 1905

Whatever the degree of distance between employers and employees, this was not necessarily matched among their children, at least when they were young and going to the same schools. Mr McManus played and went to school with the sons of the miners who were subtenants of his father. Other boys, who grew up to be farmers themselves, spent much time around the farm with the workers, learning from them as well as from their fathers. Both Mr Veitch and Mr Isbister spent most of their free time as children with their fathers' workers. There was no evidence that girls did so, although a few certainly worked with their fathers.

Economic Reciprocity among Farmers and Crofters

There was some evidence of reciprocity in several areas. Mr Veitch's family lived in Speyside in an area in which there were many crofters. At harvest time, the crofters would come and help his father bring in the harvest. In return, he claimed that the crofters could be sure that their crops would also be harvested, because they could rely on help from the farmers. Mr Henderson told us that in Ayrshire, before the First World War, if a farmer had finished his harvest work and he saw his neighbour had not, he would go and help him. During the winter, too, they would send men to each other. There was no money exchanged, since this was simply seen as a neighbourly act.

It was thought by a couple of respondents who volunteered information on this topic that things started to change at the end of the Second World War when mechanisation started to come in in the form of tractors. This made the farmers more independent, since they could get the work done much more quickly and efficiently. They commented that, even today, co-operation among farmers is nevertheless still an important feature of work-life. Mr Henderson, who still works his farm, said that on the Saturday before he was interviewed, his combine had taken fire. 'Almost that night, we got the offer of two combines off neighbours . . .'

Social Divisons, Holidays and Community Events

In general terms, the higher the social status and the better the economic position of the family, the wider the social networks

FIGURE 4.1: Farm servants, Roxburghshire, c. 1900.

expanded. Crofting interviewees were unlikely to have childhood experience beyond the croft and its immediate environs – the church and the school. Farm servants' children also had close horizons, but were likely to have experienced social life in a number of farms within an area of, say, ten miles from their birthplace. The far wider social experience of the children of farmers is illustrated by their childhood holidays further afield, their more extensive community activities, and their more varied leisure time. This experience, as well as that of going away to boarding school or university or on some youthful expedition abroad, expanded their horizons far beyond that of their contemporaries from rural areas.

The children in most of our farming families had holidays with relatives, with friends or with one or both parents in some seaside resort or other. Sometimes the holiday involved a visit of the children alone (or with a sibling) to the farm of grandparents or aunts and uncles, which may not have presented much in the way of contrast with their home situation. Mr Veitch's family took a cottage, leaving the farm in the charge of one of the employees. He himself, however, was sent to the farm of relatives in another district, where, he thought, his father 'wanted him to see what was going on in farming up there'. It is not clear whether this was an educational trip, whether Mr Veitch was keen enough on farming to forgo a holiday like the rest of the family, or whether the transport facilities and size of the cottage meant that there wasn't enough room for him too!

Two of the elite farming children remembered having holidays at the seaside. In both cases, this was not a particularly enjoyable experience for them, as they found it hard to adjust to the 'lack of having something to do', to the unaccustomed living conditions or to the coldness of the sea in which they were obliged to disport themselves.

> I had a holiday at Scarborough. In the old days we took a house down there, two families. There was no bath in the house but a big tub was put on the kitchen floor. There were three of the Smiths and six of us. I was the youngest of the lot so I got the clean water. They put me in the sea and they splashed me till I hated it. I've hated the sea ever since. In those days they didn't teach you to swim, you sort of went in and splashed about.
>
> MRS TANNER, BORN 1912

Sometimes, the parents were able to afford the time and money to take the whole family away for the day. Mr Henderson's dairy-farming family's annual treat when he was very young was a visit to the local market town in a hired car with chauffeur. Mr Veitch usually had to stay at home when the family went for a picnic because there were too many of them to squeeze into the trap. Indeed, several people mentioned problems associated with taking large families on holidays or excursions of any kind.

As they grew older, young adults who remained on their parents' farms working unpaid might well take a trip of some distance to a Highland Games, to an agricultural show or to visit some relatives. At that time, they would be given a sum of money to cover their expenses and to buy clothes.

During the first couple of decades of this century, reciprocity in rural economic life was paralleled by an inclusive (but often status-divided) social life organised around an annual round of community events. One of those who spoke most glowingly of memories of community life was Mr Gilanders, the son of a Highland sub-chieftain. Although tied to the land in social and cultural terms, they were dependent on money made away from 'home' to uphold their position. Much of his childhood was spent living away from the ancestral estates because of his father's occupation. Coming home in summer to his grandfather's estate seems to have been the high point of their lives.

The community life described by Mr Gilanders would have been enjoyed by many local people, whether they came from crofting or farming backgrounds in the Highlands, or whether they gained their livelihood in the small Highland towns. The village halls were used for ceilidhs, with local fiddlers playing the marches, strath-speys and reels. The quality of dancing was high because there were local societies devoted to country dances and to the playing of Highland music using the traditional style of bowing on the fiddle. At a special event, there might be a famous local violinist, playing 'wonderful music and sometimes he would take too much liquor, then it would be time to stop'. Mr Veitch's three sisters, who were all musical, were in much demand for their services and travelled quite long distances to play at socials like these. He himself, like many of the young men and women, particularly enjoyed dancing.

Highland Games used to be a great event locally, before the days when they became commercialised and a tourist attraction. There was little specialisation in events; one local man would play the pipes for the piping competition and then take off his jacket and toss the caber. It was more of a convivial local affair in which local people would take part in traditional forms of competition. Shinty was one of the great games involving many people as players and spectators. Shinty matches, then as now, would have stimulated competition between towns, villages and even isolated settlements, providing the means for the young men to get together.

There were more events for those at the upper end of the social ladder, which involved people travelling from further afield – dances, balls and sporting events. The Northern Meet Ball was one of the great social events of the year, at least for persons of high status. These people would also visit each other's houses for dinners and other social events, perhaps staying for days on end. In the Borders and South, there were local events which drew large crowds of country people. Several of our interviewees spoke about participating in these as children and young adults. Here, too, were the dances and hunt balls where the better-off farmers and their grown children could get together during the winter season. These were formal events where an evening suit was required. Two of our male respondents described how they had been sent to a special tailor to be properly outfitted. Both still own and wear these suits, which were made for them when they were about twenty years old!

> I've still got it yet, full garb, white tie and tails, swallow-tails, waist-coat with four buttons. The suit cost seventeen guineas, made in Exchange Square in Glasgow, by a firm called Jackson's. Ye had to get an introduction. That's where we got our good suits. They were kinda dear, ye didna get the bill for aboot a year after ye got your suit. Supposed to be, they were very well made.
>
> MR MARSHALL, BORN 1900

Mr Marshall said he went to the dances or balls in a pony and trap. He described the etiquette of taking a young lady to the ball.

> If her brother was coming he would bring her, you would take her home of course. Yer tickets were usually about 6s. 6d., 7s. 6d. per couple. Ladies never paid, they had to be invited by a partner. It was very difficult for a young lady with no brothers unless she had somebody who would ask her. The buffet. Ye could sit and eat all night if you wished. [The buffet was put on by a caterer.] Practically everybody was there at eight, went on till mebbe two [in the morning]. When you were coming out, a cup of beef tea mebbe, when ye had your coat on, ready to go out the door.
>
> MR MARSHALL, BORN 1900

There were other kinds of dances attended by Mr Marshall, 'wee' parties in other people's houses with thirty to forty people present. No alcoholic drinks were ever served.

> No, no. And not at the balls. [Drink was] sometimes talked about in the Committee Rooms, but not in public. *Because there were women present?* ... No, just not the fashion.[10]
>
> MR MARSHALL, BORN 1900

Two of the children of elite farmers were keen riders and spent much of their young adulthood riding, or preparing for point-to-point. Mrs Tanner went to a boarding school at 8, but when she was at home most of her time was spent on horses. Elite farmers probably reflected the considerable variation among upper-middle-class parents generally concerning which activities were and were not suitable for young women. Mrs Tanner commented on why she went to a private ladies' college the year after she left school.

> I think mother thought something must be done with me. I wanted home to break horses and ride horses and do everything with horses. My brother thought I should go into a domestic school and learn some sense.
>
> MRS TANNER, BORN 1912

Tennis, a popular sport among farmers, was an approved activity for both sexes. A game of tennis on a private court would provide the setting for a social gathering of old and young. Curling, a predominantly male sport, was mentioned by a couple of respondents, both of them from the Borders. Mr McManus's account of his father's interest in the sport indicates that farmers with employees had some discretion over their working hours – a privilege not enjoyed by their workers.

> My father was a great curler in those days. On a long winter's frost one time, he told me, the frost came in November and they werena able to plough till March. And the farmers got that keen on their curling that they didna bide at home and do their thrashing [laughs].
>
> MR MCMANUS, BORN 1895

Only two interviewees, Mr Gilanders and Mrs Roberts, both of whom had very well educated and relatively wealthy parents, enjoyed cultural activities as a result of their parents' influence.

He was a very keen, and expert with the classical music of the Highland bagpipes, as well as the study of the instrument and the history of it. I've followed him with that ... always been very keen indeed. Ranks with the highest form of continental music. That's not just an opinion held by modest and humble people like myself. Mendelssohn himself regarded the pibroch as one of the highest forms of classical music and compared it with the fugue ... the classical musicians and all that. In those ways, I took to my father's [interests].

MR GILANDERS, BORN 1915

This extract also exemplifies Mr Gilanders' attachment to his cultural heritage. Mrs Roberts' family lived near Edinburgh and therefore in close proximity to the 'high culture' of the times. According to Mrs Roberts, her mother was a talented pianist and might have made a career for herself as a musician had she not married.

Mother was very anxious that I should be a musician. I was taken by mother to concerts and piano recitals. I was taken to the theatre first to see *Lohengrin* when I was about twelve. Prior to that I think my mother thought the theatre was not a place to encourage children to go. They used to talk about the devil in the theatre. She used to tell a story about a friend's son who ran away to become an actor and when he returned his father said, 'You are a child of the Devil', to which he replied, 'Good morning, Papa.' Actors, actresses were certainly on the fringe ...

MRS ROBERTS, BORN 1885

Church and Religiosity

Mrs Roberts was one of the oldest of our respondents[11] and her description of household prayers recalls a time when masters and servants would meet each day for communal prayers.

We had prayers night and morning. We'd sing a hymn. My mother had a harmonium. In the morning we sang a song, some verses of a psalm. Then we read the Old Testament and the sermon. The servants, the cook, the housemaid and nurse all came in. We used to read the Bible together, and they had to read it too, poor things, because perhaps it was difficult. And then we had ... we knelt down and my father prayed. Looking back, I think that was an important thing in my life. I don't remember much about what was there in the Bible. But my grandfather lived with us. I think perhaps he would take the prayers and it was when he went away my father would take them.

MRS ROBERTS, BORN 1885

Her mother and father were deeply religious people. When there were visitors to the house, theological questions were often discussed. Her parents were also very active in local church affairs and ran the Sunday School in connection with the church. Her father was the Church Session Clerk. He had been influential in getting the church built before she was born. Her mother played the organ and conducted the choir.

Echoing the statements of farm workers' children, she commented that many people used to walk three and four miles to church every Sunday in those days. While most of the farmers' children mentioned going to church as children, and a few spoke of religious observances, such as the regular saying of grace before meals, we had the impression that church-going was somewhat less frequent than among either crofters or agricultural workers. Two of the fathers never attended at all, although their wives and children did. In a couple of other cases, attendance was encouraged by parents rather than forced on the children.

THE HOUSEHOLD
Household Composition

The household composition and division of labour within each household depended on the stage in the life-cycle, the relative prosperity of the farm, and the extent to which parents emulated the life-style of urban middle-class households.

Some of the farming family households had had co-resident grandparents during the period of our interviewees' childhood. In others, an alternative arrangement had been possible; for example, there were cases in which another farm had been bought for one inheriting son, while another son had remained in his birthplace with his parents after marriage.

Apart from three of the four 'working-family farmer' households,[12] all of the farm households had some co-resident non-kin – usually young women or men who had been hired for household, dairy or farm work. Some were local girls, possibly the young daughters of farm workers who had recently left school. The maid on Mr Marshall's farm slept in a box-bed in the kitchen and took her meals with other employees on the farm. Sometimes, there was an unrelated boy or young man living in the household. This may have been more common on the small farms where a son or daughter was not old or strong enough to carry out the necessary chores. The hired hand would stay only long enough to fill the gap in labour requirements. His replacement by a member of the family would mean a change in household composition as well as in the family's division of labour.

In the most prosperous farmers' households, there were at least a couple of servants and sometimes a large household staff whose work was confined to the house itself. For instance, the hierarchy of servants would include at least a kitchen maid and a cook. Where the maid on a small farm would be obliged to divide her day between household, kitchen and dairy (with occasional field work),[13] a large farmhouse or country mansion would employ specialised domestic and dairy staff, a gardener and perhaps a chauffeur.

In emergency situations or changes of circumstances, wives and children might well be required to take over the duties of servants, even in wealthy households. When Mrs Tanner's father died, for instance, most of the servants were discharged, and her elder sister was obliged to help manage the household and do a great deal of the housework in association with a family friend while her mother recovered from the grief of her husband's untimely death. His death created a crisis in respect of the running of the farm, since the eldest son was still too young to take over.

The Household Division of Labour

The household division of labour among farming families depended on both the type of farm, and the number and kind of servants kept. There was typically a clear division of labour by gender and by generation. The male farmer, his sons and male farm servants were unlikely to do either domestic labour or dairy work.[14] Many women and girls, on the other hand, spent most of their working time in the household or in the dairy. Although on large arable farms women 'out-workers' could comprise a third or more of its workforce, farmers' daughters were not generally exclusively out-workers, though many at some time or other worked in the fields or with the animals. The farmer and his wife managed the work and undertook the more skilled and specialised tasks which could not be delegated safely to others. They also trained their children and their servants, either in quite specific terms, or by example.

Almost all of our farming respondents spoke about the great amount of work their mothers did in the house, the dairy and in the fields, especially at harvest time. With the exception of the gentleman farmers' wives, having maidservants did not mean that farming wives and mothers had any less to do in connection with the farm and its household. The presence of domestic servants made it possible for them to engage in productive work for the market, rather than or in addition to servicing the needs of members of the household. It should be remembered that it was not only family members who had to be fed. Meals were provided on most farms for those servants who lived in. Maids and older children of the family took over many of the time-consuming child-rearing tasks which the mothers might also have done.

The most genteel mothers of children brought up on substantial farms were not involved in growing crops or rearing animals for food. Their work was the supervision of the household, but they might also be engaged in voluntary, political or social work in the community. They were ladies whose social position was buttressed by ample household staffs who performed all the necessary menial household chores and child-caring activities usually done by mothers and their older daughters. These women employed housemaids, kitchen maids, cooks, nannies and tutors or governesses.

Further down the social scale, daughters usually worked alongside their mothers and helped in the dairy. Some were involved in farm work as well. Mrs Haslitt had been born and bred in town before her father inherited a farm. She went to boarding school, but enjoyed coming home at the weekends and holidays when she milked the cows and helped her mother so that the maid could get time off work. When she was away, her father, mother and two servants milked the 30–35 cows by hand. The milk was retailed in the local town and provided cream and butter for the household. Her sister's return to the household at the end of her schooling made it possible for them to produce butter since the sister was an expert butter-maker. When she herself returned, the maid was given notice.

Mrs Haslitt did not do much work around the house at all when she was at home, though in the evening she enjoyed going to her

FIGURE 4.2: Samuelston Mains, by Haddington, 1911.

uncle's house to bath the children . Her uncle's farm had a bigger milking than their own farm and they needed the help. Her aunt was 'awful fussy' in the dairy, having learned the art of butter-making at dairy school (*c.* 1918). What suited Mrs Haslitt also suited her aunt, and saved her getting paid help. Similarly, Mrs Haslitt helped her father.

> I worked outside. At harvest . . . I helped with the feeding of the young cattle, the hens – we had a lot of hens – and ducks, and then when it was harvest-time or hay-time worked outside all the time with the men. I worked with my father. I used to say there wasn't a sheaf on the farm that hadn't gone through my hands. We tied the sheaves, it was cut by a machine, tied with straw. The seed-hay all had to be tied in individual . . . and then stooked. Every morning you were turning hay or turning stooks . . . dried and made into rucks and put into the hay shed or big hay stacks.
>
> MRS HASLITT, BORN 1906

By the time she was fifteen, the farm had become totally a family concern, with no hired hands apart from the Irish migrant workers who came to help with the harvest.

Most of the farmers' sons we interviewed eventually became farmers themselves, showing an interest in the outdoor life from an early age. Mr Henderson, for instance, started milking cows at the age of about 11 or 12, with four or five members of the family. He also fed the calves and drove horses. All his friends were farmers' sons, and they all had dogs and would go on sheep dog trials in their spare time. He did

> every job that was going. Father used to say that when I got a man's job to do ... I was nae use doing a wee job ... I could do a man's job in less time than the men could do it, but I didna like doin' wee jobs. Too footery[15] ... A man's job was a challenge. These wee jobs are fiddly [such as brushing yard, gathering wood, etc., the usual chores done by young boys].
>
> MR HENDERSON, BORN 1913

Despite the wishes of his father, who was the manager of a distillery as well as a farm manager, Mr Isbister insisted on spending a lot of time around the farm, working with the men and indulging his love of animals. Later, his father sent him to work on his uncle's farm, hoping that he would get 'scunnered'[16] with the work, all to no avail. Mr Isbister stubbornly resisted and finally got his way. His relationship with the workers on his father's island farm, his feelings for them, the animals and the land emerge clearly from his accounts of their work.

> The men were so interested in their work. They had to be first. If they saw a neighbour putting in corn, these men would be in stitches to get at it – that's the type. They didn't like to be last. These men, they treated the stock as if it was their own. When you met them out anywhere at a Show, it was theirs, they talked about their own. It made things a lot easier. Whereas if you were left entirely with a big stock and ye had men that werena caring ... it was a bad go ...
>
> *Did you follow the men around when you were at the school?*
>
> Oh, yes. Comin' home from school, many a time I would see the men ploughing, I would jump over the dyke and if they were ploughing ... Oh, yes. At that time most of these lads would start on a farm. A lot of them went away to the mainland.
>
> *You never had the notion to go away ...?*
>
> I never did. I was quite happy. If I got in among stock, I didn't care two pins for anybody. I still think about them.
>
> MR ISBISTER, BORN 1905

By the time farmers' sons had served their 'apprenticeship' under their parents – and their parents' workers – they were ready to take full responsibility for adult work at an age which we would consider very young today. Mr Henderson and Mr Isbister illustrate the childhood socialisation of boys who started their farming careers very early. In the first example, which is quite characteristic of the experience of other male respondents, there had been a long line of farming forefathers. In the second, the boy had been attracted to outside work as a result of his close associations with farm workers and animals. This was to lead to a struggle against his father's distaste for farming as a worthy occupation for his son whom he observed working alongside his men.

Mr Veitch also experienced this early socialisation. Mr Veitch's grandfather had 'cam doun frae the Cabrach'[17] to establish himself in an economically more promising area. He acquired a farm and sent his son into a solicitor's office so that he could learn about business affairs and the law. Mr Veitch's father inherited the farm when his father died. By this time, he had married the musical daughter of a family highly placed in the area and influential in the cities. The behaviour and attitudes of Mr Veitch's father, like his own, reflected the love of land and of animals expressed by many working on the land, while the outlook of his sisters and his brother more properly belonged in the category of 'elite' gentleman farmers and the urban upper middle class. His mother, however, straddled the two. The family will be discussed in more detail later.

Although Mr Isbister's childhood was very similar to that of Mr Veitch in terms of his young working life and his love of the land and animals, there had been no encouragement at all from his father, who appears to have been somewhat contemptuous of farming. Mr Isbister said:

> I suppose when I was sent to my uncle's farm [to learn about farming], I think my father had given me up. He had. I heard him say that I was fit for nothing but being at the tail end of a coo [cow].
>
> MR ISBISTER, BORN 1905

In both cases, the boys had been thoroughly steeped in the farming life and lore as a result of their daily contact with the farm workers.

At the upper end of the farming social ladder there was no early transition to a lifetime career or way of life. In general, the children of elite families did little in the household or farm, at least before they were grown up. All four of the interviews we conducted with children from elite families suggest that the usual practice was for them to be sent away for their schooling, usually to well-known boarding schools.[18] Entrance into an occupation was typically delayed by a period at university or college, sometimes followed by a fallow year. In the case of upper-class young women, entering into an occupation other than marriage was not expected. Mrs Tanner, for example, was not boarded at a private ladies' college in England to fit her for a career, but to 'learn some sense' since she was 'horse-mad'. What she was obliged to learn at a formal institution was typically experienced by other girls from farming families when they were much younger, and were taught in familiar surroundings by members of their families.

Like other children of her own class, Mrs Tanner and her brothers spent most of their childhood at boarding school. At home on holiday, most of their time seems to have been spent in play and sports. The only exception to this was the help at harvest time required of older boys home from school on holiday, but this help was very limited in comparison with the contribution made by the children of other farmers.

Leisure on Home and Farm

Social life was more varied among farmers than among crofters or farm servants. Larger homes, more disposable income and, in some cases, more time for leisure made it possible for at least some modest entertaining to be done. Many people spoke about visiting, by neighbours for instance. Mr Isbister described how his father would have friends in to play nap.[19]

> I would be in the room. Most of them smoked and it was a pipe, so it was a great game, 'Nap'. The farmers would spend hours playing it. They would be so busy [playing], they would hand me their pipe, and ye would have a wee bit draw. That's how I started to smoke a pipe.
>
> MR ISBISTER, BORN 1905

Visiting often meant extra work for wives and daughters, since much baking would have to be done. Sometimes somebody would play the fiddle, or people sang together around the piano.

Reading was popular, both individually and reading aloud to the others. Most households bought a newspaper at least weekly. Some family members enjoyed reading books. One of the adults (perhaps a governess) might read aloud to the rest. In some households, charades, cards or board games like Ludo provided entertainment whether or not guests were also present. Mr Henderson told us that his father used to bargain with the fruiterer for a case of fruit, and he remembers how they would share the apples and oranges in the evenings, with his father peeling and dividing them for the children.

Relationship between Parents and Children

We analysed the relationships between parents and children in earlier chapters in terms of the economic and cultural context in which crofters and agricultural workers lived and worked, noting that there seemed to be no particular distinctive style associated with either category. We also noted that these children had no childhood in the sense we understand the word today – as a particular special time free from the responsibilities of adulthood, deserving tolerance and indulgence from adults, and allowing time to develop one's potential as an individual. Parents had limited freedom to choose how their children should be brought up; the economic circumstances of some parents demanded that they use what resources they had to survive, in particular the services of their children in the household and wherever else they could be usefully sent to earn. Few parents could afford to give their children treats in the form of pocket money, toys or excursions, even if they wanted to. And very few parents would have been comfortable with the laxity of allowing their children to behave as they wished, not least because this would fly in the face of convention. Most parents endorsed or had reason to respect the current social norms prescribing 'good' behaviour, especially on Sundays.

To a very considerable extent we found the same situation among working family farmers. These farmers needed the services of their children from an appropriate age to provide labour in the form of domestic, dairy or farmwork, so the opportunities for individual development were narrowly defined in terms of the work which they would do as adults. In the better-off working-farmer families and the elite farming families, 'childhood' was more clearly delineated in terms of freedom from material responsibilities, but even here children were not generally a main focus of indulgent attention for their mother and father. They had toys and games which others did not have, and they had more time for play, riding, and generally making mischief, but parents remained somewhat

FIGURE 4.3:   Farmer's son, with pet lamb, Angus *c.* 1900.

distant authority figures whose expectations of obedience had to be respected.

In general, the relationship of farming children with their parents was similar to that of other rural respondents with regard to such matters as punishment and control. As we have previously commented, traditional authority was the norm practised among Scottish families at this time. In common with other interviewees, Mr Isbister, for example, considered that parents were much stricter in those days than they are now, and they expected their children to be seen and not heard – a dictum offered by several of our interviewees. Parents did not expect to be inconvenienced by their children, as this extract shows:

> If you were ever in the room when father walked in, you couldn't open your mouth. Nine times out of ten, you were told, 'That is the door, go out.'
>
> MR ISBISTER, BORN 1905

We did get the impression that farming fathers were, in general, stricter than the mothers. At least in the eyes of their children they were the boss. Some of them lived up to the stereotype of the patriarchal Victorian father. Children were not expected to get in the way of visitors, at least not when they were very young. Indeed, Mrs Tanner remembers the particular indignity of having to parade herself in front of visitors and do her party piece. She would be brought down in a 'little velvet dress' to recite a piece of poetry and then she would disappear again. This made her feel very nervous and she hated making a spectacle of herself. But as she said, 'in those days, you were brought up to be seen and not heard. You didn't answer back to anybody.' Children were not included in the visiting, strictly speaking. They might be allowed to appear in front of visitors when they were old enough, but that was all.

> ... When we were in school, oh yes. But you were never allowed to voice your opinion. No. Not at that age. Different when we started working. Oh, yes.
>
> MR ISBISTER, BORN 1905

Our general conclusion in terms of relationships between parents and children is that the traditional authority vested in parents was universally taken for granted and adhered to among all our inter- viewees. Parents were undoubtedly loved, but in many cases they were feared too, and at least sometimes, more feared than loved. When children perceived injustices, they had to bow to that auth- ority which was reinforced by school and church. Where there was a farm or croft to be inherited, adult children who wanted more spending money or freedom than their parents allowed had to weigh the balance between remaining, and leaving for an uncertain future in which their bargaining position would be relatively poor. Such decisions would rarely be reduced to simple economic calcu- lations devoid of personal loyalties and conceptions of 'the right thing to do'. Many respondents were surrounded by a chorus of beliefs about one's place in society and the duty and obligations associated with that position.

In the following extract, Mr Gilanders talks about the standards expected of him as a leader of his community and his country.

> There was in those days, much more than there is today, an absolute fetish about very strict adherence to becoming a sportsman and a good sportsman. If ever we were slack about grooming our horses or cleaning our gun, we really copped it properly. It was almost a

religion in those days, compared with now. You really weren't considered properly brought up unless you could both take part in these sports and also behave yourself to the very highest standards of sportsmanship, both in regard to the animals and the wildlife – the game – and to your neighbours in the next door...

MR GILANDERS, BORN 1915

'Playing the game' was expected of him as a gentleman. The self-discipline considered necessary in sporting activities was also expected to be employed in interaction with social subordinates, such as estate workers and domestic staff.

We were taught to respect them, to be polite. If we were ever not polite, we were ordered to go and apologise to them. We had a very very strict social upbringing in that way.

Why was it like that?

[It was] a tradition in the Highlands ... we depended on the loyalty, not just on their subservience. We depended on their friendship and their loyalty, just like in a regiment today.

MR GILANDERS, BORN 1915

He went on to describe his relationships with his men as an officer in the army, emphasising the same forms of patrimonial interaction. Mr Gilanders also commented on the entertainments put on by his grandfather for the local people, saying that all classes mixed at these events, but that there were strict rules about who sat where at table.[20] Children of elite farmers learned about their place in society from an early age and were expected to play their part in the conformist standards of early-twentieth-century Scotland. Living standards and the trappings of high status had to be maintained.

Self-discipline was imposed on both parents and children as a necessary condition of their formal education. Preparation for separation when children went to boarding school was well established early in life. Children in our elite families all had nannies, and they and their siblings went to boarding schools unless a 'suitable' school was close. Parents in families such as these did not expect to spend much time with their children even before their offspring went to boarding school at 7 or 8 years old. Parents in other kinds of families can be said to have been emotionally distant from their children; equally, elite parents and children were neither physically nor emotionally close, at least in respect of their overt behaviour, since they might see each other for only a short time each day, before dinner. Children, of course, ate separately from their parents in the nursery until they reached a 'civilised' age.

Mr Gilanders was separated from his parents as a toddler owing to his parents' involvement in the war effort. He told us that he lived in a cottage with his nanny for a couple of years in a small village, with occasional visits to his grandfather's estate. When he learned to speak, it was in Gaelic rather than English; his nanny was clearly very important to him. It is doubtful if his well-educated mother would have approved of the nanny's child-rearing methods; she ruled by fear and threat, telling him that if he was naughty and ran away down to the water, the monster (reputed to live there) would get him. It seems that Mr Gilanders' parents were relatively liberal in their treatment of their children compared to others in upper-class Scottish society of the time (Jamieson, 1978). He feels that, as children, they ate with their parents rather more than was usual at the time. He considers that his mother was exceptionally close to her children, and possibly as a result of her own upbringing in a large family, possibly also owing to her high level of education. It may be, too, that long stretches on the Highland estate would have presented opportunities for closeness which would have been considered undesirable in urban high society. Another case in which a nanny figured prominently was that of Mrs Roberts, who gave the impression of loving her nanny much more than her parents (see the interview below). Mrs Roberts visited her nanny until she died, although they spent only six years together. Her mother appeared to have had little sympathy or understanding for a daughter who could not fulfil her expectations of becoming a musician like herself.

Among the sons of farmers, there were several cases where the sons' relationships with their fathers were either cool or even stormy. For example, Mr Marshall did not stay at home to take over the farm from his father, who lived to be over 80. He managed to establish himself elsewhere. Mr Marshall's father had a problem with drink, which caused the family a great deal of embarrassment and financial uncertainty, mitigated by the fact that, when his father inherited the farm, the capital was held in a trust. Mr Marshall described how, when he was living at home, his father would always look for him when he returned from a visit to the market with the intention of chastising him on the pretext of some task which had not been done. Unlike most of the other fathers who were at pains to train their children, Mr Marshall's father seems to have been less than competent with his livestock.[21]

> I think my mother taught me more … he was a bundle of nerves…
> You know, cows calving – they sometimes needed a hand.

If he or his brother needed help, they got their mother. They would not let the father near the cow if they could avoid it because he got too excited to be helpful.

> Mother would act as midwife, ease the passage of the calf – he would be roaring and jumping about, frightening and tensing the cow. He didna train us very much at all.
>
> MR MARSHALL, BORN 1900

Fortunately, Mr Marshall's mother's brother placed him in a job. Later, he was able to get his own farm, with the help of the family trust.

Mr Henderson had a rather distant relationship with his father, whom he appears to have feared in much the same way that Mrs Geddes feared her crofter mother. Like Mr Marshall, Mr Henderson was close to his mother, 'the apple of her eye'. Father was considered domineering. He had never chastised them for not working hard enough, but everything had to be properly done. It may be that his authoritarian style was at least partly related to a health problem; perhaps also he had unrealistically high expectations of his children. At least, his children had some leeway in what chores they did, since he did not issue them with orders for each day's labour. We do not wish to imply from these two examples that these two fathers were cruel. However, they do support the hypothesis that parents who were remembered as being clearly more authoritarian than average were marginal within their own communities in one way or another. One result of being marginal was that their children were less likely to accept their legitimacy.

Earlier in this chapter we discussed the family situation of Mr Veitch, whose father had come from an area where small farms and crofts predominated. The reader will recall that Mr Veitch's mother came from a socially well-placed background. While Mr Veitch and his parents laboured on the farm together doing the menial work associated with agriculture and dairying, Mr Veitch's brother and sisters took no part in this. There is every sign that Mr Veitch was exploited by his parents, whose plans for their other children included a good education, and one which was suited to their talents. The brother was sent to an expensive fee-paying school, while two of the three girls eventually went to London in order to further their careers in music. Mr Veitch's father considered that this would never have been possible without his son's help. Indeed, Mr Veitch's schooling was neglected and he was hardly ever included in family holidays or excursions, being left at home to mind the farm. It seems surprising that he showed few signs of resentment. His interview suggests that he was proud of his sisters' accomplishments and that, knowing his future on the farm would be assured, he was not personally threatened by his brother's fortune in getting a good education. Perhaps he saw himself working with his parents in a joint project, sharing their collective ambitions for the rest of the family. His good relationship with his father was sustained both by his own perception of the situation, and by his father's expressed opinion of him as a good worker – surely a matter of pride. His situation of a long apprenticeship for his inheritance would also be visible to the local community and regarded as legitimate.

INTERVIEWS WITH THE CHILDREN OF FARMERS

We have chosen two full transcriptions of interviews with the children of farmers to let the people speak for themselves and to illustrate the points we have made. The first interview is that of Mr Veitch, who describes carefully the work done on a substantial farm in the North-East. His father was a working farmer. The energies of Mr Veitch himself were totally occupied in the farm. As was foreshadowed in the previous chapter, however, his brother and sisters were not so confined, being destined for careers elsewhere. The second interview depicts a childhood which was totally different. Mrs Roberts and her parents lived close to Edinburgh. Although her father was a farmer, he did not 'dirty his hands'. In many respects, her childhood was the same as that of upper-middle-class children growing up in cities.

Mr Veitch, born 1903, North-East

Mr Veitch, recently a widower, lives in a small detached villa in a hamlet on the mouth of the river which ran through his family property. He is retired and lives some thirty miles from the home of his childhood, which is now that of his eldest son and *his* family. Another son farms close to the river-mouth and sees his father regularly. They are all practical men, accustomed to getting their hands dirty and to participating fully in the daily and seasonal routine of the now-mechanised farm.

In his interview, Mr Veitch himself comments on some aspects of farming which are no longer practised, and gives a particularly interesting account of his childhood and youth working on the farm that would one day become his. He also has much to say about the lives of his mother and of his siblings. Mr Veitch had three sisters and two brothers. The three sisters were all musically talented and, instead of helping their mother in the household, were encouraged to practise their music, something rather unusual for a family in their position. The sons were destined for careers in cities.

The interview starts with a section on the family history. Mr Veitch's account of his kinship networks provides many clues about the basis of the more urban upper-class destinations of his siblings.

Interview with Mr Veitch

Can you tell me a little about your father? Where did he come from?

My grandfather and he came doun frae the Cabrach. Twas my grandfather took Deeside first. My father was working in a solicitor's office. When his father died he took over the farm of Deeside Mains.

So he had to have an occupation to keep him going till he could get on the farm?

Aye, yes that's right.

Would that have happened to a lot of boys?

That happened to a lot of them that wanted a little bit o' book keeping and suchlike, went into an office to get training.

I didn't get that but I saw that my son got that. He was [in a solicitor's office] in Nairn for three years before he went into farming, after he left Fettes College ... in Edinburgh. He was at

Lathallen School first for primary school and then he got into Fettes College. My brother went to Dollar Academy. And then he came home and went out to a solicitor's office in G. for three years, and then he took up farmin' . . .

Where did your mother come from?

A neighbouring farm. She was one of the Wallaces . . . [He speaks about an illustrious ancestor.] But the Wallaces were all very musical. My mother was very musical. Mrs Macduff in Nairn, that was her sister, very musical.

Did she come from a very big family, your mother?

No, they came from . . . Aberdeenshire. [He talks about family connections, Ministers, solicitors in Edinburgh – his mother's folk.]

Kin living close to you? Did most of your kin live far away?

Most o' them were, but Mrs Macduff in Nairn, ma mother's sister, she was quite near. Her father died when she was young. She was at a boarding school. The whole lot o' them, the father and a', was very musical. One o' her brothers was an auctioneer in Dundee . . . another one is oot in America, the Argentine. Another one doun in an estate in England, a factor . . . but they're a' dead.

Was your mother educated, musically? Did she have an LRAM or anything like that?

That was ma sisters. She taught ma sisters.

But did she not have training herself?

No, only self, her father died when they were very young. They were at a school in Dundee and I think they got music there, and then, I think, they jist taught music. She played the organ in church and she did a lot of training and teaching and training privately. She hadnae any qualifications that I know of, but the girls had to be up early every morning waiting for breakfast in separate rooms, practising either the piano or the fiddle. They spent every spare moment they had practising.

Did they do that because they wanted to learn or . . . because your mum wanted them to learn?

Both. They were full of it. They were aye playing. Mother and the three girls went out to concerts, entertainments, openings of different halls after the war and that, the three of them. One of them carried right on. They gave it up after they got married [chuckles] ... jist a thing that was forgotten about after that.

What about your father's relatives?

Aye, he had two brothers and three sisters, aye.

There are problems of inheritance where there are several sons. Did father buy the farm?

No, he rented it. My grandfather rented it, he took it over from the other tenant, ye see.

But they would have had to pay for stock?

... Oh, yes, yes, they used to take over everything at valuation. Ye jist pay the rent every year instead of buying it out.

Could you get put out of a farm?

There was never anybody put out unless they werena farmed up to a certain standard. Or they drank themselves out.

The standards would be set out in the lease, I presume ...

Yes, the conditions are set out on yer lease that you must keep it up to a certain standard.

What happened to your father's brothers?

One went out to Demerara to a sugar plantation and then he come home and took the farm across here. [Mr Veitch's son farms it today.] ... then he went blind ... he never married.

How did he manage the farm without a wife?

No, he had a man and his wife did for him and he just lived in the house with them.

Woman's work in many farms is of critical importance to the farm ...

Oh, aye.

What sort of work did your mother do around the house and farm?

She never stopped knitting ... the auld folks had their band round and the needles goin' a' the time [laughs]. Oh, she did a lot of cooking and kept us all in clothes, made all our waterproof coats. Ye see, we had to walk two-and-a-half miles to school. And you had to have your breakfast by eight o'clock to walk to school by nine o'clock. That was how we had to get up and milk the cows sae early in the morning. Get the breakfast over.

Was your mother involved in the milking?

— 175 —

No, she had plenty to do in the house without the milkin'.

She had other children . . .

There were three girls older than I was, then James, ten or twelve years efter the next one come along.

Did she make butter or cheese?

Oh, aye, aye. There was always cheese hangin' aboot in the loft, hangin' from boards and wires in the couples in the loft.

What else?

There was always somebody in the district killing a pig, and always somebody come round saying, what do you want?

And you would do the same?

Whenever we had a pig ready to go, we got it killed locally and everybody got to buy a bit if they wanted it.

Money did change hands?

Yes, of course, they werena very expensive then.

Some women made butter and cream or eggs for sale. Did your mother make money off her produce?

Mostly the produce was taken for paying the groceries.

So she earned money?

She earned money, but instead of them paying it out, they bought groceries in place of what . . .

She would have had to do quite a lot to cover all your groceries?

Oh, aye she did a lot. And then again, she was preserving. Afore the hens came to the broody season, she was preserving eggs and she generally had waterglass in a big jar, preserved about ten dozen eggs. Of course, they were no' used for boilin'. They had to be broken and scrambled or poached.

Or used for baking.

And then we always had a barrel of salt herring. They had to be taken out the barrel the night before and soaked in milk all night to get the salt out o' them for next day.

What about a fisherwoman coming around?

Yes, she came around regularly frae Lossiemouth. She took the train from Lossiemouth to Elgin and then out to our station. And she came round every week wi' her creel.

So you had fresh fish as well?

Oh, yes.

Now to your work. I know you had to get up early every morning to milk the cows. Was this true of your sisters as well?

No. No, they were too busy with the music!

Didn't they milk at all?

They were always . . . there was nobody lay-in in the morning, they were always up . . . they were into different rooms with their music and their mother making the breakfast . . . [chuckles] . . . she could tell them when they were playing a note wrong.

This is quite unusual because most farm girls did help . . .

No, ye see, the most of them . . . there was very few of them that I knew of, except them, that were sae musical. And ither folk were just employed wi' doin their work and keepin' things goin'. Found it difficult to keep things goin'. But she was interested in music and she kept the girls there. Then father, the man who'd work – slaved – same as a did. I niver knew anythin' else [laughs].

You seem to have worked very hard as a boy. Did you have any employees on the farm?

Yes, yes, we had three men, three pairs o' horses, y'see. We had a cattleman besides that, and an orraman besides that. Ye needed that . . . Then in harvest time oo needed eleven folk. [After the interview, Mr Veitch told me that the farm workers had perks: 10 stone boll of meal every three months, peat until coal became available, 15 cwt. of potatoes and four pints of milk a day.]

Where did you get the extra people?

Mostly from the fishing industry. The fishing stopped in the September or October and we got the fishers . . . and then they went on to do draining on the farms, after they were finished the harvest. Then they were nearly all crofters that had an acre or two of their own and a cow and calf of their own . . . that's what all the crofts round about were a' composed of. Some of them worked on the railway and some of them worked with the estates and just did work . . . some of them were doin' the fishing at the mouth of the river, and suchlike. And there was always somebody available for the extra hands that ye needed in harvesting.

And then when ye weren't able to thrash the grain . . . well, ye got

FIGURE 4.4:   Aberdeenshire, *c.* 1900.

... all the crofters came into ye that day. But then you put your men there when they had the mill, jist exchanged.

So when they needed help, they would get it from the farmers and vice versa.

Say they had a few acres to cut and they needed the mill too. When they got the mill in, they got the men from Doonside because they had already come to Doonside...

That would be very important to their self-sufficiency and to yours ... that the work got done ... What did you grow on the farm for your own use?

... There would be oats. Barley a' went to the distillers. Then the turnips for feeding the cattle and the sheep. The garden was aye looked after by the men. They just come in, grow a bit of potatoes.

What about you ... did you do any gardening?

[Laughs.] ... No, I was never very fond o' gardening. I got plenty work without it. I was always too tired to think aboot the garden, looking after the horses, if I was driving horses, looking after sheep, looking after cows and calves.

It seems to me you were very much discriminated against when you were a boy because your sisters got off pretty lightly.

... M-huh. Everything.

Did you not feel resentful?

Never, never. I enjoyed it too much ... The only other thing I might have done, I might have gone in for a vet, but I was too interested in yoking young horses, driving horses and ponies and things o' that sort. I did a lot o' horse work.

I remember when I was a little boy, the time o' the lambin' – funny to say such a thing – my father said when I was afraid to put my hand in the ewe for lambin', ye've got a fine little hand, put your hand in and turn the lamb's head.

You were doing that when you were a little boy?

Yes. Very young.

How old were you?

I don't know, mebbe 12. I was walkin' to Nairn wi' sheep before I was 12. That's nine miles.

When did you go to school?

Well, I got off school on a Friday to do that. That was a Friday market.

Was that allowed?

[Chuckles.] There was nobody else to do it . . . I got it to do . . . there was no objections made.

You were needed? Were other farm children needed? But off school?

I was going to tell you this. We were the only farm as I know – nearly every other one all up and down the river valley has gone out bankrupt, just with not being able to look after things and too much o' this. Noo every farm all up and down here is all changed . . . [He lists the bankrupt farms, all six of them.]

Why?

. . . Just the times.

Are you talking about the thirties?

Oh, before the thirties. Oh, 1931 was the worst year that anybody could have had, a bare year . . . y'know I was looking after the farm for the family then and I bought the sheep in Nairn, 500 grayfaced lambs, 12s. 6d. a head. Those sheep today are making about £60. We got £22 for an 11-hundredweight bullock – tae kill.

Talking about bullocks, do you remember using them at all to pull a plough?

Yes, uhuh. I've driven them with a horse and an ox, a big black and white steer. I've driven that.

I hadn't realised that that would have been possible.

FIGURE 4.5:   Ploughing, Aberdeenshire, 1913–14.

I'll tell you when we had it. When the mares came to the foal in the spring and we had no mare to put on, this oxen, we used him to relieve the mares with the foals. I'll tell you where they came from. They came from Orkney, Orkney had a great lot o' that. When I was at school there was a man in F. who worked his croft, used dairy cows.

To pull the plough?

Aye . . .

When you were working with your father, did he tell you what to do or did you know what to do?

Well, you were just told if you were wanted to go to the plough. Ye just went wherever they wanted . . . or harrow the grain or whatever they wanted to do. Ye just got your instructions and ye knew what to do.

So you would get your instructions just like the employees would get their instructions?

Exactly.

How did your father deal with you?

Well, I just remember him telling me that if I hadn't stuck in as I had, he couldn't have kept the girls in London.

Oh! So you were doing this all for the girls?

If I was goin' to a dance or anything I would get half a crown or something. But I never got wages. Got my keep. [He repeats what his father said about keeping girls in London.] But I got no thanks for that.

Perhaps they didn't even know, didn't think about it?

They never appreciated that. They thought it was there.

When you were learning things, made mistakes, how would your father deal with it? Would he be patient or . . . ?

Depends what ye mean by a mistake. Whit dae ye mean? D'ye mean . . . if ye did something . . .

Say ye were shearing a sheep and you sheared it too close.

Too slow?

Too close. And he felt that you ought to have known better.

No, no [chuckles]. There was never any word o' shearing them too close . . . I was shearin' sheep when I couldn't hold them [laughs].

When you were so small . . .

Aye.

That would have been terribly hard?

Some of the older men would catch the sheep for me to clip and I was shearin' sheep. I remember the biggest day's sheep clippin'. I clipped 120 in a day, black-faced ewes.

By hand?

The greatest thing was tae keep yer shears sharp, ye just ran through them [laughs].

Ye must have had some sore hands.

Never felt them!

You didn't seem to get much in the way of rewards for your work.

No.

But you also had the likelihood that you would inherit the farm?

You mean that I would follow in the tenancy?

Yes.

Yes, of course.

You say you would have liked to have been a vet. Would you have preferred to have been a vet?

[Long hesitation.] I don't know. I was very interested in animal life, very interested in ill calves and suchlike. I liked to get them better, nursin' them.

Did you ever think about this at the time, did you think about this? Do you remember?

No I don't remember. I think it came on to me too quickly when my father died. Ye see, everything was just left a' o' a sudden.

Tell me about that. What age were you?

Twenty.

He had pneumonia I think you said . . .

Aye . . .

So it would have happened within a week?

Within a very short time. I was down at the Wembley Exhibition and saw my brother off tae Australia, on to the boat, and I came back. It was on the 2nd o' September that we got word that he [had died and] was lowered at sea. And on the 24th September, my father died.

So it was a great shock?

One after . . . aye. Then we were left with a lot . . . there wasna a lot of money on the go . . . they left me to take over, if I would stay and work. It was left with the representatives and I was the one that did the work.

What about your sisters? They would be old enough to learn?

Oh, aye, but one married in the February and the ither two went music teaching. There was one of them was a teacher in Aberdeenshire. She come home every weekend. They aye came home and lived offa me.

So they didn't contribute to the household?

No, no [resigned]. And my young brother, of course, he was at Dollar Academy. He went out and into the office intae G. from school, he got an opening. My responsibility. Then I put him into a place. Then I had a bad accident with the mower and I was ten–eleven weeks in hospital. The banker came to me and asked me if I would sanction him going into a place, and that started him up.

So you took the farm from your father?

No, I took it over from the representatives of my father. My mother ... there wasna enough money for any of us to take it over, and my mother was left with the same share as I was. The girls had a fifth each and that made it up to five-fifths. I had to work under that rule till I got married.

At that point did that happen?

They had to clear out ... I got married and took over everything from then on.

Then it would be your farm then.

Yes.

Family life as a family ... Meal times ... Did you look forward to meals?

When you're working outside as much as I did you're always hungry [laughs].

Was it a pleasant time from the point of view of talking to each other?

Oh, yes, there was never anything else. The only thing was that my father was quite religious and there was a grace said every time before a meal. We said our prayers every night when we were young. On Sunday night, there was always a chapter of the Bible read.

Did everybody else take part in family prayers ... servants?

We had a servant, washed up the dishes, one of the women did the dairy to save my mother doing the dairying.

One of the wives of the farm workers?

Yes.

And the young girl, the housemaid, would she have been one of the workers' family members?

Most likely. Just started off with us about 14, 15, or thereabouts. Then she went away to some other service, and we got another in. Just a young person.

[*The interviewer suggests a pattern of young girls working first in their own home, then on a local farm, then in the nearest town as they got older.*]

[Laughs.] I think they just got married.

What age?

Some of them didn't marry till 20 or thereabouts, but there was often a young girl ... and quite a lot of them went off ... young ...

They got pregnant?

Yes.

What would happen if somebody was naughty at the table?

We were always taught to hold our forks and knives the right way and things o' that sort ... There was never anything that turned up that I can remember, never anything bad. We were nearly always all together at our meals. Canna mind anything bein' wrong. The only thing that I would say is that if any o' the girls didna like the porridge they just said, if ye canna take yer porridge, ye canna take anything else. That was their way.

Did they get it served up at the next meal?

No, no. There was never that, no.

Did you ever get smacked?

[Hesitates.] I couldna tell ee.

You don't remember?

[Long hesitation.] No, there was never anything very far wrong in the family life at all. Everybody was ... awthing was quite pleasant, a' would be daein their different things, different subjects ...

Another funny thing was, with me ... not at the table ... we had quite a number of sheep and my father was never used to work a good dog. When the sheep broke out it was me that, me had to go and put them in [laughs]. That took up many a night.

Did you have to do that all by yourself?

Aye, wi' a doggie. He couldna work the dog. The dog would work with me, but it wouldna work with him.

What age would you be then, 12?

Just a young lad. I remember takin' the horses one day, he said, I canna work yer dog, I'll take your horses. Go on and mind the sheep.

Would you be about 12 then?

Maybe 14. I was into [milking] very early ... I don't know ... I would think about eight. There was no milking machines then [he was doing this morning and evening every day of the year]. I was interested in the foals, leadin' the foals when a was jist a kid.

What about leisure?

[Laughs.] ... [Long silence.] ... The only thing that I remember about much leisure is that time when I went doun to London, opening of the Wembley Exhibition in 1924. Before that, I did get a fortnight in the summer holidays when I went up to the folk in the Cabrach, the relations.

Why did you like to go there?

I didna' like to go there any more than anything else, but there was too mony o' us to go anywhere else. You see, they sometimes took a cottage at I. and things like that.

Well, they always took the three girls with them. I went to the relatives. There was maybe another reason for that too, was that ... that he would see what was going on in the farm work up there.

So you wanted to go there?

Well, I didna want, but they always put me there. I think things maybe would have been a wee bit difficult with finance, and I was aye sent there ...

Ye don't think you wanted to be a vet at that time ... when you were leaving school?

No, if I had really been wanting to be a vet, I would have had to stick into school longer than I did.

What was your parents' attitude towards your education as opposed to your sisters'?

They was too interested in what I was able to do, to relieve somebody else, they hadna to employ more labour or anything of that sort. They got the work done. There was another thing, I think he was mebbe verra proud of what I could do. He knew that when I was put to anything, it would be done to the best of my ability whether it was right or not. Even in the time of ... when there was a bad harvest, ye had to do a lot of scything and that ... I was scything along with the men when I was 15, 16. I remember him saying, 'For goodness' sake, dinna kill yerself keepin' up with the men' [chuckles].

There must have come a point at which you got some pocket money?

[Laughs.] Are ye telling me? I got a . . . A month before he died I got £100 put into savings for me. And the solicitor took it out to divide it in the estate. Because it was only in a month. [Father put £100 into war savings, the estate wasn't big enough and the executor took it out and put it into the estate.] I wasna treated, I was abused. Wasna my father, was a cousin and the solicitor. I wasna old enough, ye see, if I had been 21, it would have been different, but I was no' old enough, they would no' give me control till I was 21.

Did you have any control over your own life as a young lad, under 21?

Although I took on what I wanted . . . I was also doing what I wanted . . . although she signed the cheques, I could go and buy or go and sell. I wasna controlled, or anything o' that sort. But I never asked for a penny o' wages or anything o' the sort, just lived, lived happily.

Did you not feel the need for something? Like a bike?

Well, I could have bought a bicycle if it was needed, out of the farm . . . but I was more interested in a pony than I was in a bike.

In fact, you got a pony out of the farm.

Yes, it was the difference between buying and selling.

If you broke a horse in, you were able to make money on it?

Aye. But I had to break it in first. That was when my father was alive, but after that I just lived off the ferm, what I was needin', I just took the money, bought cattle, bought sheep and ran the whole place. I'll tell you anither thing about the sheep, whit I did often. If I had sheep at G. at the sale and they werena makin' a certain price I often bought more and got them to the killin' house and sent them as dead meat to London . . . in the train. You had maybe taken in twenty sheep, and ye'd buy another twenty to make up a wagon and put them to the killing house . . . But that went into the farm.

You were talking about not taking money out of the farm . . . like money for groceries . . . You talked about your mother getting the groceries from the egg money . . . I think farmers tried to keep money in the farm.

That's right.

So that you would have been brought up thrifty . . . upbringing.

Oh, very. Another thing about the folk a' round about. Most of them – well the fairly big farms got a cask of whisky in turn. And ye knew who had the whisky this week or the next week . . . see, that was where everybody went! My father never joined that company [much laughter]. That's whit put them a' out.

He didn't drink?

He was never a drinker . . . never liked that [socialising]. He was too interested in making money to pay off his debts when he took over the farm, frae his brothers and sisters. And keep the girls, and pay for their education. He wasna interested in the boys' education as long as they could work. But he was interested in the girls' education . . .

What about going to dances?

Well, I cycled to some of them. Cycled to B. [laughs], as far away as that. I was never late to feed my horses in the mornin' [laughs]. I could get up. I've seen us, half past two or three o'clock before oo got home but I was aye up in the morning.

Did your father not mind you being up that late?

No, no, it didna matter as long as I wasna late in the morn.

What about the girls?

The girls were often away, and sometimes they had to be driven to things wi' horse and pony. It was a long time before they got cars, into 1920s something. We was aye driving the pony and trap . . .

Were they about to go to dances?

Yes, sometimes they drove and sometimes I drove.

And did they have to be back at a particular time?

Well, just when the dance finished.

Not chaperoned?

If they were anywhere, they might be asked to stay in a house, if they were, generally I had to drive them.

That would be when you were older? You were quite a lot younger than they were?

Just two years younger. I was more used to driving than any of them.

Did you go to church regularly? Every Sunday?

Mm-huh. When we was kids, every Sunday and sometimes the Sunday School in the afternoon, every time. Besides the church. Oo always had to turn oot to kirk . . . [Repeats.]

What would happen if you didn't want to go?

Nothing would happen, your father wasna very pleased if you didna turn oot. I remember him, in the big range – puttin' tatties into the big range to roast them, ye could keep them in yer hands . . .

To keep them warm? Cold in the church?

No heating then.

What about your neighbours?

Quite good, but ye didna see much o' them. See, they were at a' different stages in life, o' that sort. Except there was one boy who was in the same class at school. But oo were never much out except durin' the Christmas time. Christmas parties and things o' that sort.

What about first footing at New Year?

Och aye, yes we did.

And what about picnics?

[Long hesitation.] Aye, there was a little of that, not a lot. There wasna a lot of picnics until we . . . we drove down to the seaside maybe on a Saturday afternoon or something o' that sort. Took a piece with us.

The whole family?

No, depended on who was there. Mother and father and maybe the other three – could only manage six, five in the gig, only a pony and trap. We often had two ponies . . . G. was nine miles away . . . If I walked in wi' the sheep, my father came in with his pony and trap.

Mrs Roberts, born 1885, East Lothian

Like Mr Veitch, Mrs Roberts' parents – or at least her mother – had very definite plans for her future. Her parents never made any attempt to ensure she had the productive and domestic skills of most farmers' wives. She was brought up to be a young lady and her mother would have like her to be a musician. Running through the interview is her perception of her mother's disappointment in her on the one hand, and her exceptional achievements as a young woman on the other. She was among one of the first groups of women qualifying in medicine in Scotland.

Like other children from elite families, Mrs Roberts was sent away as a child. In her case it was to the home of her aunts. Her education was completed at a higher grade school in the city and then university. The fact of being sent away to school diminished any distinction between her childhood and that of urban middle-class young women.

In the other interviews there is usually some sense of the rough and tumble of childhood, at least during school years, even among children who spent much of their young lives contributing to the family in some way or other. There seems to have been little horseplay for Mrs Roberts who, apart from being able to wander through the local woods, had a sedate childhood hedged in by manners. Little else was expected from her. It was only her nurse and her aunt who seem to have had strong emotional ties with her. Brought up to become an upper-class lady, Mrs Roberts appears to have had emotionally distant parents who clearly preferred their sons, and she was denied the company of children other than the 'nice girls' approved by her parents.

When she was interviewed in 1980 by Lynn Jamieson, she was living comfortably in a very desirable part of Edinburgh and was frequently visited by family, friends, colleagues and clients.

Interview with Mrs Roberts

We could fairly easily get away into the wood and my mother didn't seem to bother about us, you know, she didn't think it was a worry to have her children wandering in the woods. I knew the woods well and where all the different things grew.

Were there farm servants living in the house?

No. We had maids, a cook, a housemaid and a nurse. The nurse was a very important person to me. She was from South Africa. She was a coloured woman. Some family had brought her home . . . they brought this woman to be nanny to their children, on the long sea voyage, and then I think they more or less deserted her. She came into our household before I was born and she was with us until I was 6 years old. She was a very important person in my life.

Did you spend more time with her than your mother?

Yes. Much more. My mother had two boys older than me and one of them was, what was very well known in Victorian days – a delicate boy – a delicate child. Nearly all Victorian families had a delicate child. A great focus for maternal anxiety. So when I came along she wasn't greatly bothered with me. She had her boys and I was handed over to this woman we called Nursie and she and I were very great friends. She taught me all sorts of things when I was a child. I remember her teaching me the Lord's prayer for instance. I could scarcely speak, I think ... when I asked her questions she would say, 'I don't know, but you could ask your aunt, she will know.' That was important because my aunt was a doctor and she was a woman doctor before I was born. She was my father's sister and she was also a great influence in my life.

Did she live in your house or did she live nearby?

No, she didn't live anywhere near. In fact, she was in China for a time ... Perhaps that was one of the factors making me want to be a doctor. When I asked questions that were not immediately answerable ... 'The Doctor knows ...'.

Did you go to a school in that neighbourhood?

There was a school within a mile to which my brother went. But my mother thought that I would get to be a very rough girl if I went. There was a great emphasis on refinement. My mother was a musician ... she wasn't a typical farmer's wife at all ...

If she hadn't married my father, I think [Mother] would have been a concert pianist. She had been educated in London and abroad in Germany. She was a very very gifted woman, gifted musician. Her ambition for me was that I should be well educated and refined and a musician. Unfortunately, she decided early on I had no capacity for music ... so I didn't go to school there, I was sent away from home to my mother's sister. My mother's sister was a spinster and she lived with a spinster aunt – that is to say my grand aunt ... just outside Dundee. I went to a girls' school there, a private school. I was away from home for two years, from 6 to 8 or 9.

How did you feel at that age leaving home?

I think I felt pretty sad about it but not explicit about it when I got home. I don't think my aunts were unkind to me but neither of them were married women and they were very anxious that I should be 'good' and learn my lessons well, and anything like telling a fib was a terrible crime ... I must have been a lonely child. The school was all right. I remember some of the people that taught me there with pleasure.

Were you confined to the house in the evening?

No, I was allowed to play in the street . . . I played with boys as well as girls. I remember being awfully thrilled when the boys as well as the girls were friendly with me.

Had you played with your brothers when you were at home, or were they too old for you?

Well, they were very much of the opinion that girls were no good. That boys were something special. I rather tagged on after them. The younger sisters tagged on after me. I think I may have been rather unkind to the younger sisters. I think that might have been a factor in them sending me away although I've never heard that said.

My next school was in Edinburgh, when we had a house in Edinburgh. Queen Street School . . . And I was there until I was 17 or 18.

Who lived in the house in Edinburgh?

My mother, brothers and sisters. My father came at weekends and in summer we went to the country at weekends. My brothers were at Watsons and my sisters went to Queen Street.

Do you remember having pocket money as a child?

Very little. I don't remember pocket money much. I always had a little money, but money went quite a long way. I remember buying a halfpenny worth of fresh dates . . . you'd get quite a packet of dates . . . I also remember getting into trouble for going into the ice-cream shop on the way home from school. My aunt had some notion that it might be poisonous. I was to never, never, never . . . there was a good deal of never, never, never do that again about that time. I had school friends.

Would you meet them after school?

No I don't think so because I came home after school. There were the children whom I played with in the street. Looking back, at least they had enough sense to let me play in the street. Of course, the streets weren't dangerous in those days.

Were some of your friends at school not allowed to play in the street?

I don't remember.

Can you remember some of the things you were never, never to do? . . . Do you remember ever getting smacked?

Punishment was quite an important thing always in those days. I think both parents and this aunt, especially this old grand aunt, she had been a schoolmistress in her day. I think she was very disapproving and it was more this very harsh look on her face. I remember that I decided I wouldn't go to school and she called me a truant and held me up to great disapproval. I also remember stealing cake out of the cake tin and I was a thief! There was great disapproval of any aberrant behaviour. They must have had an ideal child in their mind who would always be clean and good and kind and loving. My aunt ... was a great source of information, she was a well-educated woman, she actually taught school and was also a pianist and taught music ... she could answer my questions and I think I was ... I remember that very well because the old aunt used to call me 'Little Miss Curiosity' and disapprove of me. It was a naughty thing to do to be always asking questions, but the other aunt used to take things in her stride.

I think that by the time I had been with her two years, I was thought of as a very intelligent child, but I think that was because I was a better informed child. Very often at Queen Street, the teachers would put up some question and the other girls didn't know ... usually I would have more information. But I don't think I was particularly intelligent. Of course, we didn't have our IQs done in those days. If you ask plenty of questions, it's always something, isn't it?

Did you go to a Sunday School as well as a day school?

Oh, yes. From the very first. My mother and father were deeply religious people. They ran the Sunday School in connection with the church. The church was a little isolated church which is now demolished ... It was a Free Church ... Father was session clerk, was the important man in that church. He was influential in getting the church built, after the Disruption. That was forty years before I was born. I think they worshipped in a shed. He and my mother had got this church built, a very beautiful church. An outstanding architect who had been a friend of my father's. Mother played the organ and conducted the choir. And people walked for long distances to this church – three or four miles.

Did you have other religious things at home?

We had prayers night and morning. We'd sing a hymn. My mother had a harmonium. In the morning we sang a song, some verses of a psalm. Then we read the Old Testament and the sermon. The servants, the cook, the housemaid and nurse all came in. We used to read the Bible together, and they had to read it too, poor things, because perhaps it was difficult. And then we had . . . we knelt down and my father prayed. Looking back, I think that was an important thing in my life. I don't remember much about what was there in the Bible. But my grandfather lived with us. I think perhaps he would take the prayers and it was when he went away my father would take them.

Presumably you weren't allowed to play or make a noise on a Sunday of any sort?

Well, it was a farm and we weren't much restricted very much. I think that things were becoming less strict by then.

One of my early memories is of my father smoking a cigar on a Sunday. He had hidden himself away in the garden behind a hedge and was reading the *Strand* magazine. That was a wicked thing to do on a Sunday.

My father was a very good man. He was a farmer, but he had also been at Edinburgh University. He was a cultured man, and cultured people came to the house. They often had people staying who talked about the finer things of life. I was accustomed to hear people discussing serious things as a child.

When you were in Edinburgh did you go to any formal entertainment?

Concerts. Mother was very anxious that I should be a musician. I was taken by mother to concerts and piano recitals. Theatre. I was taken to the theatre first to see *Lohengrin* when I was about 12. Prior to that I think my mother thought the theatre was not a place to encourage children to go. They used to talk about the devil in the theatre. She used to tell a story about a friend's son who ran away to become an actor and when he returned his father said, 'You are a child of the Devil,' to which he replied, 'Good morning, Papa.' Actors, actresses were certainly on the fringe . . .

When visitors came to the house, were you expected to be silent?

I think they would want . . . my grandfather . . . They would be discussing theological problems. I must have been interested because I still remember about them. But we certainly wouldn't be expected to contribute.

Would it be unfair to say that your parents believed that children should be seen and not heard?

No, they weren't rigid. We sat round the dining room table and one did talk to one's parents and they would answer one's questions up to a point. But there were taboo subjects that you didn't talk about. Sex was taboo in those days. Very much so. Where babies came from and what happened in the parental situation was . . . not to be talked about.

When you got older, say about 14, were there parties and things like that?

Yes. I remember the first big dance party I went to. It was at 17 Moray Place. I remember very well because they were the first people we knew who had electric light installed in their house . . . I think I was 15. Their name was . . . [she identifies the father and his status] . . . his son . . . was at school with my brother and his daughters were at school with me, with us . . . until they got too grand and then they went off to St Leonards . . . they used to love to come out to the country in summer when we were living there. They often came out to stay with us and we were always invited to their parties.

[She comments on the lack of modern facilities in her childhood, electricity, water towers, the use of penny farthing bicycles.] I had a bicycle when I was 11. I think it rather says that my people were . . . forward-looking people. I had a bike, girls didn't have bikes.

Do you think your parents made much difference between you and your brothers?

I don't think they did [make much difference]. I think my mother was pretty open about it and my father was. I don't think they made much difference. But when it came on to going to medicine . . . going to university, I was considered . . . I can hear my mother saying, 'What a cheek she has to think she can be a doctor.' Because women . . . in Edinburgh there was one girl from George Square, the other Merchant Company school, I was the only one from Queen Street. There were only two or three Scots girls in our year. But there were quite a few from England, and some from New Zealand strangely enough . . . They were beginning to be educated as doctors in those days. I think my mother was very pleased about it. She had had her ambitions before she became my father's wife, and she was quite pleased to see me coming on and pushing my way up.

From what age did you seriously want to be a doctor?

Oh, I think perhaps all my life. From the days of Nursie. My aunt [her father's sister], she was a great influence in my childhood although I didn't see a great lot of her. Later on I lived with her. She became an idealised figure. I was leaving my mother behind as it were ... this aunt would talk to me about all sorts of more profound spiritual things. The adolescent girl wants to talk about those things. I think my mother was very matter-of-fact, and also I wasn't musical. I think in a way she discarded me because of that and then I was doing ... once I got into medicine I was doing science and she couldn't keep up with me. My aunt and I were really very good friends.

You remained living with your parents throughout university? At home?

No, I was with this aunt most of the time. But I was coming and going. My home was only twelve miles out of Edinburgh. I would go home at the weekends and that sort of thing.

By the time you had got to university, did you have a more independent source of money?

I had very little. About 5s. That had to do for your lunch and tram fares. But I used to walk. My aunt lived in Morningside and I would walk from the university. I had a bicycle at one time. We thought nothing of walking.

Once I had got into the University I got very much attached to the surgical ward and worked there at night. I didn't just do a minimum, I did a maximum. So I got to know the surgeon and he was very kind to me. He used to give me the opportunity to watch him operating. There was no degree in anaesthetics in those days and as a student, I was handling the anaesthetics for hours on end ... I'm glad to say that no-one ever died at my hand. But they might have done. [She comments on the positive value of her experience in the theatre in her later career. She was trusted.]

To go back a bit, you said that sex was never talked about? Did anyone ever explain menstruation to you?

No.

How did you feel at that time? Was it a complete shock?

Complete, yes. It was so taboo that even the girls at school didn't talk about it. Nowadays school girls talk about it of course, but I think then it wasn't a topic at school. It was very . . . there were no sanitary towels in those days . . . things that had to be washed. It was great . . . that you didn't tell your brothers. You told nobody about it. A great secret. It was very much a taboo. When my daughters were at that stage, their brothers knew about it, could talk about it . . . I remember at medical school, I remember a woman saying, 'So and so, she's a dreadful woman, she has explained to her fiancé all about menstruation before they were married.' This was shocking. You can scarcely realise how all this was taboo and shocking.

Presumably there would have been considerable reserve . . . that your brothers would never see you partially dressed, for example?

. . . No, there was great reserve about . . . the differences between men and women.

What age did you go out with a boy for the first time?

When I was going to stay with a family of cousins, when I was perhaps 12 or 13. There were two boys and they liked me very much, you know. I was very much surprised that I should be popular with the boys. Those boys were quite involved in my life, they were friends too [as well as kin]. But even when I went up to do medicine, I had a great deal of inferiority about being a girl and I was surprised if men . . .

Can you remember when you were first alone with a man?

Yes, I remember the picnic in which we first detached ourselves. I was very excited. I would be about 16.

All the time in medicine, we were very segregated from the men. They rather tended to laugh at us. 'Who did we think we were?,' you know. Although we were obviously in many ways more intelligent than they were, but there was this feeling, what cheek these women have thinking they can enter this province of medicine.

That never angered you?

I think I accepted it very much. No Women's Lib in those days. Then I went to India. I was 23 at this time, and I was very much surprised how the men buzzed round, you might say. I had quite a few men wanting to make love to me straight away, but that was quite surprising to me.

I can remember meeting a man in India who had been a medical student with me and he told me that the medical students did, they did like me, but that I was unapproachable.

Had your parents ever tried to protect you from contact with anybody? Any children you wanted to play with? Men?

At school I think there were certain girls who were considered a bit undesirable. It wasn't so much explicit as implicit, that if I brought a girl home for the weekend. Some girls, 'Oh, yes, that's a very nice girl,' and others, 'I'm surprised at you, dear, being friendly with that sort of person.' I remember feeling guilty about that, that I dropped people because of my parents ... implicit disapproval. There were nice girls and not so nice girls.

Did you think they ever worried about your attractiveness to young men? Being with men?

I don't think so. I don't think I knew enough about sex. Even as a medical student, there were great areas in which one just didn't just allow oneself to think. Knew all about midwifery and gynaecology and all that, but there was still great blanks in one's knowledge about sexual intercourse and all that sort of thing.

What age do you think you felt grown-up?

Very early. Even as a child, I felt a sort of grown-upness.

Why do you think that was?

I was the eldest of three girls. I do associate with that going to [place of her school] and coming back and going to school and feeling that I knew a lot. I was more aware of what I knew than what I didn't know, perhaps.

Did you ever feel on an equal footing with your parents?

No, I don't think so. My mother was always sure that she was in the right. She would always ... if any disaster occurred no matter how. She knocked over a jug of milk. I thought, she'll have to say now that she did something. She just said, 'You shouldn't have put it there, dear!' [laughter]. So I learned this trick of always justifying oneself, it's a very bad trick.

Were you as close to your father as to your mother?

He was always about, you know, he in the house and in the fields we

were with him. He was a bit of a puzzle to me because in the fields
with his men he spoke broad Scotch and in the house he was a
cultured man.

He was an important person in the church. He was loving and
kind. He wasn't . . . I don't remember being hugged or kissed by
either of them, but I think he accepted me as long as I didn't ask
questions about sex.

Would you have been discouraged from speaking Scots?

No, I don't think so. But Nursie, of course, was not a Scot. She was
with us till I went to [school outside Dundee]. She was very, very
dear to me. It's curious how in old age I think back to her. A
coloured woman recently became my patient . . . from South Africa
. . . and it wakened up my memories of Nursie. She was very very
fond of me. I think that she fantasised that I was her child. Even
after she had left she would come back to us for her holidays – when
she was in another situation – she was very fond of my mother and
my mother was very good to her.

What age did you lose touch with her?

Till she died. She knew my children.

NOTES

1. It is now argued that, rather than their numbers diminishing as
mechanisation inceased, mechanisation increased as their numbers diminished (Campbell & Devine, 1990: Smout, 1986).
2. In 1906, 70 per cent of rented holdings had rentals of under £50.
However, the dairy counties of the South-West and the arable farming
counties of the South-East with their larger farms had a significantly lower
proportion of holdings with cheap rents. In Midlothian, an exceptional
county because it included Edinburgh, 47 per cent of rented holdings had
rentals of over £300 – only approached by arable Berwickshire's 30 per
cent. But even in the arable eastern counties, the majority of rents were
below £300 (Campbell & Devine, 1990, p. 60). The distribution of holdings by size, like their rental, gives some indication of the typicality of a
capitalist muckle farmer.
3. Mr and Miss Mathews were siblings who were interviewed together.
They lived together all their lives and managed the farm together. They
are both counted in the total of fourteen. We are not including two cases in
which a small farm was acquired by the father later in life. Mrs Ramage's
father was the foreman of a large farm until he retired to a small farm or
croft. This had little affect on Mrs Ramage. The case of Mr Renton was

different. His father, who had been a shepherd, was able to acquire a small farm when Mr Renton was 19. Mr Renton's labour was probably a key factor in his father's success.

4. See Appendix Two for a list of the five respondents. The Mathews family and the MacPhersons family seemed to be the most modest in terms of their class connections. The Mathews family farm was described as an arable farm. They had five cows, as well as ducks, hens, turkeys and pigs. They grew oats, turnips, hay and potatoes and kept a vegetable garden. This household never had a maid or any paid help on the farm. Their less middle-class connections and aspirations are suggested by the fact that the respondent's sister spent 'all her days' in domestic service. The MacPherson family also had connections with domestic service. Their dairy farm supported 'a couple of dozen cows', suggesting it was around 100 acres or more. They took in summer visitors to help eke out their income, but were sometimes able to employ up to two men.

5. But the Marshalls also had a kin network which was more middle-class than was typical for the average crofter. Mr Marshall's brother, for example, was a lawyer.

6. They had thirty-five cows, pigs, hens and ducks and grew their own feed. Previously one man and one little girl had been employed – a ploughman, who also milked, and a girl who helped in the house and milked. Presumably, once Mrs Haslitt and her sister were working on the farm, her father did all the ploughing, as women did not do this work.

7. We have less specific details from Mr Isbister and Mr Craven concerning the size of farm and number of employees.

8. Mrs Tanner's family farmed a 700-acre arable farm which employed eight men and four or five women out-workers and a cook, a housemaid and a dairy maid. Mr Turnbull's family farmed 640 acres arable and the household staff included two maids, a cook and a nanny or governess. Mrs Roberts grew up in a farm house which employed domestic staff of a cook, housemaid and nurse.

9. In three cases, the father also had an occupation. One, Mr Gilanders' father, a hereditary sub-chieftain, had a profession, which meant that the family divided their time between their Highlands home and the place in which the father was employed. Mr Isbister's father was manager of a distillery, although he also managed the farm on which the family lived. Mr Craven's father was also a furrier.

10. We do not know whether this absence of alcoholic drink was general in public gatherings and in private socials, nor do we know that drink was served in the Highlands, as suggested by Mr Gilanders' interview. But see Smout (1986), Chapter VI for a general discussion of alcohol use in Scotland. Several of our male respondents claimed that they had never taken strong drink, or did so only at events like weddings and funerals or at New Year. In one case, the father of an interviewee had a drinking problem which resulted in the whole family's relative social isolation. In

another case, an interviewee blamed the financial failure of many local farmers on the regular drinking of whisky. Here was an interesting case of social reciprocity, for the whisky was bought by one in bulk one month and shared with others, and bought by another the next month. The interviewee clearly contrasted their immoderate behaviour with that of his father, who only imbibed at New Year and managed to keep his farm over the Depression.

11.   She was interviewed by Lynn Jamieson in 1980.

12.   That is, those farming families used exclusively family labour for part of the family life-cycle. While there were five respondents from such households, there were only four such households since two were brother and sister.

13.   Higgs (1986) looked at domestic service in and around Rochdale and found it difficult to differentiate between domestic and productive work done by servants.

14.   One farmer, Mr Marshall, was an exception in that he regularly cooked the family dinner when the others went to church.

15.   Finicky.

16.   *Scunner*: to conceive a loathing as a result of too much of something.

17.   A very hilly, stony and isolated farming area in which poor farming families had had to work very hard to try to keep their independence in the face of the encroachment of capitalism during the period 1880–1914. Although people still try to make a living by farming today, the landscape is dotted with scattered, ruined stone cottages.

18.   Boys and girls from other farming families also went to boarding schools. They were likely to leave school at an earlier age than children from elite families. The schools to which they were sent were generally less well known.

19.   *Nap*: a card game, played in the same manner as whist.

20.   Status was both bridged and preserved in social interaction at different levels of society – in the home, the neighbourhood and at local gatherings. For example, children were taught to be polite and respectful to those they nevertheless learned were their subordinates. The assuming of a local Scots dialect by Mrs Roberts' father when talking with his workers helped bridge their relative social positions, but it was no doubt generally known that he spoke something more like standard English at home – a fact which set him apart.

21.   His father was different from the other farmer fathers in many additional respects. First of all, he had farmed for some time in England. Secondly, he was enthusiastic about his garden, growing a range of vegetables which were not mentioned by others. Thirdly, he made soup sometimes and he cooked the family dinner on Sundays while the others were at church.

CHAPTER FIVE

Conclusion

———

BY SURVEYING THE RURAL SCENE from different vantage points it is possible to get a more detailed picture. The selected interviews provide a rich tapestry of individual experiences. The lives of our interviewees were unfolding in economic and cultural contexts which have changed radically during this century. To read and appreciate them is to go some way towards feeling what it might have been like to be a country child before the Second World War.

The focus has been on the children of three types of agricultural worker – crofters, farm servants and farmers. One specific aim was to explore how the degrees of freedom in individual lives are constrained by their situation from birth. Did some 'get on' and others did not, simply because they started off with very unequal lots? The economic circumstances of the family-household in which a child is brought up clearly did and do profoundly affect educational and occupational destinations. But life has never been so simple that the end could always be known from the beginning. The material presented has documented the complexities, the twists and turns of ordinary lives.

It may be that this book gives slightly too wholesome a picture of rural life. Those who speak from its pages are the stayers and the survivors. Most, although not all, lived in the countryside all of their lives. They were apparently immune or indifferent to the pejorative characterisation of 'country folk' which was pervasive in society (Littlejohn, 1963). But it is not a romantic picture. Their collective lives were in no sense idyllic, and the detailed nitty-gritty of life discussed in the interviews is no rosy-spectacled version of the past.

FIGURE 5.1:   The Law family, Kincardine, *c.* 1900. The birth of one more child would bring this grieve's family to the farm servant's average.

Economic Circumstances, Family and Household Size

There has been a great deal of debate about whether parents have typically tried to match the number of their children to their economic circumstances. The 1911 Census shows that all three groups – crofters, agricultural labourers, and farmers – typically had above average sized families. Crofters headed the table of occupations, with fertilities significantly greater than the mean in Scotland at the time. The mean number of children per couple in 1911 was 5.82 (measured when wives had reached the end of their childbearing years); crofters, agricultural labourers and farmers had means of 7.04, 6.42 and 6.20 respectively.[1]

A large family does not necessarily seem rational in circumstances where nobody could earn a great deal, and where their living could only be supplemented by a finite amount of food produced on a small stony croft. However, given limited contracep-

tive technology and knowledge, actual family size does not necessarily reflect desired family size. But a large family was not
necessarily undesired. A well-spaced family does not mean a household bursting with children. The oldest children had often left
home before the youngest were born. Poor crofting households
were net exporters of labour. Sons and daughters often went away
to work at 14 and then, rather than being a drain on the family-
household, they were a source of at least occasional income.
Younger children were able to do useful jobs on the croft from
about the age of 7, and each child, particularly the youngest, was a
potential support in old age.

Whether or not children left home was sometimes a matter of
pursuing a strategy for the benefit of the household, rather than a
matter of personal choice. Young people often knew from an early
age whether they were expected to stay or to go. For example, Mr
Geddes knew he was wanted on the croft. Mr Geddes's immediate
family was in fact smaller than average: only two out of his four
siblings survived childhood, and the family-household contained a
permanent dependent as a tragic result of his sister's meningitis.
The need to look after his handicapped sister reduced the amount
of crofting work his mother could do. Although, like his father, he
and his brother took waged work rather than concentrating their
energies on the croft, they remained home-based and able to make
some contribution to crofting. This was in spite of the fact that their
accommodation was particularly cramped in the period of the
summer when they moved out of the cottage into a barn to make
way for the paying summer visitors.

The strategy of living on the croft and being employed as a
wage-worker elsewhere would not have been possible in all crofting
districts. For some crofters' children, earning a regular wage meant
leaving the district. It may also not have been a strategy open to the
family-household with more daughters than sons, as many jobs
available on local estates and the railways were not open to women.
Unlike areas of arable and dairy farming, the local estates offered
little employment for women beyond domestic service. Hence, the
number, spacing, and sexes of children in the family, and the state
of health of individual members, had effects on the overall well-
being of the household. This was particularly true for those households that were living close to subsistence, as was the case for many
crofters. In such households, the wellbeing of the family-household

might entail migration to other parts of Scotland where employment was more readily available. Farm service and domestic service were common destinations, but for some, emigration or life at sea were the best option.

The quality of parent/child relationships and cultural ideas about children and childhood influence people's willingness to have large families. Most parents did not expect to spend hours enjoying young children and nurturing their relationship with them. A large family was rational when mother and children were fit and healthy; children were useful from a young age, and young people who were not needed left home without fuss at the age of 14 and could be recalled if required.

The Effect of Parents' Social Position on a Child's Destiny

It is the patterning of life chances at the level of groupings above and beyond the individual which causes social scientists to talk of social inequalities attributable to gender, class or ethnicity. In societies which systematically distinguish individuals and groups on these grounds forms of social differentiation have a powerful effect on shaping people's identity and life chances.

We have referred to social class at a number of points. Much has been written defining and redefining 'social class' and arguing about its current usefulness in categorising groups in contemporary society. (See for example Marshall *et al.*, 1988 and subsequent debate and contributions to *Sociology*, particularly Vol. 24, 1990.) A conventional way of allocating people to 'classes' is to use their occupation. Occupations are translated into a class position using some combination of their status, income and the degree of responsibility, supervision and autonomy involved in the work. Wide diversity on any of these indicators among those holding the same occupation works against the usefulness of occupation as a proxy for social class.

In this book we have selected people to illustrate differences with some regard to these categories. We chose women and men whose fathers belonged to occupational groupings which both represented distinct positions in the rural, social and economic ladder and, being either predominantly Highland or Lowland, represented culturally (if not ethnically) distinct parts of Scotland. There were no highly visible ethnic minorities in rural Scotland, although Scotland was not and is not culturally homogeneous. The extent of divisions could be described as ethnic differences. For example, some of our respondents did not speak English until they were forced to do so in school; they were Gaels and culturally distinct from other Scots. Then there were cross-cutting religious differences which were reflected in how the Sabbath was spent, but which also carried more pervasive and divisive meaning. At the same time it is important not to overplay these differences. There was then, as now, some shared sense of being Scottish first, rather than British.

Of the three rural occupations, farmers were particularly diverse in terms of culture, status and income. Large farmers ranked high on all indicators of social class, and it seems unproblematic to call them middle-class or upper (middle) class, particularly when they were connected through family ties to the commercial and professional middle classes – owner/managers, bankers, lawyers, ministers and teachers. On the other hand, the unmitigated sweat and toil of some farmers makes it seem inappropriate to call them middle-class. Moreover, small farmers without employees did not share the same status, income or supervisory role as large farmers, although they still had full responsibility for their farm and autonomy to get on with it as they saw fit. Crofters, while less diverse in their circumstances, are no less difficult to classify. They had responsibility and autonomy in their crofting work, but typically they also held another occupation.

Was it Mainly a Question of 'What your Father Did'?

The occupational history of farm servants, and their standard of living at the time of interview, most clearly confirmed the predictably constraining consequences of being born a son or daughter of a worker at a particular level in a local, gendered, rural labour market. Occupational destinations had a remarkable sameness for the children of farm workers, although sons and daughters went separate ways. With only one exception among the men we interviewed, the sons of farm workers became farm workers. Several told us that they simply 'followed in father's footsteps'. Most of their brothers had done the same. With some exceptions, they remained in what could be called working-class jobs all of their lives. Two out of nine, Mr Collins and Mr Renton, managed to acquire their own small holding or small farm after many years. The daughters of farm servants interviewed, with only one exception, did some form of domestic work, as residential domestic servants, day cleaners or domestic workers at home[2].

For these children of farm workers, the absence of other ambitions (on their own part or by parents on their behalf) fitted their economic circumstances and were sanctioned by their social context; many were in the same position, expecting and saying the same thing. Most had no opportunity to go on in higher education. Thoughts of university were only exceptionally raised (as with Mr Collins who would have liked to have been a vet), and even more modest ambition was generally crushed. For example, Mr Pearson cried when he left school because he wanted to stay on; Mr Linton knew he wanted to be a journalist. Both went to work on the farm like everybody else (Jamieson, 1990b). Mrs West similarly had her sights narrowed. She was constantly reminded throughout childhood that 'they', the family-household, could not afford to do without her wage coming in at the first opportunity, and she was not able to realise her desire to be a dressmaker or children's nurse. Many were unaware of how their perception of what was possible had curtailed their ambitions. It was only in later years that Mrs Doughtie could think that she might have liked to be a history teacher if she had had the chance, and May Carruthers could muse on the fact that her granddaughter's teacher, a 'big farmer's' daughter who had been in May's class at school, had never gained the high marks that she had done, yet it had been May who had never had the chance to be a teacher.

The farmers' sons we interviewed also generally followed in their father's footsteps – although those we interviewed were those who stayed on the land. Some had brothers who had entered middle-class occupations whilst in some cases all the sons had become farmers. Among some working family farmers, siblings entered working-class occupations. For example, Mr Mathews' sister was 'in service a' her days'. We interviewed very few farmers' daughters, but the small number suggests that in the case of well-to-do farmers their options were those of middle-class young women of the time: marriage, or a restricted range of 'suitable' occupations such as teaching or nursing. Crofters' sons and daughters were the most heterogeneous in their destinations. Among those we inter-

FIGURE 5.2: Channelkirk School, Oxton, Berwickshire, c. 1911. Most of these children were destined for farm work or domestic service.

viewed about a third stayed on the croft, and the occupations of the remainder ranged from unskilled manual work to the professions.

We have tried to avoid using labels like 'farm servant' or 'middle-class' as if they were explanations in themselves. The text concentrates on the processes which generate the lived reality of the categories and the meaning of these categories for people themselves. Focusing on a lower level of everyday ways of thinking and doing makes it more possible to discuss variation within as well as between categories such as 'crofter' and 'farmer'.

It was suggested in the introduction that the relevant economic circumstances of the family household were not reducible to the market position or the relationship to the means of production of the father or head of the household. To translate this into less abstract language, the important economic differences affecting the quality of people's childhoods were not simply a matter of whether their father was a crofter, a farm servant or a farmer, or of the varying incomes, statuses and positions of power that their fathers' employment entailed. These differences were important and take us a long way in predicting who gets on and who does not. But even when fathers' incomes and status is held constant, important economic differences existed between family households.

To understand, for example, how well fed a child was or how much freedom to play he or she had, it is necessary to look at the opportunities and actualities of economic activity of all the members of the household. This is particularly so when people were providing for themselves directly from the land without the mediation of money and when considerable effort was involved in transforming raw materials into a consumable form. For them, factors such as the skills and muscle power which household members could muster between them; the size and quality of land holdings; the proximity of forests, the sea, and rivers – all these were important, as well as the type of paid employment available locally, and who had which job. The skilled labour needed to produce wholesome food from restricted and unprocessed ingredients, by baking, cheese-making and the like, was no less crucial than the skills of growing, hunting or gathering.

Even a very detailed list of such economic factors is never enough to predict absolutely how comfortably a family lived and how much they toiled. For example, if two family-households were similar in the balance of their resources, their income-generating opportunities and their skills, it was possible that they would have seen and tackled things differently. A response was never determined merely economically. People drew on the ideas of their social scene and from their personal repertoire, and in this sense their response was also cultural and personal. For example, both Mr Collins and Mr Renton were sons of thrifty parents who managed to accumulate savings. Both had shepherd fathers who cherished the idea of having their own farm. But Mr Collins's parents valued education highly, and their savings allowed them to encourage their child to go to university (although Mr Collins believed they could not afford it and decided not to go), whereas Mr Renton was never encouraged to do anything other than the farm work which enabled him to contribute to the common purse and to his father's ambition. These different parental approaches clearly cannot be explained by immediate economic circumstances.

Social class has a cultural dimension. If parents believed that they were the sort of people who had to send their children on to higher education because of their social position, then they would struggle to do so even when they could barely afford it. On the other hand, such a notion might never occur to working-class parents who had managed to accumulate enough savings to make such a sacrifice possible. But there were always exceptions who were not blinkered by their immediate social-class milieu. Our respondents included individuals whose social backgrounds and ultimate destinations are apparently anomalous. For example, a crofter's daughter, Mrs Gillies, went to university; judging by her father's occupation, aspiring to a university education could not have been predicted.

Mrs Gillies has been identified as something of an anomaly, but in fact here aspirations were in keeping with the high social standing of her family in the community. Mrs Gillies and Mr Geddes were crofters' children whose fathers combined crofting with some form of income-generating work, but their economic circumstances were different and their sense of their families' social status was markedly at variance. Their fathers had inherited different resources and were exploiting different labour market opportunities. Mrs Gillies' father inherited 'the fishing' and owned his own boat as well as the croft, which included a home renowned for its quality furnishings and clocks. While Mrs Gillies talked of income from fishing providing capital for a subsequent transport business for her father, Mr Geddes talked as if the steady wage his father brought in as a railwayman was barely enough to cover necessities. Mr Geddes categorised his family as poor crofters while Mrs Gillies knew that her family were regarded as 'the Brahmins of the district'. The difference in their education seems to follow from these differences. Mr Geddes's parents did not ever advocate higher education. His father wanted him to work exclusively on the croft, but money was too tight to allow this. His wage was needed and, at this stage in the family-household's life-cycle, crofting had to be fitted in when the paid work of household members permitted.

The contrast between Mr Collins, the shepherd's son who rejected going to university, and Mrs Gillies, illustrates how the experience of economic circumstances was more than a matter of available money. Mrs Gillies's family were not wealthy by upper-class standards and she described the bursary she succeeded in winning as essential to funding her university career. Her mother's high regard for education was obviously important. Her mother was both very critical of her and ambitious for her – a combination which, as with Mrs Roberts, seems to have spurred Mrs Gillies into trying very hard to do well academically. This determination, in turn, helped her overcome the disadvantages suffered by Gaelic-speakers taught only in English – a language which they had to learn from scratch when they started school at the age of 5. Determination was also needed to gain a bursary – a financial contribution towards the costs of carrying on in education, awarded to the winner in a competitive examination. Mr Collins's parents did talk of university, and he attended what we would now call a secondary school for a year rather than leaving elementary school at 14 years old, as most of his peers did. On the other hand, he did not go to university despite encouragement to do so.

Mrs Gillies and Mr Collins both had parents who had educational ambitions for their children, but they were in differing economic circumstances. The differences were both an objective matter, and a matter of how 'the facts' were subjectively experienced and interpreted in the community and by the respondent as a child growing up. One was the child of an exceptionally prosperous fisherman/crofter. She knew that the croft, its furnishings and apparel were 'theirs' and had been for generations; she knew that 'everybody else' knew what they had, and she had a strong sense of being better-off than the rest. It did not seem strange to her that she should go to university when most of her peers did not. The other, the child of a thrifty shepherd who always lived in tied cottages, had, like 'everybody else', little visible signs of his parents' quietly accumulating savings. He thought of going to university as extra-ordinary, and too much of a sacrifice for his parents to bear.

These examples illustrate that children's futures were sometimes negotiated by parents and children, each of whom might refer to examples and inspirations beyond the household. Each parent brought his or her own biography to the business of bringing up children, and each may have had aspirations and visions beyond local horizons. Each parent might also take into consideration how others educated their children – others whom they perceived to be like themselves, or to be the way they would like to be. The views of each parent and their child may have been blended into a single vision, or may have remained distinct and even contradictory. With reference to some households it was possible to talk of a collective strategy in which children's destinies were orchestrated to suit the common good. Typically it was the parents (or some-times a single parent, usually the father) who imposed their vision of 'the common good'. But sometimes children also had a voice.

Children often had some input into the direction of their future even when they were not formally consulted. Mrs Roberts, an elite farmer's daughter, had no say in being sent to boarding school at a young age but her education and experience away from home gave her ideas of her own. By the time she was in her teens, she knew that she wanted to be a doctor. Although her mother scoffed at her plan, she was not actually opposed in carrying it out by either of her parents. Mr Veitch, a farmer's son, knew he loved working with animals from an early age. Had he not so obviously loved farm work, then his father may not have sanctioned his absence from higher education, while he was educating his daughters and keep-ing them 'in style'. His father must have weighed up the fact that he himself had had a training as a lawyer before being settled on a farm, and that he was ignoring family precedents by not similarly educating this son. It was expedient to sacrifice Mr Veitch's edu-cation, because his labour on the farm made it possible to keep the girls, but this strategy would never have succeeded without Mr Veitch's enthusiastic compliance.[3]

Sometimes parents had aspirations for their children that did not obviously derive from their own experience or social world. For example, Mr Collins's parents wanted him to be a vet, despite never having had any higher education themselves or any freedom in their own biographies for occupational choice. However, his father had always wanted more for himself and his family than being a shepherd. Despite saving all his life, he was never to achieve improvement in his own position. His son's proven ability at school seemed to trigger alternative hopes for achieving social mobility vicariously.

Gender and Destiny

Whether a child was labelled boy or girl and brought up with the trappings of masculinity or femininity had profound consequences for adult social destination. Economic, cultural and personal factors have to be seen through the prism of gender. One can return to any one of the detailed interviews and ask if the individual's destiny would have been the same had he or she been born the opposite sex; the answer is usually an emphatic 'no'. Even Mrs Roberts, who had an exceptionally successful career for a woman at that time, had initially been pushed in particular 'suitable' directions for a girl.

Among farm servants and crofters, girls and boys shared the same elementary schooling but at school age they were already doing 'women's work' or 'men's work' out of school hours. Both boys and girls learned that housework was 'women's work' unless no woman was available, and they learned that activities like ploughing and fishing were only done by men. The degree of overlap and flexibility that existed amongst the various tasks on crofts and family farms was not reflected in vacancies for paid employment. On leaving school, boys and girls were generally in different job markets; the situations they sought involved jobs done exclusively either by women or by men. In general these divisions of labour were ones which favoured young men and gave them the more skilled, more prestigious and better paid positions. Both young men and young women might anticipate marriage at some stage, but it had very different consequences for each sex. Marriage for women meant withdrawal from full-time paid work in favour of housekeeping and child-care. For men, becoming a husband/father meant establishing a household in which they were the main earners. While the work of both husband and wife was essential to the survival of many households, women's greater financial dependence provided the conditons which made it possible, although not inevitable, for men to treat wives as servants. Among farmers' children at the lower end of the social scale the picture was much the same, but the daughters of the more elite farmers might be educated as ladies who never expected to take paid employment. Sons, on the other hand, had to learn to earn a living in commerce, the armed forces, the professions or farming.

As with social class, the effects of gender are not a simple matter. This can be illustrated further by returning to the comparison between Mr Collins and Mrs Gillies. On the face of it, the latter was more advantaged despite her sex; it was Mrs Gillies, not Mr Collins, who actually went to university. But then when Mr Collins decided against university his prospects for farm work were very different from those of Mrs Gillies. This would have been the case even if both had been the children of farm labourers or crofters. Mr Collins rejected the vision of becoming a vet, not only because of worry about the financial burden this would impose on his parents, but also because of the intrinsic attraction of farm work to him. At the age of leaving school Mr Collins was already keen on being a shepherd. From his intimate knowledge of his father's work, he could see a future which involved skilled work, autonomy, responsibility and perhaps some prospect of advancement.

It could be said that it was Mr Collins's personal preference to become a shepherd – but personal preferences are shaped by visible opportunities, as well as by intellectual space and stimulation encouraging alternative visions. Girls did not leave school wanting to be shepherds, as this was not an option available to them. While Mr Collins's environment made him aware of the attractions of being a shepherd, it did not promote serious consideration of going to university. Mrs Gillies had a sense of being socially above her neighbours, in which she located the idea of going to university; she had no positive image of immediate local employment to counterbalance the prospect. She could have stayed on the croft, but the role available there was one of helping, often under the close and critical supervision of her mother. Staying on the croft might have been a more attractive immediate option had she been a young man. Young men staying to help on the croft were often doing so in the knowledge that it would eventually become theirs. Young women with brothers interested in the croft could only stay for life at the behest of their brother. Crofting communities often offered no local alternative to agricultural work for women. In less prosperous families than Mrs Gillies', when girls were not needed by the croft and/or the girls themselves wanted to get away, the 'solution' was domestic service.

The different destinies of girls and boys were particularly marked in the detailed accounts given by the two selected respondents from farmers' families. Mr Veitch's hard working life was entirely different from that of his sisters, who were brought up as 'ladies'. Mrs Roberts' parents were also concerned with her gentility, and would not send her to the local school like her brother. Speaking broad local Scots and 'being rough' was an asset for a prospective working farmer with no loss of gentlemanly status, provided he could also, like her father, switch at will to speaking 'properly' and being genteel. Such skills were not considered assets in a young lady.

Comparing Mr Veitch and Mrs Roberts, again it was the young woman rather than the young man who had the privilege of going to university. But again this has to be seen in the context of the alternatives available to a young woman who (to a much greater extent than Mrs Gillies) was regarded as too socially superior to be eligible for the main sources of rural women's paid employment – domestic service or farm work. No possibility of being a farmer was ever open to Mrs Roberts: only men were farmers; she was to be a lady, and then a wife. The fact that she became a professional woman rather than making a profession of being a wife was the consequence of a number of quirks in her biography, including the role model of her professional aunt. Not all farmers' daughters were brought up as 'ladies'; some were expected to milk alongside the dairy maid, and even to supersede the dairy maid and do a great deal of other work. But despite getting their hands dirty and sharing some of the everyday toil, they were no closer to a destiny of a farmer. Their relationship to farm work could only be consolidated by becoming farmers' wives.

Economic and Cultural Influences on Parenting

This brings us to some general observations concerning parenting. We have explored differences between the children of fathers from three occupational groups. Social science literature itemises a number of ways in which occupations interact with personal life. For example, the household division of labour which allocated housework and inside work to women mirrored the segregation of women into less skilled, less prestigious and more domestic employment in the labour market, and fitted with the withdrawal of women from the labour market on marriage. Men as workers had higher expectations of autonomy and status in paid employment than women; men as husbands had the opportunity to exercise financial control over wives and children. In such a society, authors have suggested, it was those fathers whose occupations placed them in particularly subservient or brutalised positions who were likely to be the most domineering and brutal at home. Following this reasoning, we would expect to find more authoritarian fathers among the more supervised and less autonomous farm servants than among crofters or farmers. Any suggestions of this order were tentative, and overall the similarities in how parents treated their children were more striking than the differences. But this is not surprising because farm servant fathers do not qualify as down-trodden deferential workers; rather, they were men established in skilled jobs, respected in their own community as superior to the odd job men and the casual workers.

A degree of distance and deference between fathers and children was the norm across all classes and occupational groupings. Many mothers were also rather distant figures, preoccupied by the daily toil of producing meals, cleaning clothes and maintaining a clean home. But even in better-off households with paid help, mothers did not necessarily regard spending time with their children as a priority. How close parents and children were, how much affection they showed each other, how much time they chose to spend together was not dependent only on how much money, time or energy parents had for children. It was profoundly influenced by pervasive ideas about parental authority and the place of children (Jamieson & Toynbee, 1989). At this time children were generally expected to be deferential and grateful to adults to whom they owed service; adults rarely regarded themselves as being at the service of their children. For example, Mrs Roberts' mother and father were relieved by domestic servants and paid workers from toiling all the hours of the day, but she does not remember being cuddled or played with a great deal. Like many middle-class children, she spent more time with her nurse than with her mother.

In most households, while children were of school age the norm was that they automatically obeyed parents, and 'speaking back' or spontaneously offering opinions was not only discouraged but actively forbidden. However, the faithful of the more austere and severe Protestant churches were probably the strictest parents in these respects. Most parents accepted that children ultimately had to lead their own lives, although some continued to exercise financial control over their children long after the age of 21. Among our interviewees there are several sons and daughters who worked late into their adult lives for their parents without any payment. Most explained that they wanted to do it. Although in this period parental authority was rarely overtly challenged, children had at least a little power in the situation, and what happened between them and their parents involved some degree of give and take.

Only a minority of the better-off parents in this study did not assume that their children would leave school at the minimum leaving age of 14. Encouraging children to develop their own talents and preferences as a means of helping them choose what to do in life was a luxury rather than a necessary part of parenting for the vast majority. Many parents needed their children to obtain the best paid job they could as soon as possible. Only those who could afford higher education seemed prepared to support or encourage children in making a job choice informed primarily by personal preference. But even in the households of the more middle-class farmers, where parents were educated and it was assumed children would be too, children were not always encouraged to express themselves or develop their individuality. For these parents, too much self-expression would have threatened the respect that they expected to receive from their children.

Recent Change

It should not be assumed that these parents were particularly strict or distant from their children for the period. City children were also often expected to 'be seen and not heard'. In both town and country, children were predominantly regarded as legitimately being at the service of adults. Parents were not necessarily child-centred in the way many parents now organise their domestic lives. Precisely when, where and how 'good parenting' has come to include spending a lot of time with children, enjoying being with them and fostering all aspects of their psychological, social, and intellectual development is a matter of debate. While there have always been exceptional parents who wanted to be a friend to their children rather than an authority over them, we have argued elsewhere that the general abandonment of a more traditional style of authority is a feature of the post-Second World War period (Jamieson, 1983; Jamieson & Toynbee, 1989). In so far as these changes have been associated with increased affluence, the cult of leisure, the development of mass consumption, mass media and mass culture, is there any reason to suppose that the parents and children of crofters, farm labourers and farmers have been left behind?

Radio and television have become ubiquitous in rural Scotland. Crofters in the Western Isles can daily absorb the same popular culture as urban dwellers do, albeit they also have access to a few hours a week of broadcasts in Gaelic. But for their young people there are limited opportunities for participating collectively in a consumer youth culture which in cities centres on clubs, discos, gigs and pubs.

It is beyond the scope of this book to make definitive statements about parent/child relationships in rural Scotland from the Second World War to the present. But one reason for not expecting any very distinct rural pattern today is the transformation in the composition of the rural population. While some Border towns have become dormitories for city commuters, all of rural Scotland has provided holiday and retirement homes for prosperous 'incomers', and much of the tourist industry of the Highlands and Islands is now run by entrepreneurs 'from South'. In many parts of the Western Isles, for example, the incomer population of migrants from the town, many of whom are English, outnumber the indigenous population. In the time that our interviewees grew up, many city dwellers still remembered their roots in the country. Many living in the country will presumably now remember their roots in the town.

NOTES
1. Fishermen crofters, shepherds and 'others in agriculture' were all listed separately with means of 6.93, 6.35 and 6.25 respectively.
2. This was despite the availability for some of farm work. We interviewed six daughters of agricultural labourers. Mrs Ramage cleaned and

did general domestic work for a local woman when she left school. Mrs Doughtie spent the first year after leaving school at home helping her mother, before working for a gamekeeper's wife. Mrs Aikman kept house for her father. Her mother had been seriously ill since she was 12, and was in and out of hospital until she died when Mrs Aikman was 17. May Carruthers kept house for a year before going into residential domestic service in prefrence to farm work (Jamieson, 1990a). Mrs West left her first job on the farm to go into domestic service in the hope that she would have more money for herself. Mrs Alison Allison was the only one who never did domestic service; she was a dairy maid.

3.   Although he was not downwardly mobile in terms of his occupation, Mr Veitch was less connected to a middle-class world than his parents. Mr Veitch made friends of his father's workers and spent time with them from an early age. His contacts with more middle-class worlds were restricted to the rural social scene of balls, etc. and contact with kin as a visitor to their farms. Both his father and mother had potentially wider social circles developed through university, and in his father's case through previous work as a lawyer. However, his father's preference was to concentrate most of his energies on the farm, and he was happy for this to be his son's life. His mother maintained wider social connections and musical ambitions for her daughters, but did not attempt to encompass her son in this world.

APPENDIX ONE

Getting the Information

IT IS IMPORTANT that readers should know how much faith can be placed on the validity of the information we have gathered and the reasons lying behind our sampling procedure so that they may judge for themselves the degree to which our findings may be trusted.

Sociologists use a wide variety of methods to carry out their research, sometimes using several different methods in a single project, for example, interviewing combined with observation of some kind, together with the use of records. The best known method is the survey, i.e. an investigation in which a number of relevant questions are put to a carefully selected sample of people, either on a face-to-face basis or through a self-completed question-naire. Surveys are primarily concerned with gathering information on which generalisations can be based. If valid generalisations are to be made, some form of random sampling[1] is necessary. Such a survey was not possible or suitable in the case of this research. There is no list of living people born in a particular year and brought up in rural Scotland from which to draw a random sample. Little is known about growing up in Scotland during this period since scant research has been devoted to the topic, so in-depth detailed ex-ploratory interviews were more appropriate than a list of standard questions. Instead of asking *only* a determinate number of questions in a specific way and in a pre-determined order, we deliberately encouraged our interviewees to introduce topics *they* thought would be relevant. In this way, we were able to discover aspects of family life which we had not considered as a result of our previous re-search. There were, however, questions we always asked based on the earlier and more general study of Edwardian childhood by Paul Thompson (1977) and modified by our own previous work as oral historians.

Our qualitatively-oriented research is exploratory rather than definitive. We make no claims to have covered all types of family-households which existed in rural Scotland in the early decades of the twentieth century.

Sampling Design

Exploratory studies such as our own typically employ some form of non-random sampling, usually based on what the researchers consider to be categories of special importance.

Before inviting anyone to take part in our project, we made a number of decisions about the selection process. We decided to include people who had been brought up in areas where large-scale, profit-oriented farming was well developed, and regions virtually unaffected by large-scale farming, such as some crofting areas. This distinction was important because many aspects of everyday life are influenced by the local mode of production and its associated employment structures, opportunities and demands. Since we were interested in gender, both men and women needed to be included, preferably in equal numbers. To keep our data comparable with that of other oral historians, we tried to confine our interviewing activities to those who had been born before 1912, a date used by other researchers. Each of our categories included sufficient interviewees to make sure that the information we were getting was consistent and representative, as far as this was possible with such methods.

At the outset the categories of farmer, farm servant and crofter were attractive as a way of covering very different economic and cultural contexts. Put simply (and unfortunately too simplistically, as we will explain), sons and daughters of fathers pursuing these occupations would be growing up in sufficiently different worlds to make interesting comparisons. However, in each of these occupational groupings there was a considerable range of life situations, from relatively rich to relatively poor, from socially respected to marginalised or isolated, and so on. This was particularly so for farmers. As the chapter on farmers explains in some detail, there was not one type of farmer. While landowning and farming were traditionally separated from each other, the term 'bonnet laird' referred to small landowners who farmed their own land – although the overwhelming majority of farmers were tenants. However, among tenant farmers there were enormous variations. At the top of the social and economic hierarchy were the 'gentleman' farmers who did not dirty their hands with menial work, and whose wives and children were not involved in production. In the text we refer to them as 'elite' farmers. In the middle were farmers who worked alongside the labour force they employed, while their wives worked in the house and dairy. They are refered to as 'working farmers' in the text. Some farmers, typically on the smallest farms, did not employ labour on a regular basis, but rather, all members of the family household were involved in production, including children who worked from an early age. These farmers are referred to in the text as 'working family farmers'. Our interviewees represent the children of each of these three types of farmers, but the majority were 'working farmers'. Interviewees were drawn from both the southern Lowlands and the north-east Lowlands, and one interviewee was the son of a Highland laird.

The term 'farm servant' covers a number of specific occupations and these are discussed in greater detail in the chapter on farm servants. The majority of interviewees in this category were the children of ploughmen, cattlemen and shepherds – the typical established jobs for married men among farm workers. While each of these jobs had its own particular demands and rewards, they had a number of conditions of service in common. Generally the lot of married male farm servants was much more homogeneous than that of farmers. Again, interviewees were drawn from both the southern Lowlands and the north-east Lowlands.

The variations amongst crofters were not as great as those amongst farmers, since even large well-endowed crofts were too small to make a decent living. Crofters are, technically speaking, those whose land was tenanted under the Crofters' Act of 1886 and the Small Holding Scotland Act of 1911. The latter allowed land holdings of not more than 50 acres or with a rent less than £50 a year to be registered as crofts. 'Crofting' was a very particular life-style with its roots in Gaelic culture which nurtures a community feeling of attachment to the land (Hunter, 1976; Smout, 1986, pp. 65–70). Economic differences between crofters concerned not just the size of the croft, but also the local opportunities for alternative ways of making a living. There was also a cultural difference between crofting in the West Highlands and Islands, where Gaelic was still the first language of many, and the crofters of the North-East who were more akin to small farmers. Our interviewees are mainly children of crofters from the West Highlands and Islands, but crofters from the North-East are also represented.

As well as variation within each category, there was also a problem of overlap between categories. For example, we had some difficulties with classifying agricultural workers or their children who eventually bought their way into a farm or croft later in life, perhaps when the children were grown up. We finally decided to classify cases like this on the basis of the situation of the family during most of our respondents' childhood.

In Appendix Two, we provide some background information on all of our interviewees and their parents.

Finding and Meeting our Interviewees

Reading and advice from others led us to believe that for both theoretical and practical reasons it would be wise to concentrate on three broad geographical areas from which to draw our sample: the south-east Lowlands, particularly the Borders, and two parts of the Highlands, the North-West and Islands and part of the North-East – an area including Speyside and Morayshire. There, we would be most likely to find the people conforming to our criteria.

We knew that we were unlikely to find difficulty in locating the children of farm servants in the Borders, given the very large numbers of them who had laboured there around the turn of the century. We hoped, too, that some of the children of their employers might still be living around the general area. We knew that we would be likely to find the children of crofters in the contemporary crofting areas of the Western Highlands, where children from some families would have remained to carry on the croft, or married in the immediate vicinity of their childhood residence. We hoped to find enough survivors from families which had been involved in subsistence farming in isolated pockets of Morayshire. Here too, there might be some children of one-time crofters.

Personal contacts were used to help find suitable respondents. In the Borders some contacts were initiated by a radio programme in which Lynn Jamieson explained the aims of the study. Several people responded. As in the Highlands, our initial interviewees recommended others with the same kind of background as themselves.

Because place of residence in old age does not necessarily reflect place of childhood, we encountered appropriate respondents who had moved to other parts of Scotland. For example, we have a number of interviews with people brought up in the Western Isles although we did not go there ourselves. The county in which each of our interviewees was brought up is given in Appendix Two, and Map 2 shows the old county boundaries.

Since we decided to interview people still living in the rural areas, our sample is biased towards those who stayed, who were inevitably those least likely to have wanted to leave.[2] This limitation is mitigated by the fact that the majority of our respondents were able to give us information about brothers and sisters who did leave the croft or farm.

Evidence on crofting was provided by twenty of our interviewees. Not all of them were from crofting families, as explained above, but all of them were brought up in areas where crofting was vital to the survival of the majority of the population. There were eleven people who had been brought up on crofts and one interviewee became a crofter as a young woman (see Appendix Two); three others lived in crofting areas in cottages with large gardens (Mrs MacAndrew and Mrs Scott, blacksmith's daughters, and Mrs MacAlister, a gamekeeper's daughter) which arguably were not large enough to be crofts. Information on crofting was also supplied by agricultural labourers' children who grew up in crofting areas, by people who grew up on family farms, and in one case, by a laird.

There were difficulties in finding enough crofters to interview, partly because of the short time available for searching them out in isolated parts of the country. Children from crofting families had probably been less likely to remain in the area of their birth than others, because of lack of employment opportunities. This made things difficult for us. Three of our crofters were born too late to satisfy our age criterion – one very substantially so.[3] However, the information obtained from the younger respondents was perfectly consistent with that provided by the older men and women.

The youngest interviewee was a woman who had been born in 1951. While readers may feel that our decision to draw on some of her comments about crofting life is unreasonable, her childhood in fact closely resembled that of other interviewees brought up on Lewis, despite the forty years which separated her experience from other respondents. Her taped interview, which runs for about two hours, is full of clearly articulated, highly detailed descriptive material on a wide range of subjects. It also includes valuable insights about the changing nature of childhood based on her experience as a mother of teenaged children. We have used a single Christian name to distinguish her from all the others.

We had difficulties balancing our desire to find enough crofters to include them in our research, and confining our sample to people born before 1912 – the date selected by Paul Thompson and by ourselves as the upper limit for our respondents' date of birth. Thompson was interviewing in the early 1970s, Jamieson in the late 1970s and Toynbee (in New Zealand) in the early 1980s, while the interviews on which this book is based were gathered in the autumn of 1986, so mortality accounted for many of our problems.

We had no difficulties whatever in finding children of farm servants in the Borders, and had to call a halt to interviewing them long before we had exhausted the 'possibles' list.[4] We recorded interviews with fifteen farm servants (see Appendix Two). It was somewhat more difficult to locate farmers, although we did interview thirteen tenant farmers and one laird. While we feel that we had enough cases of profit-oriented farmers, we would have welcomed a few more from the top end of the social scale – people who had been brought up in large country houses or mansions. Their numbers would have been proportionately very small in any case.

Using a sampling method of this nature, it is not possible to say that the people are representative of their group. However, even cursory reflection will convince the reader that it is not possible to take a representative random sample which requires that a carefully calculated proportion of each group be drawn from *all* of the set to be sampled, in this case people born before 1912. A very high proportion of the people in each of our groups would have already died, gone to the cities, or migrated overseas when they were young adults, and were therefore unavailable.

In any case, researchers who use our kind of sampling method do not seek to make definitive generalisations about what they find.

Rather, they are interested in making more tentative suggestions about social processes, seeking some understanding rather than full explanations. They try to find informants whose experience appears to be typical of the group or groups being studied, continuing to interview people until a high level of consistency is achieved in order to ensure that the collective account of their lives accords with whatever other information is available. This we have done.

Interviewing took place during the months of September, October and November of 1986. In all, we conducted some thirty-five interviews, mostly on a one-to-one basis,[5] most of them conducted by Claire Toynbee. A couple were conducted jointly, and ten were conducted earlier by Lynn Jamieson as part of the fieldwork for her Ph.D. We experienced few refusals to take part.

Oral History as Method

Oral histories have much in common with what sociologists call semi-structured interviewing – a respected technique for gathering qualitative data. Minimally structured interviewing is commonly used where the sociologist wishes to avoid imposing his or her own ideas on an area of social reality which is not already well researched. A topic list, rather than an elaborate interview schedule, allows informants to introduce information which could not be elicited by a long list of detailed questions composed by the researcher. We took a middle approach between minimal structure and very elaborate schedules. Detailed questions were necessary to cue people to the fact that we considered certain mundane aspects of life interesting and worth talking about and to ensure a fairly even coverage of topics across interviews. At the same time we always 'played it by ear', modifying and reordering questions in order to accommodate what the respondent seemed to wish to discuss.

None of the interview sessions which we conducted took less than a couple of hours, though we did not usually tape record more than about forty minutes of that time. When our respondents were first contacted it was almost always on a face-to-face basis, rather than by letter or telephone. We always told them what the aims of the study were and the sort of questions we were likely to be asking. When we arrived on the appointed day we were invariably offered tea to refresh us after our journey and usually spent the first hour or so asking about the topic area, the person's life in general terms, or answering questions about our own lives. After the taped interview there was always some more refreshment. During this time, it was common for new information to arise out of the conversation.

Our oral histories differed from many semi-structured interviews in that, instead of asking people about recent events, we were asking about segments of their lives relating to fifty to eighty years ago. This difficulty is inherent in the method and has been discussed at length by the practitioners of oral history. Paul Thompson (1978, pp. 100–113) defends the interview which is retrospective over a long time span by citing evidence from psychological research which shows that much of what is discarded from memory is lost relatively soon after the event. Memory is in fact more profoundly selective than this suggests, as Thompson recognises. Memory is not a simple store-room of all that a person experiences. What is noticed or perceived in the first instance is inevitably selected, so what is available in the memory-bank for recall is far from total. What is more, the image of storing the inert is inappropriate for the purposes of social science; since memories are constantly available for modification, the past can be reinterpreted.

The selectivity of memory can, in some circumstances, become valuable information in itself. Thompson, for example, argues that: 'The discovery of distortion or suppression in a life-story is not, it must be emphasized, purely negative; it may provide an important clue to the family's psychology and social attitudes' (Thompson, 1978, p. 110). We do not necessarily claim these as virtues since we have no way of assessing significant absences or distortion in the content of an interview. Where specific instances arise out of the oral testimony, we bring them to the attention of readers who may wish to judge for themselves. We have done our best to ensure that the interviews are internally consistent and that details of specific places and events do not contradict other respondents' accounts.

Whatever the problems associated with the use of oral histories, they also have great merit, especially when used for gathering information about the commonplace – family life, the everyday life of ordinary people. They can reveal more of the quality of everyday life for more sectors of the population than most documentary sources can, which are usually compiled by officials of some kind, or by people belonging to the higher levels of society. In the case of our research, it is the child's point of view which comes to the fore, or rather the interviewees' perceptions and memories of childhood. We believe that careful questioning about details of everyday life at particular ages and stages does allow some recapturing of what it was like to be a child.

Methods of Editing and Presentation

The tape-recorded interviews were transcribed by the interviewers themselves on to computer to aid in analysis and writing-up. Since then, they have been checked, edited and indexed. Those which are presented in full have been especially carefully checked, edited and rendered in a form which makes them acceptable in a literary sense (ums and aahs, except where they were considered especially meaningful, have been ironed out), and where absolutely necessary the order has been changed to provide a more readable account. The words of the interviewer are typed in italics to distinguish them from those of the interviewee. The full transcripts were selected on the basis of their interest and their representativeness. These particular interviewees were also notably articulate.

In order to preserve the anonymity of our interviewees we have chosen pseudonyms to disguise identity. We have also taken what we consider to be excusable liberties with place names for the same purpose, using the real place names only where they refer to a general area.

NOTES

1. Random sampling is a statistical term, indicating that choice of respondents has been based on established techniques which make sure that every person in a specified population has an equal chance of being selected. For this to be possible, a complete list of all the people in the population has to be made.
2. Some of our interviews were conducted with people living in towns and cities, either because they had retired there, or because they had been interviewed by Lynn Jamieson as part of her Ph.D. research.
3. The average date of birth for all interviewed crofters was actually 1912. However, the statistic for crofters from the West was 1918, and from the East 1909. We did obtain interviews from a couple of very old crofters, which helped balance our very young one. The average date of birth for farm workers was 1908, and for farm owners 1902. (In one case we omitted to ask for the date of birth. Observation would suggest that the person would have been born in about 1906.)

4.   Although it should be noted that men were easier to find than women, presumably because in the rural areas where we looked the facts of mortality had been balanced by the differential out-migration of women.
5.   There were a few exceptions, for example, when the respondent had a visitor, or when two siblings lived together and took it for granted that they would and should be interviewed together. While it would sometimes be desirable to insist on one-to-one interviews, it was crucial that the respondent felt at ease and that the interviewer did not stretch hospitality. In any case a third person can further stimulate conversation to the benefit of the enterprise.

APPENDIX TWO
Interviewees and their Work History

—————

Name	Father's occupation	Date of birth	Place of childhood	F[1]	E[2]	Work History	I[3]
Landowner							
Mr Gilanders	Lawyer and laird	1915	Inverness-shire	?4	?	Armed services, laird	C
Farmers							
ELITE OR GENTLEMAN FARMERS							
Margaret Roberts[5]	Farmer	1885	East Lothian	5	23	Doctor of Medicine	
Mrs Tanner	Farmer	1912	Berwickshire	3	19	Year at college, then at home	C
Mr Turnball	Farmer	1911	Berwickshire	6	?17	18 months in accountant's office, then farmer	C
WORKING FARMERS							
Mr Craven	Furrier/farmer	1897	Aberdeenshire	10	14	Civil servant	L
Mr Henderson	Banker, then farmer	1913	Ayrshire	3	?18	3 yrs. agricultural college, then farmer	C
Mr Isbister	Farmer/manager of distillery	1905	Western Isles	5	13	Farm work/farmer	L
Mr McManus	Farmer	1895	Ayrshire	2	14	Worked on farm/farmer	L
Mr Veitch	Farmer	1903	Morayshire	5	15	Worked on farm/farmer	C

Name	Father's occupation	Date of birth	Place of childhood	F[1]	E[2]	Work History	I[3]
WORKING FAMILY FARMERS							
Mrs Haslitt	Merchant, then farmer	1906	Ayrshire	3	16	Worked on farm and in house	C
Mr MacPherson	Farmer	1916	Inverness-shire	4	14	Worked on farm/farmer	C
Mr Marshall	Farmer	1900	Ayrshire	3	15	Worked on farm/farmer	C
Miss Mathews	Crofter, then farmer	1912	Morayshire	3	14	Worked on farm and in house	C
Mr Mathews	As above	1916	As above		14	Worked on farm	C
Crofters							
Mr Campbell	Crofter/estate worker	1910	Inverness-shire	1	14	Hall boy, forestry worker	C
Mrs Currie	Farm servant, crofter/distillery worker	1917	Morayshire	13	14	Domestic servant	
Mr Firth	Crofter	1899	Wester Ross	9	14	Gillie, forestry, railway worker	C
Mr Fleming	Crofter (foster father)	1907	Wester Ross	n.a.	14	Domestic service	C
Mr Gillies	Crofter/fisherman/shopkeeper	1899	Western Isles	9	21	Teacher	C
Mr Geddes	Bank clerk; small farmer; crofter	1900	Inverness-shire	6	14	Estate worker	C
Miss Gibb	Crofter/blacksmith	1909	Morayshire	2	14	Kept house	C
Mr Gibb	As above	1911	as above	2	14	Crofter/blacksmith	C
Mr McClelland	Crofter/fisherman	1925	Wester Ross	4	14	Handyman; navy; crofter	C
Mrs MacDiarmid	Crofter/fisherwoman	1929	Western Isles	4	14	Worked on croft and in house	C
Mairi MacKay	Crofter/seaman	1951	Western Isles	8	15	Hotel work	C
Mrs McLeod	Horse contractor	1905	Inverness-shire	n.a.	n.a.	Crofter	C

Farm Servants

Name	Father's occupation	Date of birth	Place of childhood	F¹	E²	Work History	I³
Alison Allison	Ploughman	1900	Midlothian	6	13	Dairymaid	L
Mrs Aikman	Shepherd	1918	Midlothian	2	14	Kept house	C
May Carruthers	Ploughman	1905	Caithness	11	14	Kept house, then domestic service	L
Tom Collins	Shepherd	1906	Berwickshire	10	14	Shepherd	L
Mrs Doughtie	Cattleman	1912	Berwickshire	10	14	Kept house; day servant	C
Mr Duncan	Ploughman	1900	Roxburghshire	4	14	Farm labourer	C
Mr Humphries	Ploughman	1901	Selkirkshire	3	14	Farm labourer	C
Wullie Linton	Ploughman	1989	Berwickshire	10	14	Orraman; ploughman	L
Alec Pearson	Farm worker	1898	Midlothian	9	14	Electrician	L
Jean Ramage	Cattleman; farm manager	1913	Inverness-shire	6	?	Domestic servant	C
Davy Renton	Shepherd	1912	Peebles-shire	8	14	Farm worker; shepherd; small holding	L
Mr Ritchie	Grieve	1905	Easter Ross	11	14	Farm labourer; roads; ploughman	C
Mr Walker	Farm foreman	1899	Berwickshire	6	13	Ploughman, steward	C
Mrs West	Dairy cattleman	1921	Aberdeenshire	3	14	Farm worker; domestic service	C
Mr Yuill	Farm steward	1922	Midlothian	3	14	Farm labourer	C

Other Rural Workers

Name	Father's occupation	Date of birth	Place of childhood	F[1]	E[2]	Work History	I[3]
Miss Fraser	Driver/chauffeur	1913	Midlothian	3	14	Mill worker	C
Mrs McAlister	Game keeper	1927	Inverness-shire	4	14	Domestic service	C
Mrs McAndrew	Blacksmith (foster father)	1900	Morayshire	n.a.	14	Post woman	C
Mrs Scott	Blacksmith	1899	Morayshire	3	14	Domestic service	C

NOTES

1. Number of children in the family, counting the interviewee and his/her brothers and sisters.
2. Year in which s/he left full-time education.
3. Interviewer: C=Claire Toynbee, L=Lynn Jamieson.
4. ? indicates that this information was not clear from the interview.
5. A first name is used as well as a surname as extracts from this interview have already been published by Lynn Jamieson using this fictitious first name. The exception is Mairi MacKay. In this case her first name is used in the text to alert the reader to the fact that she was an exceptionally young interviewee.

References

ANDERSON, Michael (1988) 'Households, families and individuals: some preliminary results from the national sample from the 1851 Census of Great Britain', *Continuity and Change* 3 (3) 421–38.

ANTHONY, Richard (1989) 'Scottish farm labour 1914–39: aspects of continuity and change', unpublished MA dissertation, Department of Economic and Social History, University of Edinburgh.

ANTHONY, Richard (1992) 'Labour mobility and turnover in Scottish agriculture, 1900–1939', paper presented to the Economic History Society Conference, Leicester.

ANTHONY, Richard (forthcoming) 'The market for farm labour in Scotland 1900–39', Edinburgh University Ph.D. thesis.

ARMSTRONG, Alan (1988) *Farmworkers: A Social and Economic History 1770–1908*. London, B.T. Batsford.

BANKS, J. (1954) *Prosperity and Parenthood*. London, Routledge & Kegan Paul.

BANKS, Joseph A. (1981) *Victorian Values: Secularism and the Size of Families*. London, Routledge & Kegan Paul.

BATHGATE, J. (1901) *Aunt Janet's Legacy to her Nieces*. Fifth edition, Selkirk.

BOARD OF AGRICULTURE FOR SCOTLAND (1920) *Report of the Committee on Women in Agriculture*.

BRITTON, D. K. & HUNT, K. E. (1952) 'Agriculture' in M. Kendall and A. Brudford Hill (eds.) *The Sources and Nature of the Statistics of the United Kingdom* vol. 1. London, Oliver and Boyd.

BUCHAN, Margaret (1983) 'The social organisation of fisher girls' in Glasgow Women's Studies Group (eds) *Uncharted Lives: Extracts from Scottish Women's Experience*. Glasgow, Pressgang.

BUCHANAN, R. H. (1984) 'Box-beds and bannocks: the living past', *Review Of Scottish Culture* 1, 65–9.

CAMERON, David Kerr (1987) *A Kist of Sorrows*. London, Victor Gollancz Ltd.

CAMPBELL, R. H. (1984) 'Agricultural labour in the South West' in T. M. Devine (ed.) *Farm Servants and Labour in Lowland Scotland, 1770–1914*.

CAMPBELL, R. H. & DEVINE, T. M. (1990) 'The rural experience' in Hamish J. Fraser & R. J. Morris (eds.) *People and Society in Scotland*, 46–65.

CARTER, Ian (1979) *Farmlife in Northeast Scotland 1840–1914: The Poorman's Country*. Edinburgh, John Donald.

CLARK, G. (1983) The Agricultural Census – United Kingdom and United States, *Concepts and Techniques in Modern Geography*, No. 35.

COLLINS, E. J. T. (1987) 'The rationality of surplus agricultural labour: mechanisation in English agriculture in the nineteenth century'. *Agricultural History Review*.

CORR, H. (1990) 'How distinctive is Scotland? An exploration into Scottish education' in Hamish J. Fraser & R. J. Morris (eds.) *People and Society in Scotland*, 290–309.

CORR, H. & JAMIESON, L. (eds.) (1990) *The Politics of Everyday Life*. London, Macmillan.

CRAFTS, N. (1985) *British Economic Growth during the Industrial Revolution* . Oxford, Clarendon Press.

DAICHES, David (ed.) (1981) *A Companion to Scottish Culture*. London, Edward Arnold.

DEVINE, T. M. (ed.) (1984) *Farm Servants and Labour in Lowland Scotland, 1770–1914*. Edinburgh, John Donald.

DEVINE, T. M. (1984) 'Women workers, 1850–1914' in T. M. Devine (ed.) *Farm Servants and Labour in Lowland Scotland, 1770–1914*.

DEVINE, T. M. (1988) 'Urbanisation' in T. M. Devine & R. Mitchison (eds.) *People and Society in Scotland*: Volume 1, 1760–1830.

DEVINE, T. M. & MITCHISON, R. (eds.) (1988) *People and Society in Scotland*: Volume 1, 1760–1830. Edinburgh, John Donald.

FENTON, Alexander & OWEN, Trefor M. (1981) *Food in Perspective*: Third International Conference of Ethnological Food Research. Edinburgh, John Donald.

FENTON, Alexander & WALKER, Bruce (1981) *The Rural Architecture of Scotland*. Edinburgh, John Donald.

FENTON, Alexander (1976) *Scottish Country Life*. Edinburgh, John Donald.

FENTON, Alexander (1986) 'Food on Sunday', *Review of Scottish Culture*, No.2. Edinburgh, John Donald Publishers and the National Museums of Scotland, 53–8.

FENTON, Alexander (1987) *Country Life in Scotland: Our Rural Past*. Edinburgh, John Donald.

FEWEL, J. & PATERSON, F. (eds.) (1990) *Girls in their Prime: Scottish Education Revisited*. Edinburgh, Scottish Academic Press.

FINN, M. (1983) 'Social efficiency, progressivism and secondary education Scotland, 1885–1905', in Humes, W. & Paterson, H. (eds.) *Scottish Culture and Scottish Education 1800–1980*.

FRASER, Hamish J. & MORRIS, R. J. (eds.) (1990) *People and Society in Scotland*. Vol. II, 1830–1914. Edinburgh, John Donald.

GIBB, R. S. (1927) *A Farmer's Fifty Years in Lauderdale*. Edinburgh, Oliver & Boyd.

GILLORAN, A. (1985) 'Family formation in Victorian Scotland', Edinburgh University Ph.D. Thesis.

GORDON, E. (1990) 'Women's spheres', in Hamish J. Fraser & R. J. Morris (eds.) *People and Society in Scotland*, Vol. II 1830–1914, 206–35.

GORDON, E. & BREITENBACH, E. (eds.) (1990) *The World is Ill Divided: Women's Work in Scotland in the Nineteenth and Early Twentieth Centuries*. Edinburgh, Edinburgh University Press.

GRANT, I. F. & CHEAPE, Hugh (1987) *Periods in Highland History*. London, Shepheard-Walwyn.

GRAY, J., McPHERSON, A. and RAFFE, D. (1983) *Reconstructions of Secondary Education*. London, Routledge & Kegan Paul.

HIGGS, Edward (1986) 'Domestic Service and Household Production' in Angela John (ed.) *Unequal Opportunities: Women's Employment in England, 1800–1918*.

HUNTER, James (1976) *The Making of the Crofting Community*. Edinburgh, John Donald.

HUNTER, James (1991) *The Claim of Crofting: The Scottish Highlands and Islands, 1930–1990*. Edinburgh, John Donald.

HUMES, W. & PATERSON, H. (eds.) (1983) *Scottish Culture and Scottish Education 1800–1980*. Edinburgh, John Donald.

JAMIESON, L. (1983) 'A case study in the development of the modern family: urban Scotland in the early twentieth century', unpublished Ph.D. thesis, University of Edinburgh.

JAMIESON, L. (1983) 'Growing up in Scotland: Class and Gender', in Glasgow Women's Studies Group (eds.) *Uncharted Lives: Extracts from Scottish Women's Experience*. Glasgow, Pressgang.

JAMIESON, L. (1986) 'Limited resource and limiting conventions: working-class mothers and daughters in urban Scotland *circa* 1890–1920', in J. Lewis (ed) *Labour and Love*.

JAMIESON, L. (1987) 'Theories of family development and the experience of being brought up', *Sociology* 21 (4) 591–607.

JAMIESON, L. (1990a) 'Rural and urban women in domestic service', in E. Gordon and E. Breitenbach (eds.) *The World is Ill Divided*.

JAMIESON, L. (1990b) '"We all left at 14": girls' and boys' schooling 1900–1930', in J. Fewel and F. Paterson (eds.) *Girls in their Prime*.

JAMIESON, L. & TOYNBEE, C. (1990) 'Shifting patterns of parental control', in H. Corr and L. Jamieson (eds.) *The Politics of Everyday Life*.

JONES, D. T., *et al.* (1926) *Rural Scotland during the War*. London.

KEMMER, D. (1990) 'The marital fertility of Edinburgh professionals in the later nineteenth century', Edinburgh University unpublished Ph.D. thesis.

KENDRICK, S. (1983) *Industrial and Occupational Structure*. Social Structure of Modern Scotland Project (SSRC HR 6948), Working Paper 2.

LASLETT, Peter (2nd ed.) (1971) *The World We Have Lost*. London, Methuen & Co. Ltd.

LENEMAN, L. (1989) *Fit for Heroes? Land Settlement in Scotland after World War I*. Aberdeen, Aberdeen University Press.

LEVITT, I. & SMOUT, T. C. (1979) *The State of the Scottish Working Class in 1843*. Edinburgh, Scottish Academic Press.

LEWIS, Jane (ed.) (1986) *Labour and Love*. London, Blackwell.

LITTLEJOHN, James (1963) *Westrigg: The Sociology of a Cheviot Parish*. London, Routledge & Kegan Paul.

MacDONALD, D. (1984) 'Lewis shielings', in *Review of Scottish Culture*, No.1. Edinburgh, John Donald Publishers and the National Museums of Scotland.

MacFARLANE, Alan (1978) *The Origins of English Individualism: The Family, Property and Social Transition*. Oxford, Basil Blackwell.

MacLAREN, A. A. (1976) *Social Class in Scotland Past and Present*. Edinburgh.

McCRONE, D., BECHHOFER, F. AND KENDRICK, S. (1982) 'Egalitarianism and social inequality in Scotland', in D. Robbins (ed.) *Rethinking Social Inequality*. London, Gower.

McPHERSON, A. (1983) 'An angle on the geist: persistence and change in the Scottish education tradition', in W. Humes and H. Paterson (eds.) *Scottish Culture and Scottish Education 1800–1980*.

MARSHALL, G., NEWBY, H., ROSE, D., & VOGLER, C. (1988) *Social Class in Modern Britain*. London, Hutchison.

MILLS, C. W. (1970) *The Sociological Imagination*. Harmondsworth, Penguin.

MITCHISON, Rosalind (1978) *Life in Scotland*. London, Batsford.

MORRIS, Angela (1989) 'Patrimony and power: a study of lairds and landownership in the Scottish Borders', Edinburgh University unpublished Ph.D. thesis.

MORRIS, R. J. (1990) 'Urbanisation in Scotland', in Hamish J. Fraser & R. J. Morris (eds.) *People and Society in Scotland*. Vol.II, 1830–1914, 73–102.

MURRAY, Charles (1927) *Hamewith and Other Poems*. London, Constable & Co. Ltd.

MUTCH, A. (1991) 'The "farming ladder" in North Lancashire 1840–1914: myth or reality?' *Northern History* XXVII 162–83.

O'DOWD, Anne (1991) *Spalpeens and Tattie Howkers: History and Folklore of the Irish Migratory Agricultural Worker in Ireland and Britain*. Dublin, Irish Academic Press.

ORWIN, C. S. & WHETHAM, Edith H. (1971) *History of British Agriculture 1846–1914*. Newton Abbot, David & Charles.

PATERSON, H. (1983) 'Incubus and ideology: the development of secondary schooling in Scotland 1900–1939', in W. Humes and H. Paterson (eds.) *Scottish Culture and Scottish Education 1800–1980*.

PREBBLE, John (1963) *The Highland Clearances*. London, Secker & Warburg.

RAPP, Rayna (1982) 'Family and class in contemporary America: notes toward an understanding of ideology', in Thorne, B. & Yalom, M. (eds.) *Rethinking the Family*, 168–187.

Review of Scottish Culture, No. 2, (1986). John Donald Publishers and the National Museums of Scotland, Edinburgh.

RICHARDS, Eric (1982) *A History of the Highland Clearances: Agrarian Transformation and the Evictions, 1746–1886*. London, Croom Helm.

Report to the Board of Agriculture for Scotland by Sir James Wilson on Farm Workers in Scotland in 1919–20 (1921). Edinburgh, HMSO.

Report of the Committee on Farm Workers in Scotland (1936). Cmd. 5217.

Report of the Royal Commission on the Housing of the Industrial Population of Scotland Rural and Urban (1917). Cmd. 8731.

ROBERTS, E. (1984) *A Woman's Place: An Oral History of Working-Class Women, 1890–1940*. Oxford, Basil Blackwell.

ROBERTSON, B. W. (1973) 'The Border farm worker, 1871–1971: Industrial Attitudes and Behaviour', *Journal of Agricultural Labour Science*, II, 65–93.

ROBERTSON, B. W. (1978) 'The Scottish farm servant and his union: from encapsulation to integration', in Ian MacDougall (ed.) *Essays in Scottish Labour History*. Edinburgh, John Donald.

ROBERTSON, B. W. (1990) 'In bondage: the female farm worker in south-east Scotland', in E. Gordon and E. Breitenbach (eds.) *The World is Ill Divided*.

ROBSON, Michael (1984) 'The Border Farm Worker' in T. M. Devine (ed.) *Farm Servants and Labour in Lowland Scotland*.

ROSS, E. (1983) 'Survival networks: women's neighbourhood sharing in London before World War One' *History Workshop* 15.

Royal Commission on the Employment of Children, *Young Persons and Women in Agriculture*, Fourth Report. Parliamentary Papers 1870, XII.

SAMUEL, R. (1977) 'Workshop of the world: steam power and hand technology in mid-Victorian Britain', *History Workshop* 3, 6–72.

SMOUT, T. C. (1972) *A History of the Scottish People, 1560–1830*. London, Fontana.

SMOUT, T. C. (1986) *A Century of the Scottish People, 1830–1950.* London, Collins.

THOMPSON, Paul (1977) *The Edwardians: The Remaking of British Society.* London, Paladin.

THOMPSON, Paul (1978) *The Voice of the Past: Oral History.* Oxford, Oxford University Press.

THOMPSON, Paul (1983) *Living the Fishing.* London, Routledge & Kegan Paul.

THOMPSON, Paul (1984) 'The family and child-rearing as forces for economic change: towards fresh research approaches', *Sociology* 18 (4) November, 515–30.

THORNE, Barrie & YALOM, Marilyn (eds.) (1982) *Rethinking the Family: Some Feminist Questions.* New York, Longman.

TOYNBEE, Claire & JAMIESON, Lynn (1989) 'Some responses to economic change in Scottish farming and crofting family life', *Sociological Review* 37 (4) 89.

TOYNBEE, Claire (1986) 'Her work, his work and theirs: the household economy and the family in New Zealand, 1900–1925', unpublished Ph.D. thesis in Sociology, New Zealand, Victoria University of Wellington.

WILSON, J. (1902) 'Half a century as a Border farmer', *Transactions of the Highland and Agricultural Society, 5th series,* XIV 35–48.

WILSON, P. & PAHL, R. (1988) 'The changing sociological construct of the family', *Sociological Review* 36 (2) 233–266.

WITHERS, Charles W. J. (1988) *Gaelic Scotland: The Transformation of a Culture Region.* London, Routledge.

WOODS, Robert (1982) *Theoretical Population Geography.* London, Longman.

Index